JAMES STIRLING   MICHAEL WILFORD   and Associates

For MARY and ANGELA

JAMES STIRLING MICHAEL WILFORD
AND ASSOCIATES

BUILDINGS & PROJECTS

1 9 7 5 – 1 9 9 2

INTRODUCTION BY ROBERT MAXWELL
ESSAYS BY MICHAEL WILFORD AND THOMAS MUIRHEAD
LAYOUT BY THOMAS MUIRHEAD, JAMES STIRLING, AND MICHAEL WILFORD

1 9 9 4

T H A M E S   A N D   H U D S O N

In memory of James Stirling 1926–1992

Introduction

Michael Wilford

There were 38 projects in Volume 1 of this monograph, encompassing James Stirling's university thesis, his early competition entries and unbuilt work, followed by the projects carried out with James Gowan during their 1956–63 partnership, and work done later under his own name, leading into the James Stirling/Michael Wilford partnership. Volume 2 includes the 58 projects designed by us since then until Jim's death in June 1992. Taken together, the two volumes therefore comprise a continuous and complete documentation of the James Stirling *œuvre*. Apart from a short interruption in 1963 after completion of the Leicester Engineering Building, when the Stirling/Gowan partnership dissolved, Jim and I worked alongside each other, in the same room, for the 32 years from 1960 until 1992. We ran the practice together in true partnership, discussing and sharing all aspects of the projects in the closest possible collaboration.

Throughout every stage of the design process we draw every probable option for each part of the project. All our staff are creative architects who think and invent as they draw and because there is a minimum of mechanical drafting we find that computers, which cannot think laterally, are of little use to us in the creative process.

We begin with a series of alternative conceptual studies and schematic outline drawings, and when a single concept has been agreed with the client we develop a full range of plans, sections, elevations, up or down-view axonometrics, isometrics, perspectives, etc. The actual viewpoint from which we decide to 'see' and draw a building as we design it is of course critically important, and can often only be determined after experimentation with different drawings.

Drawings are prepared in several alternative versions which allow us to make comparative evaluations and to ensure that our decisions are based on full knowledge of the design problem. Initial sketches are made using felt-tip or pencil; Jim's own favourite tool was the red "Bic", of which the office always kept an abundant supply. All other drawings start out as pencil "underlays" using graphite leads in clutch pencils. As these are refined and finalised, we change to fine 'Rotring' pens and black ink, on tracing paper or film.

The appearance of our drawings is deliberately hard, spare, restrained, and scientific in character, meticulously to scale and as accurate as hand and eye can make them. They are meant to convey information clearly and with immediacy, and to be restricted to the task in hand. For clarity, we therefore omit much information from drawings and retain it instead in our mind's eye; thus what is not shown on a drawing may be just as important to the design process as what we decide to draw. The image on the paper represents the absolute minimum necessary to convey the maximum amount of useful information about the project, in the clearest possible way.

Stripping away extraneous information is done by overlaying tracing paper on an underdrawing and re-drawing it, often many times, until the scope and detail are pared down as required. We use the smallest sheets of paper possible so that the eye can encompass the whole image without any need to scan and search across the page. This also eliminates the temptation to incorporate extraneous or irrelevant information. When completed, our design drawings convey, to the practised eye, a correct and factual architectural understanding of the building – not a confusing and subjective 'artists impression'.

Although they are of course made by the many different hands and personalities who work on a design, all our drawings are highly consistent in style and technique. By remaining strictly within the limits of this shared discipline of drawing, we find that the individual creativity of each architect can be expressed far more effectively and comprehensibly to the others because we are all communicating in the same visual language.

We have a partiality for axonometric drawings because they enable us to set out the spaces, surfaces, and volumetrics of a design in a single image which has no distortion, and gives an accurate reading of the building. The vertical and horizontal planes are both represented at the same scale (what Reyner Banham once described as 'all-dimensions-true'). This facilitates our design decisions by making explicit what the consequences of these decisions will be and by clarifying how complex assemblies, interlocking functions and construction sequences will actually work. We have therefore developed the 'axo' as one of our key working tools and also often find it useful in explaining the more complex parts of a project to our clients.

For the same reasons of accuracy and lack of distortion, our use of perspective drawings is extremely limited. Occasionally we might find that to get the best understanding of how a particular interior space will feel, simple one-point perspective drawings enable us to study what the surfaces enclosing the space will look like, and to ensure that all lighting, air conditioning and other details are properly considered in the room as a whole.

We make use of three-dimensional exploratory drawings to study details or special elements of construction because by using single, simplified images we can grasp the essence of an idea in a way which normal orthographic projection can only achieve using several images, and often with far less clarity.

There are certain architectural concerns which inform all of our work and which extend across the 40-year time-span and wide range of project types encompassed by the two volumes of this monograph. To the observant reader, some underlying elements of continuity will be apparent: a strategy of breaking down each building into a number of discrete parts, each expressed separately and clearly; clarity and dramatisation of pedestrian circulation within and between these separate parts; an interest in the contrasting relationships between solids and voids (i.e. between "mass and membrane"); the exploration of non-rectilinear, oblique, and curvilinear geometries; the use of a limited range of materials and colours; and especially, the predominance of formal and spatial objectives over structural and technological systems.

In many projects throughout our *œuvre*, the larger, more important elements of the building are expressed as autonomous forms of individual identity, assembled to make various arrangements of hierarchical, three-dimensional composition responding to the functions of the Brief and to the context of the place. Of itself, this fragmentation might only create confusion, whereas we want our buildings to be easily readable and welcoming. Our architectural language therefore deliberately makes use of a recognisable, obvious, and even playful vocabulary of shapes, finished in a palette of a few materials such as stone, glass, or plaster rendering.

One of our concerns is that modern architecture should be able to regenerate urban space. In the contemporary tendency to resolve the complexitites of large built organisms by enclosing all their functions in a single rectilinear block, leaving shapeless leftover open spaces around the edges, we see a withdrawal from architecture's responsibility to consider the public realm. In our own architecture we work to express differentiation and complexity, and we consider solids and voids together as compositions of interrelated interior and outdoor spaces.

According to the number and relative size of the elements which comprise a project, a sense of architectural order may either be inherent in how we combine them or be achieved by introducing additional organising elements. This is seen for instance in a comparison between the Düsseldorf and Stuttgart projects, in both of which the gallery rooms are contained in strong three-dimensional figures (what we refer to in office parlance as 'doughnut' and 'horseshoe') dominating the composition and linked with smaller elements in supporting roles.

The Cornell Performing Arts Centre for example, consists of large discrete volumes containing theatre, studios, foyer and workshops, all about the same size though of varying shape. To hold together the variety of these 'pavilions' they are arranged behind a grand loggia which also provides a processional route along the site. This dominant figure establishes a clear identity for the project; at the same time, the pavilions interact with the scale and geometry of adjacent buildings and streets to integrate the project into the context.

These "urban" projects are intended as a re-reading and commentary on the complex patterns and textures of the city. They derive their form and character not merely from functional and physical constraints, but also through the incorporation and/or definition of new boulevards, plazas, courtyards, pathways and other open spaces which enrich the life of the public realm. Our intention is that they can transform the pre-existing situation into a richer dialogue between past and present, and this is done neither by the use of ingratiating historic pastiche nor by undue deference to the *status quo.*

The housing designs for Runcorn and Lima, and the Paternoster redevelopment scheme for London make use of repetitive grids or repeating patterns to rationalise and resolve complex programmes; but for large projects on green-field sites, we prefer to avoid these expedients. Instead, we analyse the brief closely and then seek a strong individual formal expression for the various parts, giving each a sense of architectural individuality. In the Bayer Research Centre competition entry for example, we organised the blocks of laboratory buildings as clusters, grouped in various ways to give each research department its own identity. Overall cohesion was achieved by means of a radial plan which focused all the departments on a central garden with a symbolically-placed administration building at its centre.

This use of an architectural image (rather than an abstract planning geometry) to organise large projects is again evident in Temasek Polytechnic, Singapore, where four separate schools acquire individual identity through an overall organisational strategy based on a 'horseshoe' entrance plaza enclosed by the main administration facilities common to all the schools. Other large projects, such as the Siemens Research Centre or the Florence Administrative Centre are also planned as a series of clear parts within a strong overall image on the ground.

Occasionally, we use collage and "pasted together" pieces of architecture to make up a plan. We explored this in our suggestions for modifying Nolli's plan of Rome and developed it further in the Berlin Wissenschaftszentrum project and the British Telecom HQ at Milton Keynes. In these designs elements of the project are accommodated in familiar building forms or fragments, some of which are positioned in response to objective constraints and the rest randomly disposed around a garden or plaza, overlapping as required so that the necessary functional connections can be provided between them.

Sometimes the need for phased construction is a significant factor in designing the basic organisation of a project so that it can accommodate either planned or unpredictable future additions. In such circumstances we develop an organisational diagram which will provide functional integrity, architectural image, and character when the first stage of construction is finished but which allows for later addition without disrupting that functionality and character. These strategies range from providing for delay of a building element in a pre-determined overall composition as in the university arts centres for St. Andrews, Cornell, and the Braun factory; the use of incremental linear systems in the Dorman Long HQ, the Olivetti Training Centre, and the Siemens Research Centre; and radiating systems in the Bayer Research Centre and Temasek Polytechnic. These incremental types are designed to allow outward expansion from fixed central or end cores by additions at the extremities. The degree of initial and ultimate integrity required between original and added parts, and the extent of

reorganisation which can be tolerated at each stage of expansion, determines which strategy is adopted.

Depending on the particularities of brief and context, we use different strategies to organise the composition of parts, but in all of them, pedestrian circulation is the dynamic and motivating element. (This is deliberately in contrast to the 'plan libre' approach in which all kinds of activities and circulation mix together inside neutral, all-embracing skins.) The public and institutional nature of many of our projects has led us to concentrate on development of the *promenade architecturelle* as a fundamental concern. In projects for museums, arts centres, and theatres, which are used by large numbers of people, our primary aim is to establish coherent processional routes along which people will move, organised with as much richness and subtlety as possible. To achieve this we use sequences of rooms, ramps, stairs, and transparent lifts to guide people through the buildings and the spaces between them. Even on sites where the space for manœuvre is very constrained (as at the Clore Gallery, London) we organise and pace the sequence of arrival and entry so that visitors are gently guided through level and direction changes, encouraging the eye and mood to change in readiness for the specialised and controlled environments of the interior.

Between the late 1970s and 1980s we designed a series of L-shaped additions to older buildings. Our interest in responding to the specific attributes and particularities of site and context led us to generate buildings which, in massing, detailing, and use of materials, reflect those of their neighbours. At Harvard, the Sackler extension to the Fogg Museum wraps its L-shape round a corner of the site to make a more coherent city block. In Texas, our extension to the Architecture School at Rice University encloses a sheltered outdoor space, interlocking with the older building to form a larger and more significant whole. The L-shape of the Clore Gallery in London creates a courtyard in front of the entrance.

In one or two cases, the additions to existing buildings on very narrow sites has led us to use a strategy of "façade" buildings, as in the designs for the Berlin Hotel and the Theatre Workshop addition in Stuttgart in which a thin strip of new accomodation is superimposed like a veneer and provides a new street façade.

In earlier years we felt reluctant to become involved in projects for refurbishment and restoration, a field in which we had no experience and which requires a high degree of specialised knowledge and expertise; however we eventually succumbed. In accepting an invitation to design the extension to Rice University School of Architecture we discovered that to integrate the new with the old and incorporate large public spaces at the centre, we would also need to intervene on the existing fabric. We were permitted to do this and in the event discovered how the interplay between old and new can produce rich architectural results. Since then, we have carried out other projects involving modification of existing buildings. At Jesse Hartley's classic Albert Dock in Liverpool, the need for conservation was greater than

at Rice. In converting the 19th century iron and brick warehouses to accommodate new galleries for the Tate Gallery, the needs of modification, conservation, and restoration had to be reconciled and much of our work had to be carried out in close collaboration with specialist architects and engineers familiar with Hartley's buildings and conversant with the correct techniques of preservation.

In Milan, the 18th-century Palazzo Citterio had undergone far-reaching and partially complete transformations by the time we were appointed to convert it as an extension to the Brera Museum. It was thus possible to modify the existing building in places as well as adding a new extension, and this gave us the freedom to create an interplay between old and new. However, in converting the most important surviving monumental spaces of the building, we will be consulting closely with local experts.

In these three cases, restructuring and refurbishment works were possible because the buildings were not in the most strictly protected category of historical and architectural importance. Provided we worked sensitively and in consultation with the experts, we were permitted to make limited alterations, inserting new public spaces and circulation routes into the interstices of the pre-existing buildings without destroying them. We have done this in a manner which clearly expresses where we have intervened, by contrasting our new elements against the original fabric. In this process we have overcome our earlier reticence and discovered a strong parallel between such conversion projects and the task of teasing new public buildings into the established urban fabric of cities.

The architects who have worked with us in the office were selected with great care and we were fortunate to be able to bring together teams of talented and dedicated designers, all of whom were encouraged to exert their influence on the architecture. Their names are all credited in the résumé of projects, and the two volumes of the monograph are a testament to their contribution. Jim's untimely death means that working in the office can hardly be the same; but his spirit remains with us and we will endeavour to continue the task of producing buildings of quality, vigour and unpredictability, as the best tribute to the inheritance he has left us.

The two volumes of this monograph cover James Stirling's entire œuvre from 1950 to 1991. Volume 1 (with Léon Krier) and Volume 2 (with Thomas Muirhead) were prepared under Jim's personal attention, and then under my own when he died leaving Volume 2 partly completed. The two volumes are thus the complete official record of his work, presented as he wished. My sincere thanks to Mary Stirling for her kind assistance, to Tom Muirhead for his passionate interest in the work, to the many architects who collaborated on the projects, and to Gerd Hatje for his patience and expertise. – M.W.

The Work of James Stirling

Robert Maxwell

Reviewing the catalogue of a recent exhibition of the work of Karl Friedrich Schinkel at the Victoria and Albert Museum, a show which covered all aspects of Schinkel's designs, one is struck by the variety and spontaneity of the work, which at the same time never ceases to be recognizably Schinkelesque. Whatever the genre, the work is imprinted with a characteristic luminosity and logic. It combines exuberance with precision, experiment with control; it is so positive, so adventurous, so architectural, that one's feeling for the possibilities inherent in architecture is renewed. It seems that Schinkel simply loved architecture, loved doing it, and discovered such enjoyment in it that it radiates the energy that he gave to it. Much has been made of Mies van der Rohe's inheritance of Schinkel's mantle, on the assumption that Schinkel's direction would take him through the industrial austerity of the Building Academy design to the discovery of steel and glass. But this is to interpret Schinkel as nothing but a precursor, and Mies as nothing but a system of minimalist austerity. It seems to me that by comparison with his early projects, Mies later allowed his native inventiveness to be constricted by technological necessity, or by his need to plead technological necessity. After he moved to America his work seems to succumb to an ideological straitjacket: only the Farnsworth House stands out as a truly lyrical event. The architect who best parallels Schinkel's exuberance of invention in the twentieth century is, rather, James Stirling.[1]

This is a large claim, and it may be made out of prejudice as much as of insight; and the critic will be dead long before he has been proved right or wrong. If Le Corbusier's name were proposed, these doubts would not arise, but it is difficult to see in Le Corbusier anything approaching the geniality of Schinkel – the early nineteenth century figure *he* calls to mind is Beethoven. Whether Stirling's work is as great as Schinkel's is a moot point: the rate at which History is all the time speeding up may contribute to its being sooner forgotten.

Reviewing the work Stirling has produced since 1972, it is not difficult to see it as imbued with a geniality akin to that of Schinkel. One is struck by its variety and spontaneity, by its positive character, by a certain luminosity and logic that mark it, and by the sense of enjoyment that emanates from it. In addition, we find a willingness to embrace a use of the classical axis as a structuring device, while combining it with more or less accidental features. This combination evidently affords him great satisfaction: The classical is at the same time affirmed and denied, but its very presence as a point of reference is an aspect of his work which carries us back to Schinkel. One does not speak of Stirling as a classical architect – he is plainly a modern – but the awareness of classical or neo-classical antecedents is a recurring motif of his designs.

If we speak of the classical in Stirling it is not to imply any kind of revivalist tendency, but rather to suggest that he was interested in the idea of a sort of generic classicism, of the kind that Colin Rowe claimed to find in the work of Le Corbusier. Indeed, it is likely that Rowe's interpretation of the classical as a recurring incitement to mannerism, was adopted by Stirling as a *modus vivendi*: while he never hesitated in welcoming modernism, and aimed to be an exponent of it, and was fascinated by Le Corbusier as an exponent of it, he envisaged a modernism that had evolved out of classicism and was still imprinted with rational principles. These are expressed as a preference for the right angle, the regular grid, clear-cut hard-edge forms and a sense of frontality and measure. On occasions this preference results in large broadly symmetrical and even neo-classical layouts such as that for Bayer AG (1978). Frequently it results in the use of a dominant axis of symmetry, as in the project for the Bibliothèque de France (1989), with its overtones of Ledoux [*Ills.* 1 and 2].

In the design for the Sainsbury Wing at the National Gallery in London, there is a definite preponderance of the classical [*Ill.* 3]. It is clear in the plan that all the important spaces are arranged on a single north-south axis, which is also orthogonal to the main building, and only the ground level departs from this principle by the placing of the entrance at right angles, facing back to the main building, and leaving the central axis to terminate with a bay window. Thus the main axis is plainly stated, and the turning of the axis is achieved within an axial convention, if rather brusquely. In addition, the presentation of the plans, with a shadow-line emphasizing the wall masses which are filled in with pink, speaks of a continuing respect for – and so interest in – the nineteenth-century classical tradition.

However, this brusque turning of the main axis is profoundly anti-classical, and there are other anti-classical features such as the blocking of the axial space by a square column placed on the diagonal in both the entrance bay and the bay window. Most important, too, is the method of articulating the various elements of the volumetric layout, so that the volume nearest the street may appear as detached and wholly directed towards the main building. The coved cornice, similar to that employed in the Staatsgalerie, adds emphasis to this mass, but is restricted to the walls parallel to the street, and discontinued across the "side" which contains the entrance. Although all these elements are thoroughly organised around the classical parti, they do not follow the classical rules of composition, but contradict them at many points. Classicism reappears, but at the service of a more abstract language of form. At one level, the classical is denied; at another it is renovated.

The freedom to play with classical forms without conforming to strictly classical principles is the basis for much of Stirling's work, and this has led to its being labelled as post-modernist. But this label ignores the intensive relationship that he cultivates between classical and anti-classical elements, which suggests rather a

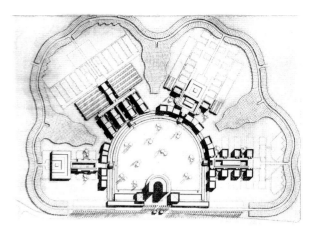

1. James Stirling and Michael Wilford
Headquarters for Bayer AG, Monheim, Germany, 1978
Layout plan

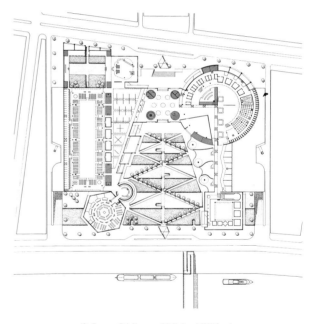

2. James Stirling and Michael Wilford
Bibliothèque de France, Paris, 1989
Layout plan

continuing fascination with the aims of mannerism as expounded by Rowe: that is, to achieve the satisfaction of breaking the rules. This satisfaction cannot exist if the rules are flaccid and yielding to begin with; in Stirling's case the rules are plainly stated, indeed presented with a strong sense of discipline, before being broken. They are respected for themselves, and for what they represent. This respect for the rules suggests an acute awareness of

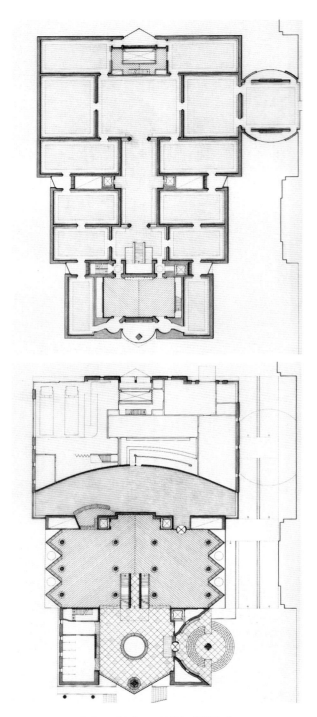

3. James Stirling and Michael Wilford
National Gallery Extension, London, 1985
Sainsbury Wing, ground and first floor plans

the art of architecture as it has evolved over the centuries, and it is this awareness, and his intimate knowledge of architecture as an evolving art form, that gives his work an intellectual edge and raises it to a level where one can begin to think of a master like Schinkel. This is equivalent to calling him a master of mannerism. In addition, the character of his work has changed – in step with the times, certainly – as interest has shifted to the civic role of architecture.

Whereas his early works were often on the margins of the university campus, or on green-field sites, his continually more important commissions have led him to consider the special demands of urban sites, and thus to become involved with the urban context, both in terms of the surrounding buildings and the history of the site. And this has also brought him to consider urban values that may be as much symbolic as factual, and that relate to the imponderable character of human institutions. That he should identify these conditions as requiring a "positively civic and populist" approach[2] indicates that he is interested not only in satisfying function in the narrow sense, but also in communicating civic qualities to the people who use his buildings as elements of the city.

The new importance given to civic qualities begins with the competition designs prepared for a number of German cities, starting with the Düsseldorf project of 1975, continuing with the project for the Wallraf-Richartz Museum at Cologne in the same year, and culminating with the 1977 design for the Staatsgalerie in Stuttgart, a successful design which has been built, and for which there are currently plans to extend it through the development of the adjacent site with buildings for the Music and Theatre Academies. This complex if completed will amount to a major contribution to the urban design of Stuttgart, providing definition to the northern margin of the central park in which is situated the State Opera House, and creating for the latter a civic garden in which a local monument – the Schicksalsbrunnen or Fountain of Destiny – will be placed on the axis of

4. James Stirling and Michael Wilford
Stuttgart, Staatsgalerie, Music and Theatre Academies, 1977–1987
Photo of model

the Opera House, thus ending a long exile during which it was preserved on a temporary site within the park. This is clearly a project with great importance for the rounding out of the civic space of Stuttgart [*Ill.* 4].

These projects show an extremely sensitive understanding of the place of architecture in the public realm, and of the degree to which civic dignity should be confirmed or challenged by a building thrown up by contemporary conditions. The Opera garden is no less marked by Stirling's hand than the other parts, but is comparatively restrained and even subdued. In contrast, the spaces contained by the individual institutions are full of a dynamic tension between the axial demands of the institution and the contingent demands of public access through the site. The public footpath "invades" the Staatsgalerie in its apparently most sensitive part – the central rotunda – which is also left unroofed, so that it belongs to the urban landscape rather than to the interior of the museum; similarly, a public footpath will emerge into the courtyard formed between the new Music and Theatre Academies, and erupt diagonally into the central park. The right of access is thus juxtaposed with the axiality of the institutions to provide, at a symbolic level, a statement of democratic values. In a similar way, important details of the buildings such as the Museum entrance hall and all the porches constructed of steel members are conceived in a free and uninhibited way using elements of modern technology, expressive of youthful irreverence rather than of aged dignity. Stirling sees his work up to this time as oscillating between extremes of *abstract* and *representational* elements –

"...but significantly, in recent designs (particularly the Staatsgalerie), the extremes are being counterbalanced and expressed in the *same* building... We hope the Staatsgalerie is monumental, because that is the tradition for public buildings, particularly museums. We also hope that it is informal and populist – hence the anti-monumentalism of the meandering footpath, the voided centre, the colouring and much else."[3]

In identifying two extremes in *abstraction* and *representation* – extremes between which his work has oscillated – Stirling is naming the poles of a dialectic which bears considerable resemblance to the famous dialectic acknowledged by Le Corbusier when he defined a man as "a brain and a heart, reason and passion..."[4] The abstract forms to which Stirling refers are by his own definition specifically modern, sometimes technological or "high-tech"; the representational forms are "obviously" so, that is are familiar, even traditional. Modern abstract forms are derived from the analysis of new opportunities and problems thrown up by material progress; a process of *reason*. Representational forms are derived from precedent, they depend on a degree of familiarity to be recognizable or to suggest the thing they represent; a process of memory and of identification with the human condition, the preconditions for *passion*. In the current evolutionary phase of modern architecture, the rational pursuit of a technological destiny is the force behind high-tech; while traditional values, with the

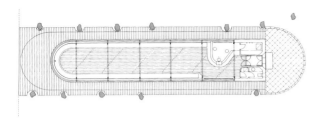

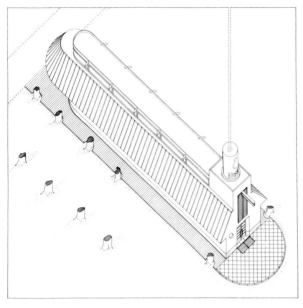

5. James Stirling and Michael Wilford, Thomas Muirhead
Electa Bookshop in the Biennale Gardens, Venice, 1989
Plan, axonometric projection

attempt to exclude all abstract thought, are responsible for a wave of classical revivalism. In practice, neither approach can be entirely free from some element of the other, given the fact that both are inevitably steeped in the rhetoric of presentation, but it is still significant that Stirling is able to admit to his system of thought two extremes that are popularly considered to be mutually exclusive – and particularly to the extent that they have given rise to a public polemic in England with two opposing parties for each of which the other is anathema. Moreover, it is highly significant that, whereas in Stirling's work these extremes were formerly present in different projects, they are now seen to be present together, being "counter-balanced and expressed in the *same* building".

This dialectical balance can be seen as a deepening and widening of the mannerist "game" of simultaneously stating and breaking the rules, which we have suggested is fundamentally congenial to Stirling. What, at the beginning, was more of a personal preference has now been acknowledged as part of a polemic, allowing him to present each work in a framework of values that are accessible to a wide public, while also remaining within a narrow history of architecture as an evolving art. What has not changed is the underlying interest in the tensions of a dialectical opposition. This allows us to see that Stirling, in adapting to the contextualism brought in by post-modern conditions, remained true to his innate view of architecture as a play of forms.

There is one recent project that seems to embody within itself this enjoyment of internal tensions, and that by its very compactness encapsulates the ambiguity within a small compass. That is the Biennale Bookshop at Venice [*Ill.* 5].

Since Venice is synonymous with water and the site faces the lagoon, it is natural that the metaphor of vessel – it is a "boat-shop" – should apply. This metaphor allows the design to be inwardly intensive and self immersed – as befits the ruminative occupation of browsing among books – and yet to take up the natural axiality of a vessel with clearly defined stem and stern. The light modular structure is like one of the steel loggias turned in on itself; while the entrance front, the stem or bow in nautical terms, declares its unique frontality in a purely architectural way, being uncompromisingly civic in character. While the sides and rear "float" in the park of trees, the front is anchored towards the approach path like a sort of pilgrimage chapel. It raises itself to a cupola in the form of a cylindrical volume bearing a sign, which also launches a single laser beam towards outer space. Whereas the concept of the "boat-shop" is integral, and governs the outcome tightly, many alternatives were considered for the entrance front. The least differentiated would have been the one that completes the roof overhang with a square end, to contrast with the rounded end, and it is interesting that this approach ("less-is-more") was rejected in favour of one that stresses the civic status of the building. There is no literal narrative here, we don't need to see only the boatiness of the form. With the increased vertical volume, due to the addition of a servicing room and a gantry for dealing with plant, we are instead given a second metaphor – a reference to the canal architecture of Amsterdam, with its civic frontage combining bourgeois pride with practical necessity – another restatement of the continuing dialectic that we have identified in Stirling's work. That so much should be packed into such a small building without overloading it is a mark of the ease with which he operates and the integral nature of his thought.

Apart from the dialectical method which controls the system of oppositions that are to be found to a greater or less extent in all the works, the Venice bookshop also embodies certain Stirlingesque characteristics that are present in all of them. There is a relaxed quality that responds directly to the function. The control of the natural lighting by the projecting eaves produces an intimate scale reminiscent of the early work of Frank Lloyd Wright. The eye is directed down to the continuous shelf of books on display, for which the light falls from the high clear-story above, but at any moment it can rise for relief to look out into the leafy park and the esplanade, just as the all-round windows in the *vaporetto* allow one to scan the watery horizon. The metaphor of boat-shop is thoroughly integrated with the function of book-shop. An intimate scale of use predominates, and many users will enjoy a pleasant experience without even being aware of the architectural reverberations that surround them. The exact definition of space through the placement of the peripheral display and the reception desk are reminiscent of the young Stirling who enjoyed the design of tight spaces within a small compass.

Yet, as with Schinkel, we are dealing with an architect who will never hesitate to embark on a large-scale project, and go in search of novel effects that can be unexpected and even stupendous in their impact.

Thus, to balance the intimacy of the little opera-house at the Cornell Centre for the Performing Arts, Mozartian in its scale, we can adduce the grand throw of the auditorium for the Los Angeles Philharmonic hall, with its complete circle of projecting balconies of seats at different levels. We *know* that Stirling did not proceed to offer a philharmonic hall without preparing himself by a study of precedent, including of course Scharoun's Philharmonie at Berlin. The play of distinct ranges of seating challenges Scharoun's concept of the interior to be read at the scale of a landscape, without violating classical principles that prefer it to be geometrically symmetrical and complete; but outside the auditorium he does not hesitate to employ escalators arranged asymetrically in a dynamic group that reflects the excitement of the crowd moving informally in the interval. The evident enjoyment of the movement system that challenges the static consequences of construction is again a recurring theme. We find it clearly expressed in the inclined spiral ramp of the Cultural Centre atrium in the Kyoto Centre competition entry, for example, where it plays against the huge suspended volumes to create an atmosphere of futuristic excitement suitable to a populist institution. All such emphasis on the intrusion of the populist element – as with the public ramp at the Staatsgalerie – seems to me to carry us back to the Corbusian use of the ramp at Poissy, where it both breaks and reaffirms the central axis of a classically ordered composition. Where Schinkel may be thought to stand for Stirling as a figure of emulation, Le Corbusier must stand more intimately as the point of departure.

Whether the projects are small or huge in scope, there is one Stirlingesque quality that seems to remain constant: this is the desire to play with space both internally and externally. In really large ensembles, we do not find all the space sucked into one massive interior, but a balance between what is required to make a satisfactory culmination internally, and what is required to provide units of building that can be allowed to express different characters, allowing the complex as a whole to be absorbed into a city environment. Thus in the Kyoto Centre, we are given a whole group of buildings: Cultural

Centre, department store, hotel, each one has a distinctive character, and though they combine to form a line of development along the railway tracks, they are organised in relation to the two new bridges that span the tracks and that aim to draw together the two parts of town separated by the chasm of the railroad. Unlike some of the competing designs, there is no intention to dramatise the new development as a "wall" of separation, but rather as a seam of junction. We may note also in this design that a Japanese character is employed for the gateway that leads into the Cultural Centre, but this is not a pastiche of the traditional form but a reinterpretation of it in terms that might have been found by a contemporary Japanese architect. Thus context, whether cultural or physical, is always the source of particularity in the proposals.

Perhaps the most important example of the way that Stirling operates within a space of his own creation is the recently completed complex for the Braun headquarters at Melsungen. Stirling has made a number of designs for industrial clients: the Dorman Long headquarters of 1965; Siemens AG, Munich, 1969; Olivetti headquarters, Milton Keynes, 1971; Bayer AG, Mannheim, 1978; British Telecom, 1983. All of these remain projects, and their forms constitute a rich repertoire of possibilities, yet remain sketches rather than fulfillments. With Braun Melsungen we are dealing with a first phase of construction which nevertheless is essentially a complete building. How do Stirling's ideas, with their recurring themes that are both architectural and civic, translate to the realm of private enterprise? The answer must be: triumphantly. Although the client is private, and the scheme conceived within strict economic constraints, the results enlarge rather than merely reflect the fundamental Stirling preoccupations. This is not to deny the contribution made in this project by Walter Nägeli, formerly the

architect in charge of Stirling and Wilford's Berlin office, here a collaborator, which may in part account for its freshness. It is also, as functional programme, completely up-to-date, largely autonomized and controlled, even to the details of production, by computer. Representing the most typical building programme of advanced technological society, the project demands our close attention.

The complex is situated in a broad and shallow valley. Entering the locality one passes under a magnificent concrete railway viaduct, and the strange harmony between a clean technological form and an idyllic rural setting has evidently been one source of inspiration for the architects. The spreading layout of the complex generates long horizontals that put one in mind of bridges and dams, and bridge and dam are celebrated in the form of this building.

The layout is strung out in the form of a giant T. The head cross-piece, which backs on to one side of the valley, is the long shed for production, only about one-sixth of which is yet constructed [*Ill.* 6]. The stem, at right angles, takes the form of a giant double concrete wall containing staircases, which gather up newly arrived pedestrians from seven levels of car parking concealed behind it. This wall also serves to conceal the goods distribution centre, which occupies the bulk of the site, of which about 80% is already constructed. At the far end, an elliptical loading shed feeds twenty-two trucks backed into separate bays. The wall is clearly a "Wall", and in its metaphoric rôle acts as a sort of dam controlling the pent-up pressure of products. The circulation that parallels it takes the form of a glass-enclosed bridge spanning the valley on angled timber supports in full view of the approaching visitor, and commanding a full view of the front of the site. This glazed circulation space is clearly the equivalent of the colonnade at Cornell (and proposed in the library for Latina), it performs the same rôle of symbolizing the public realm and embracing the landscape, placing the building metaphorically, as well as actually, in a setting of earth and sky.

The terrain which it embraces here is deliberately treated as an ideal landscape within an English tradition where landscaping implies no less than the aesthetisation of life, artifice enclosing reality. The bubbling lake is fed by a sinuous canal that at the same time defines the car circulation, so gathering up the approach roads into an ideal landscape form. The two roads, separated by the canal, are functionally differentiated, one being the public route to the parking building, the other leading to the main entrance and strictly controlled. This juxtaposition, not obvious to the casual visitor but evident to the frequent user, provides an additional twist of meaning within the suavity of the form. Artifice encloses a reality that is already marked with difference and discrepancy – a further example of Stirling's enjoyment of mannerist opposition.

From this bald description it will already be evident that the layout encompasses both practical and metaphoric aspects, making this factory both a direct

response to the programme of capitalist management and at the same time an attempt to transcend its own instrumentality and lay claim to an existence-mode appropriate to a work of art.

While the wall which conceals the parking building clearly creates a front and a back, there is another frontage implied by the convex face of the administration building, which screens the production shed from the north-east. That this is another case of front-and-back is evident when we realise that the administration building, raised up on stilts, is concave in form where it looks back across the countryside to the mediaeval town of Melsungen, where the Braun family began their saga over a century before. This curved building is remarkable in every way: it comes solidly to ground at both ends, so that it embodies the idea of an arch, perhaps a triumphal arch.

The stilts in a single row[5] that support the offices, however, are a far cry from the standard cylindrical columns dear to Le Corbusier: they are the conical capitals of such stilts, already beloved of Stirling, now enlarged and supported on squat cubic bases clad in dark brick [*Ill.* 7]. These supports thus consist only of base and capital, the intervening shaft having dissolved into nothingness. In many conditions of light even their function as supports is dematerialized, the two parts disconnect, and the capitals appear rather to depend from the building as enormous funnels from which, it appears, surplus information not required for the computer centre is collected in containers placed beneath. Or they can be seen as strangely animal in character, like a reincarnation of the Roman wolf mother. Modern information systems are thus given a mythic connection to the founders of Rome as the first instigators of a political system organised through privileged information and the division of society into distinct classes. Or at least, the forms permit, if they do not sanction, such a reading. They need and invite interpretation.

Every part of this complex building has been designed in a way that, while fulfilling its immediate technical or

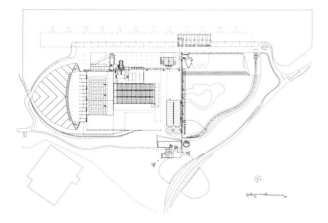

functional requirements, goes beyond the rational satisfaction of needs, which characterises the modern style, to adumbrate a universe of metaphoric equivalences. The parts, dislodged from their ordinary meanings, become signs in an obscure and suggestive language. Those signs cohere, if indeed they do, by no patent rational narrative, but by another more mythic narrative whose import is as clouded as the forms that point to it are strong. Stirling thus positions himself far from Robert Venturi, who prefers to employ weak forms that, while suggestive, remain clearly fragile and emblematic. The paradox that is raised by the use of "strong" forms is that their strength, which appears to resist any attempt to dismiss them as "merely" decorative, at the same time invites the possibility that the whole material reality of the building is to take on the destiny of a work of decorative art, a figment of the imagination.

Perhaps the clearest example of this adumbration of a new language is the principle facade of the production shed. This is intended to be, on completion, a long building, the sort that the Italian rationalists liked to propose for universities on greenfield sites. The structure is big, since the interior of the shed must be column-free, so we have a kind of impressive giant order. Yet each bay must harbour a cylindrical container for the plastic granules that are the raw materials of manufacture, held under pressure, and distributed to the work points by compressed air. These vats block the classical bays, "spoiling" the neo-classical reading of the ensemble. They are exposed not only as a visual device but because they have to be regularly replenished by machines which naturally work from the access road. Yet this rational and empirical disposition forces them, as it were unwillingly, to articulate the bays of the production shed, to be pressed into an architectural service that has the rhythm of a neo-classical museum.

In the excess of expression, and perhaps beauty, over utility, the architects have essayed to define a technically competent modern architecture that goes beyond utility into a mythic past, not only an architectural one, so that its forms provide an echo of the history of man and a guess as to his destiny. In these terms, the industrial basis of the programme does not produce a result weakened by practical constraints, but rather tested and strengthened by them. By passing this test the work becomes the more profoundly representative of modernity in architecture, and takes us to the edge of that modernity, where it yields to the cultural limitations that place all rational efforts within an interpretative – that is, within an hermeneutic – tradition. Here the subtleties of the Biennale Bookshop, so effective in the small scale, are enlarged to a point where they become globally significant, and globally representative, of the conditions of architectural practice.

In all this richness of large and small projects, while admiring the vision and will which produces them, one inevitably has preferences. I am particularly impressed by the Staatsgalerie, which I visited only in 1990, and by the Cornell Centre for the Performing Arts, which I

visited in the same year. The experience of these buildings exceeds their promise, and both have achieved a clear popular success. One is aware of a genial quality in the outcome, a genuine concern for the user and for function as a source of new form; yet always there is also present a sense of exploration in the purely architectural realm, that is, in the discourse of architecture as an essential part of the expression of an epoch. It is extraordinary to find in one firm's work such a versatility in dealing with circumstances, and such a steadfast pursuit of the purely architectural.

Footnotes

1 In this essay I have used the name Stirling to refer to the work of James Stirling, Michael Wilford, and others, as well as in discussing the characteristics of Stirling's personal style and philosophy. Without special knowledge, it is impossible to determine the contribution of each partner, and this work must be left to the care of some future historian. Obviously, Michael Wilford is an equal partner in the firm, and his contribution must be acknowledged as important and in many cases, crucial.

2 Stirling: *Design Philosophy and Recent Work,* in: *Architectural Design,* Special issue 1990, London, Academy Editions, p. 8.

3 "Our work has oscillated between the most 'abstract' modern (even High-Tech), such as the Olivetti training school, and the obviously 'representational', even traditional, for instance the Rice University School of Architecture. These extremes have characterised our work since we began, but significantly, in recent designs (particularly the Staatsgalerie), the extremes are being counterbalanced and expressed in the *same* building.
   Prior to 1975 our buildings were mainly in the semi-private category – schools and university buildings – often in greenfield or suburban sites. It is only with the more recent museum designs that our architecture has, I hope, become positively civic and populist." Stirling: Opus cit., pp. 7, 8.

4 "...a man is a brain and a heart, reason and passion. Reason knows only the absolute of current science, while passion is the vibrant force which tends to attract whatever is at hand." Le Corbusier: *In Defense of Architecture: letter to Kanel Teige,* tr. George Baird et al., in: *Oppositions 4,* I.A.U.S./Wittenborn, New York, October 1974; originally published in: *Stavba 2,* Prague, 1929; original French text in: *L'Architecture d'Aujourd'hui,* No. 10, 1933, p. 38.

5 The single row of stilts, as invented by Le Corbusier in the Swiss Hostel, Paris, is a motif we find in Stirling as early as 1950, when his Thesis at Liverpool University featured a single row of conical stilts that diminished downwards to a tight base on the ground.

MODERNISM AND THE URBAN TRADITION
Stirling's mature architectural method in four museum projects of the 1970s

Thomas Muirhead

She and I ... both being loose in New York for the afternoon, went to a museum together. It was a new one, recently completed after the plan of a recently dead American wizard ... my companion and I dutifully wound our way down the exitless slope, locked in a wizard's spell ... suddenly, as she lurched backward from one especially explosive painting, her high heels were tricked by the slope, and she fell against me and squeezed my arm ... John Updike, *Museums and Women*

The continuous spiral of Frank Lloyd Wright's Guggenheim Museum is often condemned as his wrong-headed way of making it impossible for people to look at paintings properly. Frontal vision of the pictures is impeded, and visitors are obliged to perform gyrations and circumlocutions which allow only fragmentary, interrupted glances at whatever is on show, reducing the art to something seen *en passant*. As ever with Wright, functional correctness was only part of the higher exigency of creating dynamic space, and anyhow, the way the Guggenheim Museum works is simply an acknowledgment of reality. We perceive our surroundings by way of fleeting and confused impressions much more than from logical analysis and clear observation; in fact, we often don't really listen or look very carefully at all. This is now allowed by contemporary thinking, as in *Le Plaisir du Texte,* where Roland Barthes frees himself of cultural *angst* by confessing that he reads erratically (and erotically) – deliberately missing out whole chunks of Proust. After thinkers like Barthes we need not worry if our enjoyment and understanding of art, music, or architecture is fragmentary, incomplete, and chaotic. According to mood or time of day, we sift and select, ignoring this, editing that. Wright's design for the Guggenheim is therefore no more than an acceptance of reality and an admission that when you and I go to a museum for the afternoon, we do not behave "functionally".

The subtly erotic experience at the Guggenheim, described by Updike, recounts how we go to such places perhaps because we have time on our hands, or we seek gratification of some vague desire; what we have in mind may be more complex than just looking at works of art. Dallying, flirtation, seeing and being seen, are important parts of our life, and just as a *beau monde* always admired itself at Versailles, Sabbioneta, Palazzo Pitti, today we display ourselves in places where there is nothing more to do than stand around and socialise, at events whose declared purpose may be little more than an excuse for looking at, and commenting upon, the behaviour of others. So we still need places which have no specific function and which lend themselves to people-watching,

whether it be in hotel lobbies, departure lounges, or street corners; but people-watching is at its best when given a good setting, perhaps in fine rooms adorned with works of art – in museums.

James Stirling knew this, and the importance of his architecture may in fact prove to have been his ability to express how we fragmentarily inhabit, perceive, and enjoy the world as our perceptions of it present themselves in casual, superimposed, distorted, imprecisely understood ways on which order may temporarily be imposed but which exist independently of our volition, in a confusion which can have no final resolution. Recognizing this, what he did in his work was to divulge – out of a most personal kind of erudition – the numerous architectures he found inhabiting his mind and which it never occurred to him to banish for the sake of some flat purism.

Earlier projects of the 1960s (illustrated in Vol. 1 of the present work) show him breaking away from the somewhat conventional "regional modernism" of earlier years and venturing into a much more problematic and unclear world, where ideology would not work and stylistic correctness would fail to reassure. By the early 1970s (where this second Volume begins) he was experimenting with an open architectural style which strove to appear both rustic and sophisticated, popular and elitist, monumental and informal, modernist and traditional, all at the same time, not entrenching itself in any fixed aesthetic. Terms such as *both/and, inclusion, contamination, ambiguity* became some of his favourite expressions.

For such a *forma mentis,* there could hardly be a more congenial typology than the museum, repository of accumulated image banks, of collected paintings and sculptures, through which to wander in contemplation, enjoying the continuously shifting viewpoints afforded by stairs and ramps as they rise and fall, strolling in conversation through *enfilades* of formal rooms with long vistas and unexpected close-ups; the city in microcosm.

Under the influence of his teacher Colin Rowe, Stirling had taken as given that architecture's wider purpose is to make cities. Rejecting abstract planning for its destruction of urban values, he relied instead on actual experience (following Camillo Sitte's pragmatic method in *The Art of Building Cities*) and assumed that modern architecture's paramount task is to carry the urban tradition forward, using new languages to make buildings which create proper urban space around themselves.

Prior to 1975 (where this volume begins) Stirling had worked only in England on projects for enclosed places like university colleges, set apart from the larger community and not easily accessible to a more general populace; this, as it turns out, was a limitation, and an attempt to escape from it was first seen in the cosmopolitan grandeur of the plaza for the city of Derby (*ill.* 1), surely more borbonic Naples than the centre of a rain-swept English town. That this was never built is perhaps because it shows an attitude to urban transformation which is anything but timid.

1. James Stirling and Michael Wilford
Derby Civic Centre competition, 1970
Perspective of the plaza

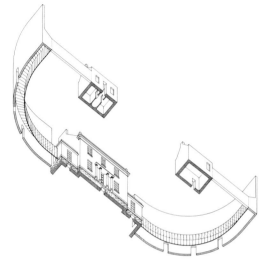

2. James Stirling and Michael Wilford
Arts Centre, St. Andrews University, 1972
Up axonometric of the courtyard

3. Sir John Vanbrugh
Castle Howard, Yorkshire, 1725
Bird's eye view from the north
(from Colen Campbell's *Vitruvius Britannicus*)

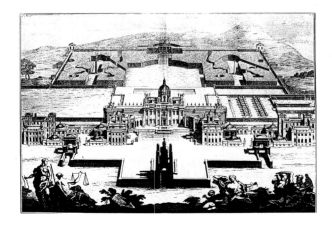

4. Sir Edwin Lutyens
Heathcote, Ilkley, Yorkshire, 1906

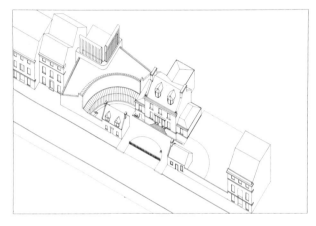

5. James Stirling and Michael Wilford
Arts Centre, St. Andrews University, 1972. Axonometric

6. James Stirling and Michael Wilford
Arts Centre, St. Andrews University, 1972
Comparative location plans

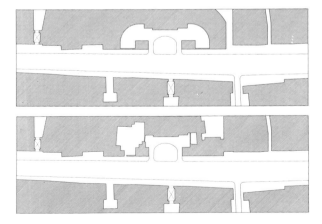

St. Andrews

A similar energy characterises his first project for an art gallery (*ill.* 2) in the Scottish university town of St. Andrews which, significantly for his subsequent work, had a densely urban location. The distorted palladianism of the layout continues an English tradition of reinterpretation which saw Palladio's ideas modified by Lord Burlington, their baroque inflation in the hands of a Vanbrugh (*ill.* 3), and their subtle infiltration into modernism through the work of such architects as Lutyens (*ill.* 4). Such distortion was congenial to Stirling and St. Andrews continues in the same vein; the palladianism, licentious and disobedient, allows itself to be violated by hints of other architectures which reappear in strange guises and happily interfere with one another as Palladio gets mixed up with suggestions of Scottish Baronial and echoes of Adam.

In spite of this, the scheme is mostly conscious of itself as a piece of modern architecture (*ill.* 5); the video projections, the smoothly curving walls, the high-tech rise-and-fall mobile partitions dramatically expressed on the roof, announce that Stirling, who grew up in Glasgow and Liverpool, was expressing the spirit of Revivalism not to break faith with modern architecture but to contextualise it in the history of the city. The before-and-after location plans of the St. Andrews scheme (*ill.* 6) show how by means of an appreciative, though irreverent, re-reading of the values and meanings of the existing buildings and spaces, they can be reorganised to extend the space of the street into a new courtyard, introducing a focal point which completely transforms the situation.

Thus the St. Andrews project is informed by a serious intent to rework urban form, more urgent than mere considerations of style or *décor,* showing that – when carried through with erudition and boldness – pursuance of a modernist image of the city can be not only believable but highly auspicable. This scheme was not built either, perhaps once again because its architecture, although respectful, refuses to be subservient and insists that the transformation must be radical; an attitude which reached maturity of expression in the three German museum projects illustrated at the beginning of this book.

Düsseldorf

After 1945, almost nothing remained of the great historic cities of Germany, a tragedy compounded by postwar traffic engineering and weak attempts at "historical reconstruction" so that by the 1970s, the only thing left was regret for what had been lost. For Stirling, with his convictions about modernist urban design and his awareness of history, the situation was ideal. His connoisseurship (modernist collector of historical allusions) became enhanced in response to the new *milieu* and his interest in the past, his enthusiasm for the museum as a type and its heroic origins in neoclassicism (particularly

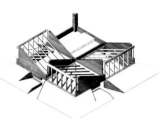

7. James Stirling
Table exhibited at the Institute of Contemporary Arts, 1951

8. James Stirling and James Gowan
School assembly hall, Camberwell, 1958–61
Axonometric of the roof construction

in Germany) combined with the need to make modern cities as beautiful as the old, led his architecture into transformations he himself could hardly have anticipated.

For Stirling's generation the inspiration was Le Corbusier, and much of his work adopted the *parti* of Le Corbusier's Salvation Army Hostel in Paris; in his student hostel in Oxford or the training centre for Olivetti, an expedient worked out by Corbu was borrowed to split the accommodation into two: a large building containing repetitive rooms and a smaller *avant-corps* for communal facilities such as dining rooms and assembly halls. *Not* derived from Le Corbusier is a four-square arrangement (its origins are unclear) used to plan projects as diverse as a table (*ill.* 7), an assembly hall (*ill.* 8) and the Expandable House (1957) (*ill.* 9) to which a circular core is added. The plan of the Nordrhein-Westfalen Museum in Düsseldorf was generated by these devices, adapted to the genius loci by allowing them to be suffused by the neoclassical flavour of Schinkel's Altes Museum in Berlin (*ill.* 10).

First stage   Second stage   Third stage   Fourth stage

9. James Stirling and James Gowan
Expandable House, 1957. Phases of expansion

10. Karl Friedrich Schinkel
Museum am Lustgarten, Berlin, 1823–30. Plan

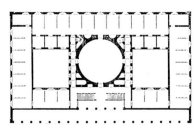

Using the corbusian *parti,* the museum is split into a large block with a smaller one in front (*ill.* 11). The four-square motif plus cylindrical core establish the building as a quadrilateral with four trees in a courtyard. The result is a playful version of the centralised plan (*ill.* 12) which recalls the stability of neoclassical prototypes of the museum, but erodes and subverts them until they collaborate in expressing a contemporary feeling. Saturating his modernism with vague echoes of reproduced Schinkel and Le Corbusier (which would not have amused either, one feels) Stirling caricatures both whilst ensuring that the building exhibits an appropriate *gravitas.*

The axonometric view shows the square mass of the main block pushed back to leave space for a plaza, embedding itself in the city block and engulfing in the process the remnants of a neoflorentine palazzo (*ill.* 13) which, no doubt to its surprise, finds itself palladianised by the addition of a pair of somewhat truncated *barchesse.* Allowing an autocthonous repertoire of forms to be blurred, corrupted, and contaminated by these external circumstances, Stirling's building is in turn violated by a public pathway which undulates along the reversing curve of the entrance, through and under the museum, crossing the courtyard and zigzagging out into a back street: the museum invaded by the city.

Other projects of the mid-70s show Stirling making use again and again of the same elements. The layout of his gigantic project for Florence (*ill.* 14) is composed of two squares, one turned off-axis. In the Düsseldorf project the same squares reappear and invert each other; the larger one, and its circular courtyard, reverses itself (void to solid/solid to void) to make the front pavilion, which is skewed obliquely to create the picturesque effect of large and small volumes juxtaposed. Its neoclassical associations weaken as it turns to face the city, marking the head of a main street and announcing the museum's presence from as far away as the river (*ill.* 15).

As relief from this dialectic, the space between the museum and the entrance pavilion is occupied by the lobby, completely enclosed in glass. In this free-form place of arrival and departure, formal itineraries of the museum relax and loosen, replacing the introspection of the galleries with the relaxation of an informal meeting place which looks out to the plaza.

With resolute intelligence, the Düsseldorf museum project seizes responsibility for reconstructing the centre of the city. Recognizing the neoclassical origins of the museum type, Stirling establishes an archaeological vocation for modernism which extends its range.

Thus nourished, he demonstrates how a generous and hospitable architecture can endow the city with the amenities of a modernism informed by erudition and taste. This museum would have enriched Düsseldorf by adding a plaza raised above the traffic, where people would have strolled and socialised, enjoying spectacular outlooks across the park and along the street. It demonstrates how such buildings can create an open, informal, and cordial relationship between culture and the city.

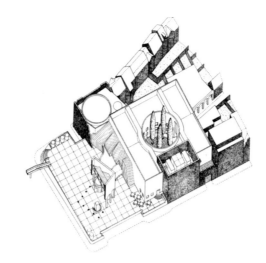

11. James Stirling and Michael Wilford
Nordrhein Westfalia Museum, Düsseldorf, 1975. Axonometric

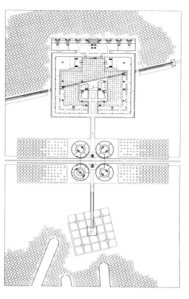

14. James Stirling and Michael Wilford
Business and Administrative Centre, Florence, 1976
Plan at plaza level

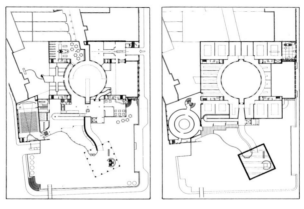

12. James Stirling and Michael Wilford
Nordrhein Westfalia Museum, Düsseldorf, 1975. Plans

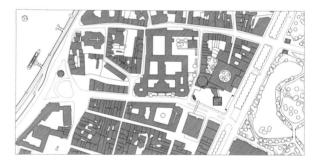

15. James Stirling and Michael Wilford
Nordrhein Westfalia Museum, Düsseldorf, 1975
Location plan

13. James Stirling and Michael Wilford
Nordrhein Westfalia Museum, Düsseldorf, 1975
Side elevation

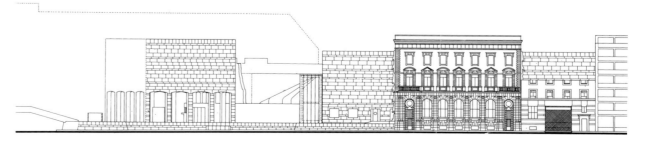

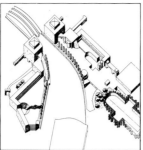

16. James Stirling and Michael Wilford
Wallraf Richartz Museum, Cologne, 1975
Axonometric views

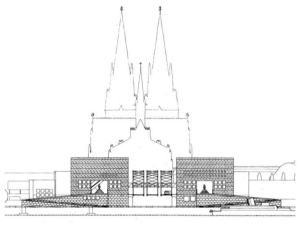

17. James Stirling and Michael Wilford
Wallraf Richartz Museum, Cologne, 1975
Elevation to the river

18. James Stirling and Michael Wilford
Wallraf Richartz Museum, Cologne, 1975
Shadow plan

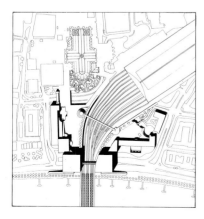

Cologne

In three dense urban sites (Düsseldorf, Cologne, and Stuttgart) Stirling introduces elements from his repertoire in ways which allow him to reinterpret the circumstances without obliterating them, engaging the functions and form of the museum in colloquium with the context, revitalising both, exploring new territory for urban design. The two bird's-eye axonometric drawings of the competition entry for the Wallraf-Richartz Museum in Cologne (*ill.* 16) show how an attentive reorganisation of bombed city centre land can be the place for introducing a *city-in-the-city* endowed with the intimacy, richness of incident, and sense of place which, captivated by the conviviality of Italian hill towns, modernism has been working to recover.

Elements of the Düsseldorf project reappear here in a different form. The circular maze is now a conical ziggurat, the cube-shaped block doubles up to make a pair of pavilions which, in Stirling's "vaguely-palladian" way, frame the railway bridge in one direction and the cathedral apse in the other (*ill.* 17). The poplar trees taken from the Düsseldorf courtyard are regrouped as a row along the edge of the plaza. Along with other inventions, these elements are shifted around, altered in scale, and massed in response to the existing buildings, engaging them in the logic of the new organisation (*ill.* 18). They are arranged in a picturesque setting of cuboid, rectangular, and cylindrical volumes containing different departments of the museum, and generate set-piece vistas which lead the eye out to the Rhine and beyond, or towards the magnificent cathedral apse.

The functional requirements of the museum are interpreted as the pretext for making a group of buildings of various size and shape overlooking a public space and with setbacks, ramps, and alleyways which create a variety of urban experience, according to precepts of city design which Camillo Sitte would certainly have endorsed and which would have lent themselves admirably to the kind of juggling, fire-eating, and general showing off which (in far less conducive circumstances) take place in front of the Centre Pompidou in Paris. From the long external ramp climbing up the front of the museum, visitors could have looked over the crowd, through the trees, to watch trains entering and leaving the station. The richness of these architectural experiences would have made Cologne into a more important place and was a lost opportunity only partly compensated for by the success, further south in Baden-Württemberg, of the extension to the Staatsgalerie in Stuttgart.

Stuttgart

The authority of the Stuttgart museum has evoked a high level of critical response, including semiological analyses concerning the signifying power of the PoMo trappings with which the building is ingratiatingly festooned; but Stirling had a deeper purpose as well. The

raison d'être of the project is to re-create in the contemporary situation, spaces and forms fit to sustain a congenial and dignified urban existence. Part of a tryptich with Düsseldorf and Cologne, the Neue Staatsgalerie is intended as a place where a heterogeneous crowd can mingle and promenade through the interior or exterior spaces of a miniature city composed of buildings of different shape and character, brought together in a tightly-knit arrangement whose outer boundaries carefully make interfaces sympathetic to the scale and character of the surroundings.

In eccentric fashion (mixing appreciation and irreverence) Stirling's plan pays homage to the existing neoclassical Staatsgalerie whilst seeming to caricature it at the same time; as before, Schinkel and Le Corbusier appear in ambiguous, unclear ways. From above, the layout looks like a giant hook grasping at bits and pieces heaped together to make an *avant-corps* of entrance door, bookshop, and foyer; these are intersected by ramped pedestrian routes rising and circumambulating through or around the famous rotunda (*ill.* 19).

The museum was constructed of *in situ* concrete and then embellished with stone cladding, Egyptian cornices, *De Stijl* canopies, romanesque or Loosian windows and the other stylistic frills which continue to stimulate so much discussion: a connoisseur's random selection of remnants of abandoned architectures, echoing through Stirling's modernism in fragmented, insubstantial ways which only indistinctly describe the epochs or places to which they might originally have pertained. And there he leaves them suspended in an ideological void, where they mingle in nonchalant accumulation, setting off dissonances which Stirling himself could not control, transcending architecture to invite philosophical contemplation of our unstable modern condition.

This essay first appeared in the catalogue of an exhibition held in Bologna in 1990, curated by Thomas Muirhead and Francesco Dal Co and entitled I Musei di James Stirling, Michael Wilford and Associates. *In fulfilment of a wish expressed by James Stirling it appears here, somewhat modified, in English. – T. M.*

19. James Stirling and Michael Wilford
Neue Staatsgalerie, Stuttgart, 1977–84
Music School and Theatre Academy, 1987
Model

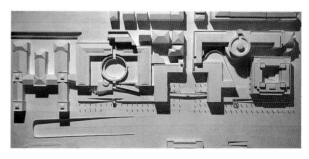

Selected Projects 1975–1992

General view showing the overhead district heating system

View of a three-storey terrace

Two and three-storey terraces

Pedestrian footways

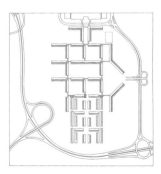

Overall plan

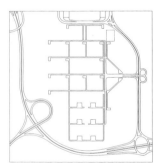

Vehicle access roads

Landscaping plan

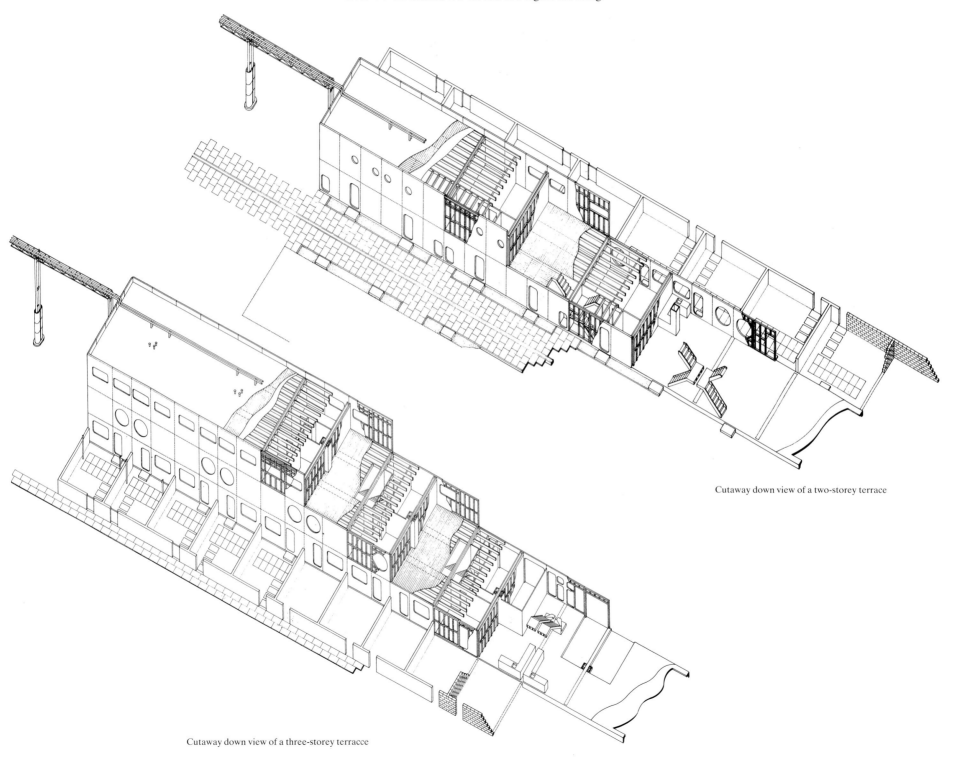

Cutaway down view of a two-storey terrace

Cutaway down view of a three-storey terracce

Internal street   Gardens and small-scale pedestrian spaces   General view

This is Phase Two of the earlier scheme illustrated in Volume One. It consists of low-cost, low-rise housing two or three storeys high and comprising about 250 dwellings arranged in terraces around tree-lined squares, in the same planning arrangement as the earlier scheme.

Each house has its own small front yard. Construction is based on the use of prefabricated glass-reinforced polyester panels with windows and doors included, assembled on timber frames. Colours are banded vertically in contrasting primary shades.

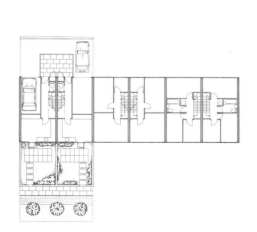
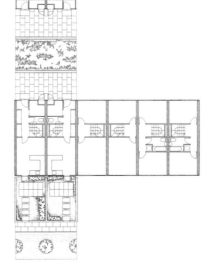
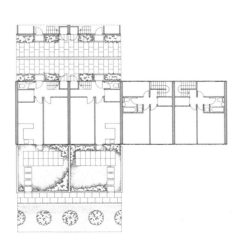
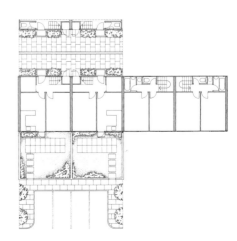

Typical plans of two and three-storey housing units

20

1972–77 Runcorn New Town: Southgate Housing

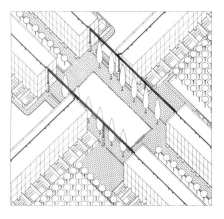

Pedestrian streets and public spaces

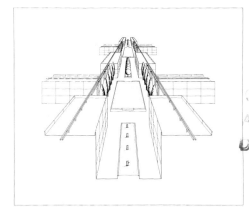

Pedestrian boulevard

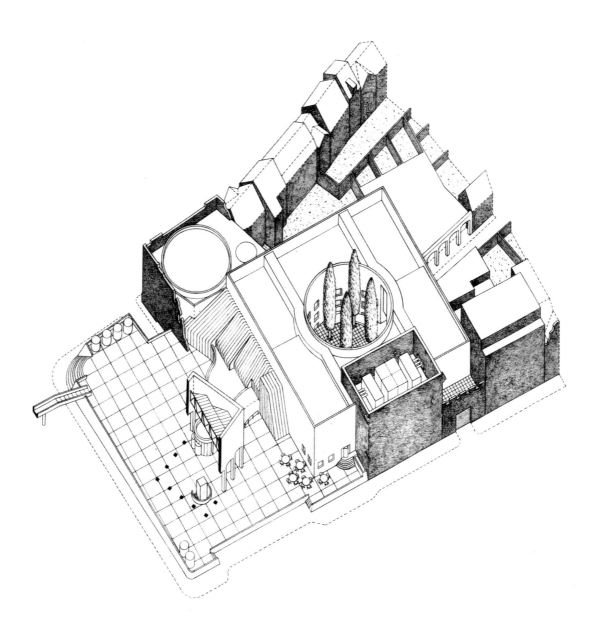

Down axonometric with the entrance pavilion partly cut away to show the lift
and steps up from the car park, and the main entrance to the museum

Location plan

The new museum responds to the conflicting scales of the surrounding buildings in contrast to the box-and-slab appearance of much modern architecture; existing façades are retained without compromising the new museum. The raised plaza extends through the museum as a succession of architectural events. A pavilion marks the entrance, the car park steps, and the walk through the courtyard. As a place for people to congregate we think of this as a more elaborate version of the steps of the Metropolitan Museum in New York or the portico of the British Museum.

Düsseldorf in 1975. The site for the museum is at the centre of the photograph

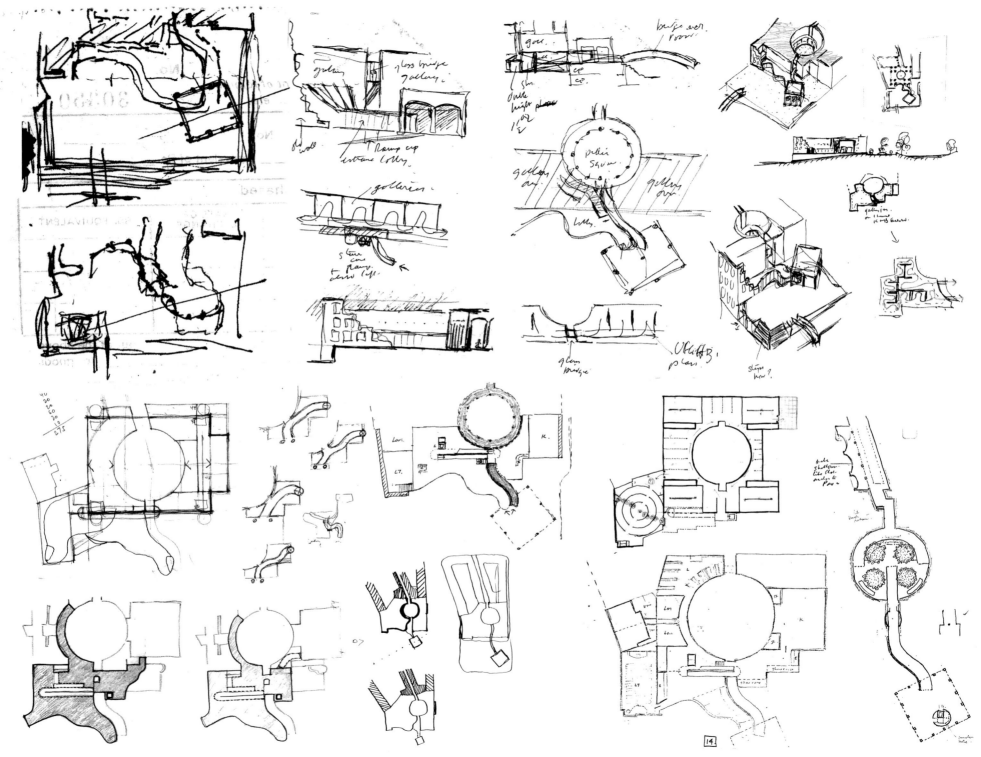

Concept sketches

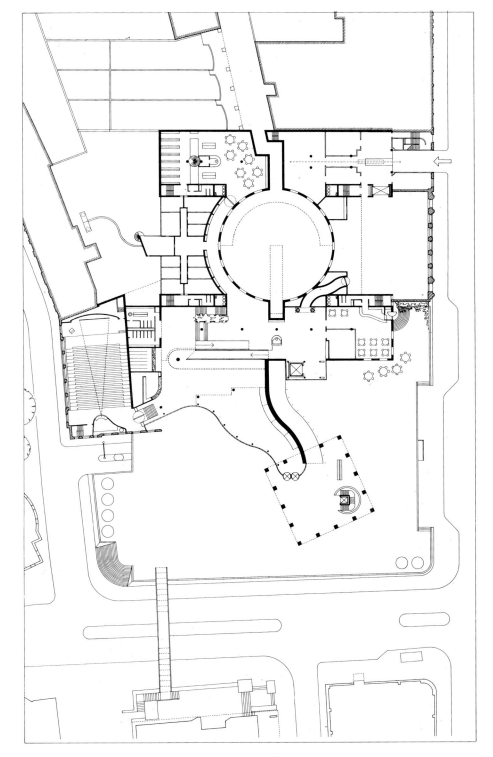

Plan at entrance level

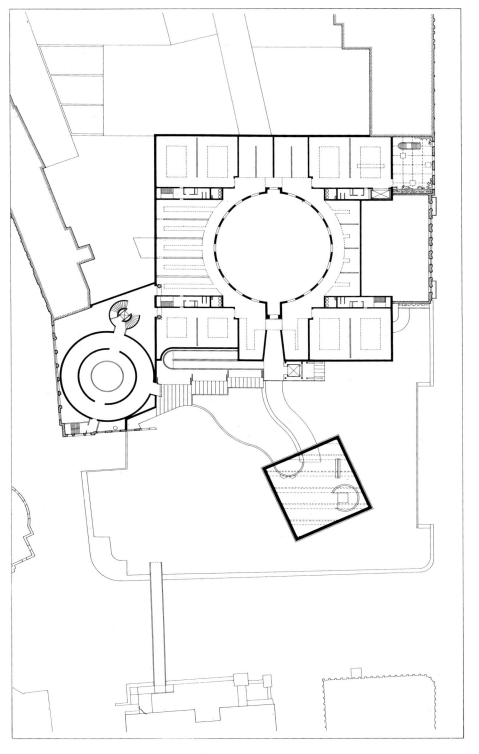

Plan at gallery level

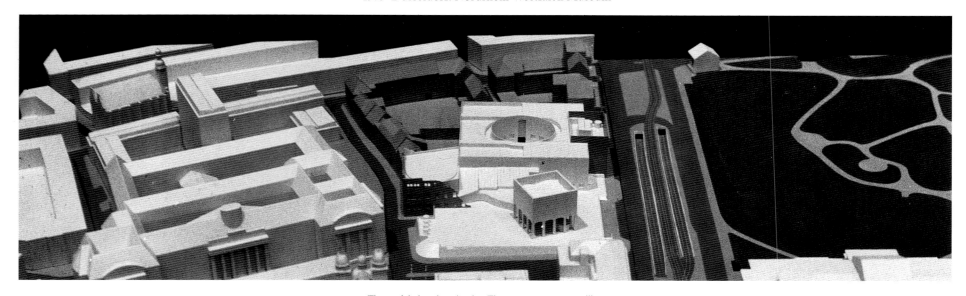

The model placed on the site. The square entrance pavilion
looks along the main street and across the highway to the park

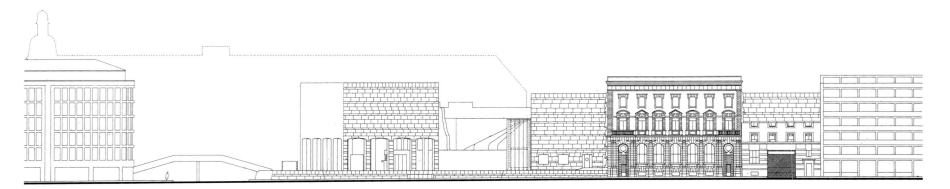

East elevation showing the raised plaza with the entrance pavilion,
the restaurant, and the retained shell of an old *palazzo*

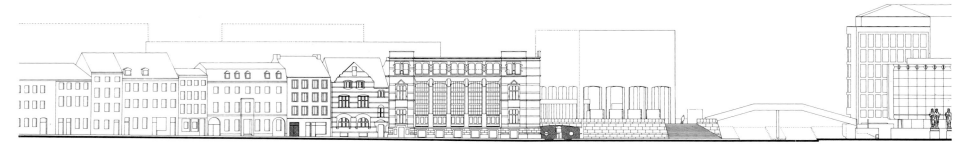

West elevation showing the entrance to the carpark under the raised plaza.
The old façade to the left of it conceals the circular galleries behind

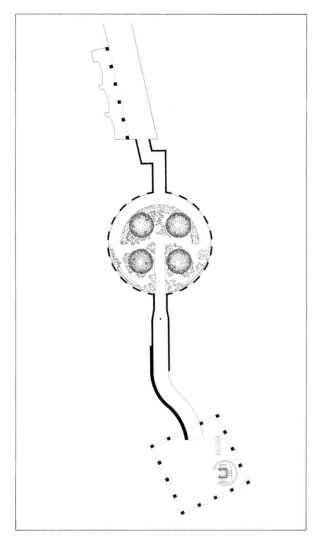

Plan of the public pathway through courtyard

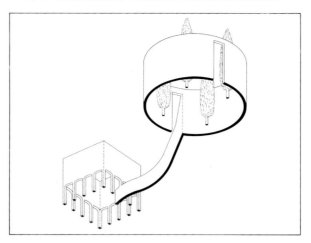

Up view of the entrance pavilion and courtyard

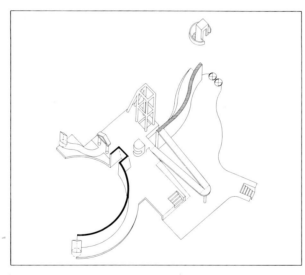

Part axonometric of the entrance hall looking down

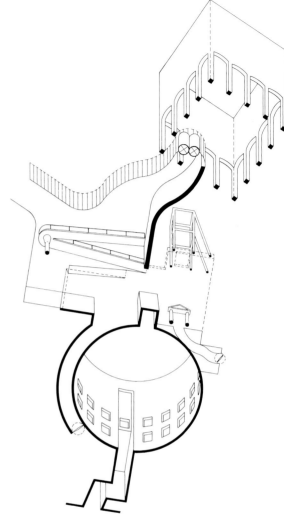

Up view of the entrance and courtyard

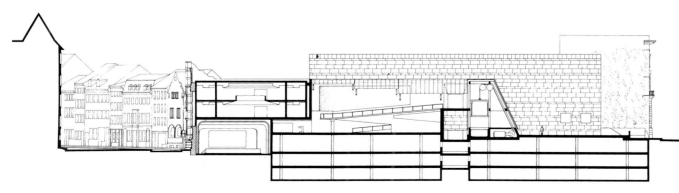

Cross section showing the circular galleries and auditorium (left), the glazed entrance hall,
and the public pedestrian walkway leading underneath into the rotunda beyond

1975 Düsseldorf: Nordrhein-Westfalen Museum

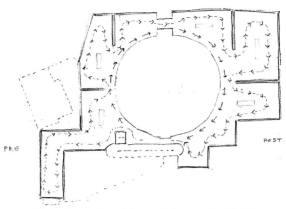

JS doodle showing a visitor's path through the galleries

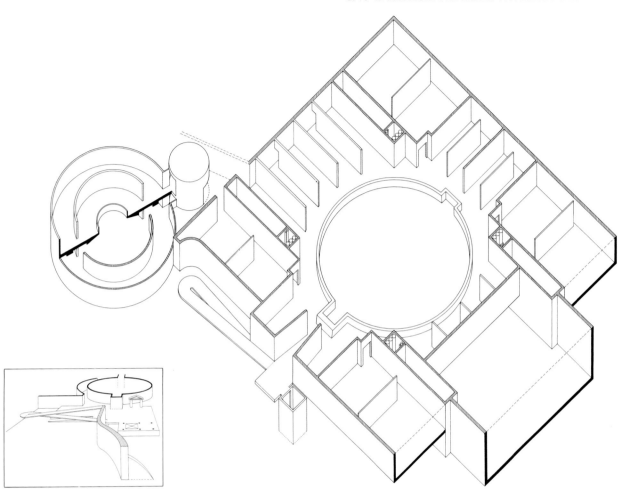

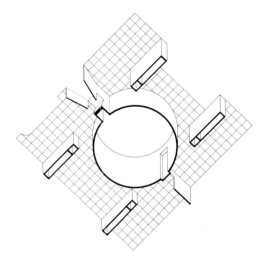

Perspective of entrance hall

Down axonometric of the galleries

Schematic up view of courtyard and the gallery ceilings

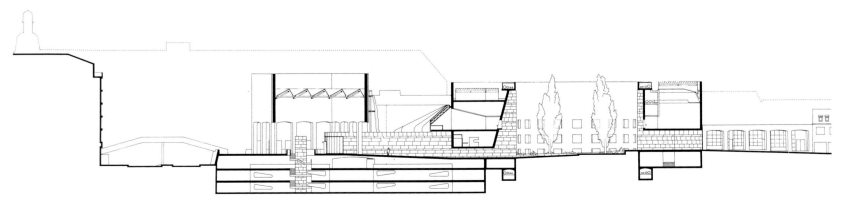

Longitudinal section showing the public route through the entrance pavilion,
under the museum, across the rotunda, and out into the street

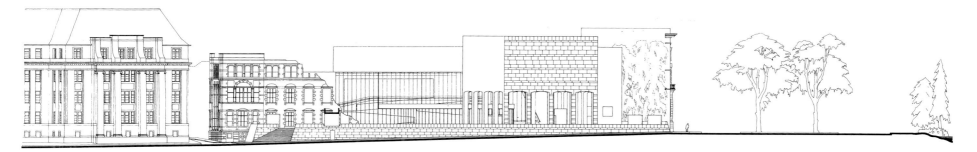

Front elevation showing the public terrace, the entrance pavilion and the glazed foyer beyond

Cologne in 1945 after destruction by Allied bombing

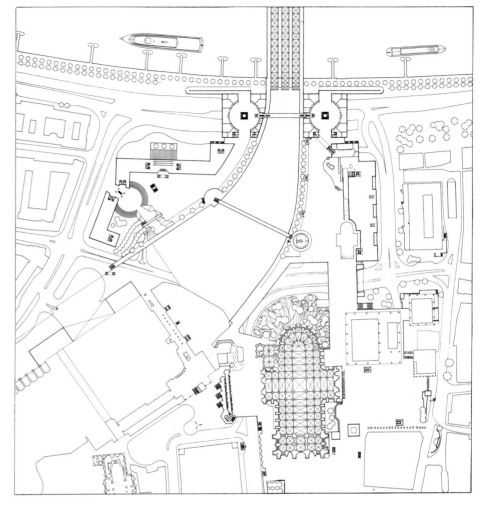

Plan at the plaza level

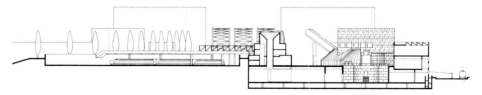

Cross section through the sunken sculpture court

This is a complex of buildings grouped in deference to the cathedral and other buildings nearby, gradually building up in height to the bridge. On the station side are an hotel, sports centre, and offices, linked across the railway tracks to the museum by a footbridge ending in a "ziggurat" in which an electrical substation is concealed. Pedestrians enter the plaza from basement car parking, the railway station, the cathedral, or up ramps from the river, and walk towards two "gateway" buildings framing the bridge, with viewing balconies over the Rhine, and shopping courts containing equestrian statues of Wilhelm II and Friedrich. One of the two gateway buildings forms part of the museum. It contains two administration floors over the shops and a 200-seat three-level flexible auditorium, connected back by escalator to the double-height

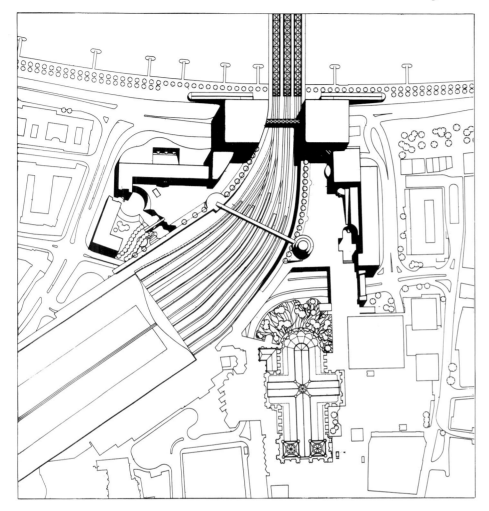

Roof plan with shadows

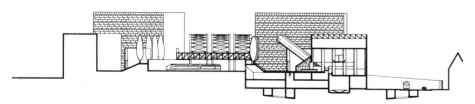

Cross section. The peristyle entrance hall to the museum is on the right

Model. Note the sunken sculpture court and ramp up to restaurant

entrance hall in the main building. The lower part of the entrance hall is an irregular-shaped glass enclosure with a "peristyle" of columns, with a ramp descending to artificially-lit temporary exhibition rooms, directly connected to the delivery dock, and a sunken sculpture court. From ground level the peristyle leads into three levels of flexible exhibition space with natural top and sidelighting, with a restaurant at the uppermost level (with good views of the cathedral) and an exit ramp leading back down into the plaza. The plaza is defined and enclosed by these buildings and by trees screening the railway tracks. By framing and unifying the separate monuments of the cathedral, the railway station, and the bridge over the Rhine, and offering connections into the city on all sides, it was intended to be a first step in regenerating this focal area of Cologne.

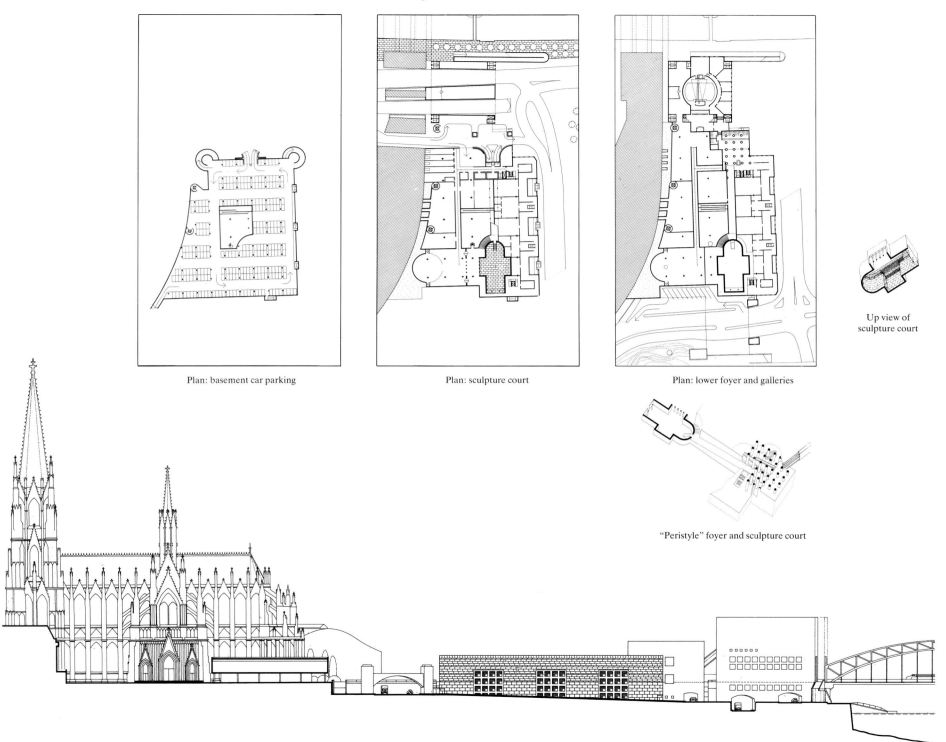

Plan: basement car parking

Plan: sculpture court

Plan: lower foyer and galleries

Up view of
sculpture court

"Peristyle" foyer and sculpture court

South elevation of the gallery building

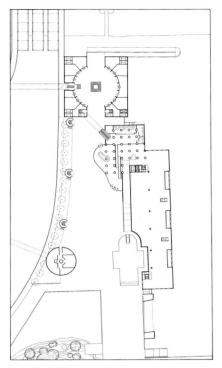

Plan showing peristyle entrance hall

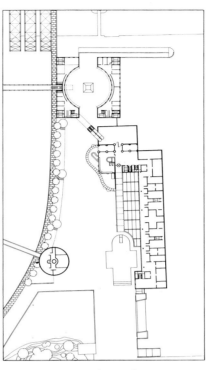

Restaurant and external ramp

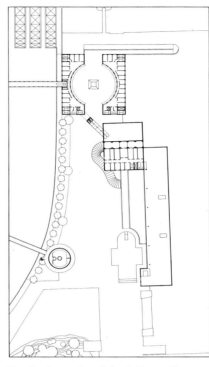

Plan showing escalator link to bridge pavilion

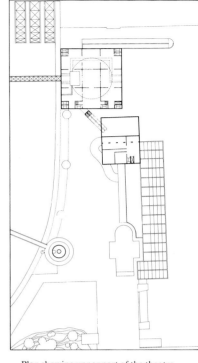

Plan showing upper part of the theatre

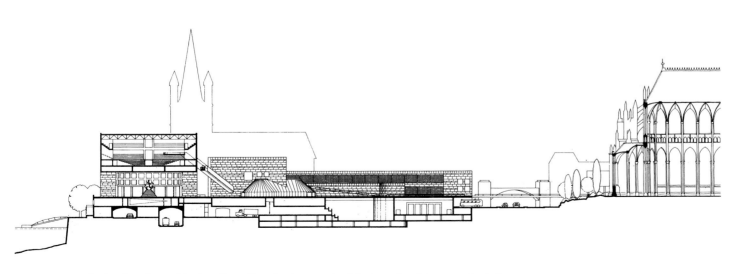

Section through one of the riverside pavilions showing upper-level theatre and escalator connection to the museum

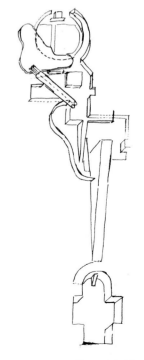

Concept sketch

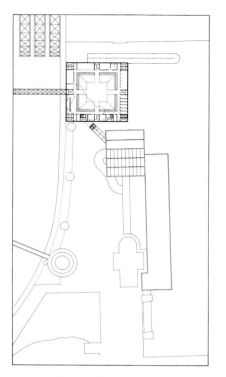

Plan at auditorium foyer level

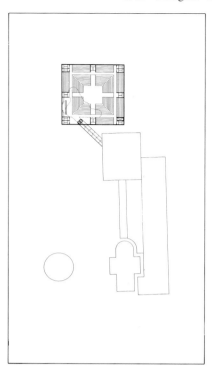

Plan at lower auditorium foyer level

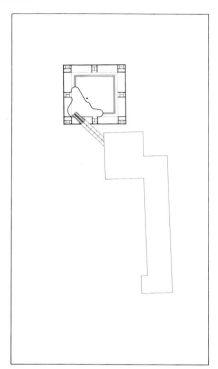

Plan at auditorium balcony level

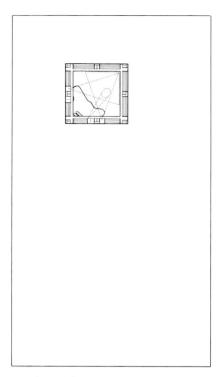

Plan at auditorium upper balcony level

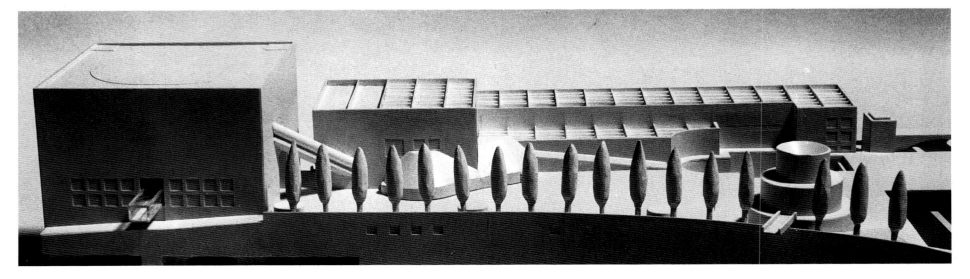

The model as seen from across the railway tracks. The river is on the left, the cathedral to the right

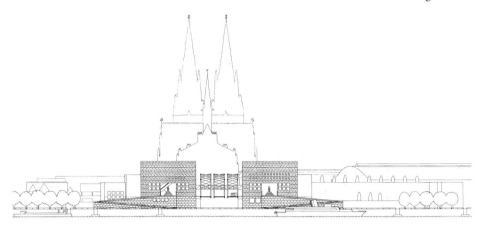

Section through the Rhine railway viaduct framed by the two new pavilions

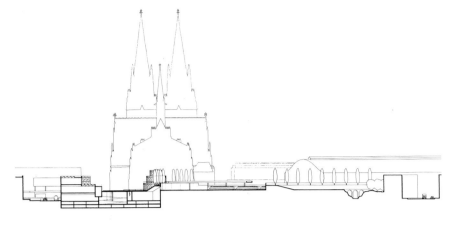

Cross section through the plaza

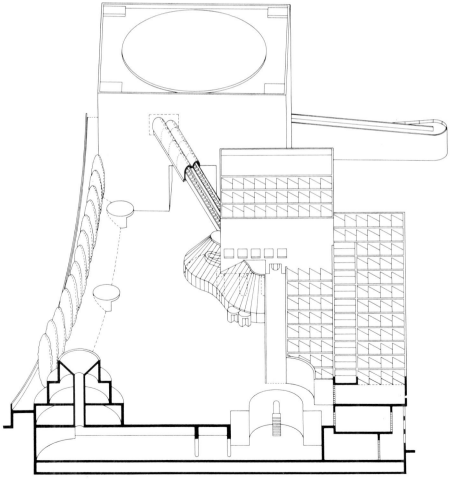

Sectioned axonometric

The model in context (the right-hand pavilion flanking the bridge has been removed)

Photomontage

Meineke Strasse exemplifies postwar damage done by gross modern architecture and commercialism: an over-scaled multi-level garage, and the street corner reduced to a petrol filling station. To restore a pleasant, mixed character we interposed a new "contextual" building, containing small shops, flats, and maisonettes and turn-ing the corner as a hinge. The window and door open-ings, gables, balconies, masonry, and rendering rework the established language and materials of this street. Two new paved gardens are accessed from openings at street level and the garage continues to function, served by a new archway through the building.

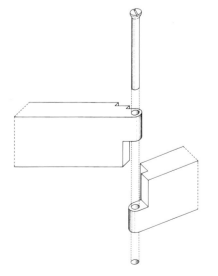

The "hingepin" concept

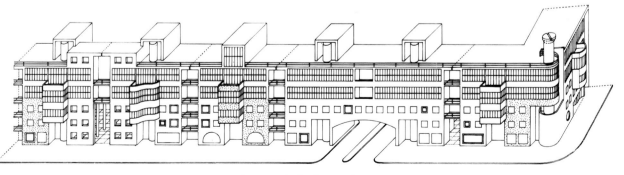

Axonometric after intervention

1976 Berlin: Hotel in Meineke Strasse

The existing situation

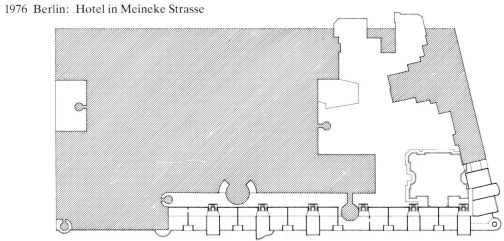

Typical upper level plan

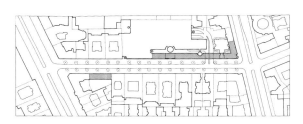

Location plan after intervention

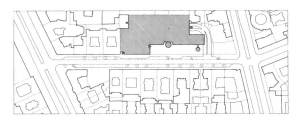

Location plan before intervention

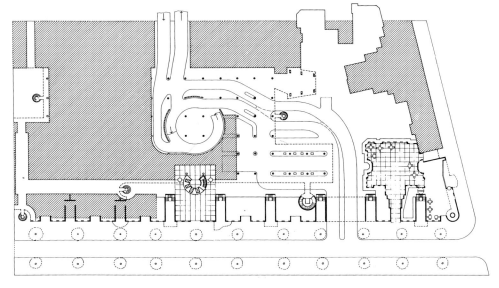

Plan at street level

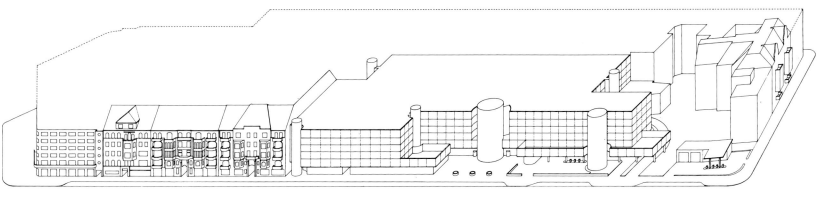

Axonometric before intervention

Elevation along the *corniche*

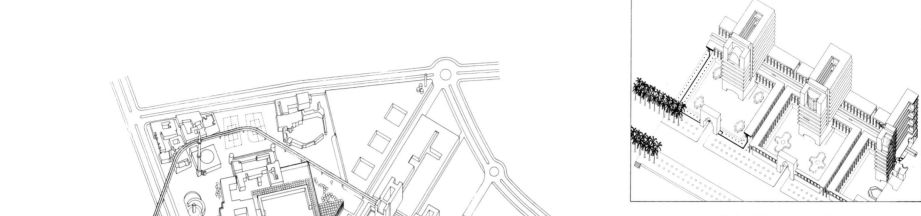

Sectioned down axonometric

Additions to the Emir's palace include a raised formal garden overlooking the *corniche,* and a ceremonial courtyard looking along a tree-lined mall of government ministries. These twelve-storey buildings are served by underground parking and interconnected by a transit system. Each has an arcaded water garden with balconies overlooking the mall, from which the public can view official motorcades and processions. Shaded walks lead through from the mall to a shaded shopping street at the back with banks, cafés, kiosks, health clinics, mosques, and welfare facilities. The ministry buildings can expand by bridging across this street to give extra shade. They are entered from courtyards cooled by sea breezes, with stairs and lifts leading to ministerial suites at the top of each building, with splendid views over the Gulf.

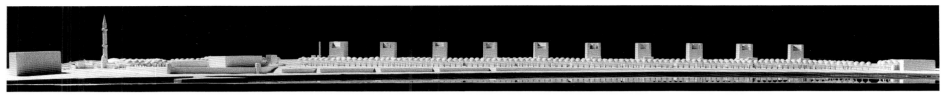

Night view of the model seen from the sea

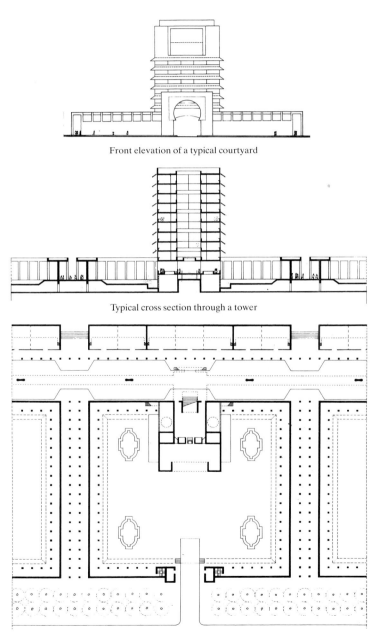

Front elevation of a typical courtyard

Typical cross section through a tower

Typical plan showing courtyard and shopping street

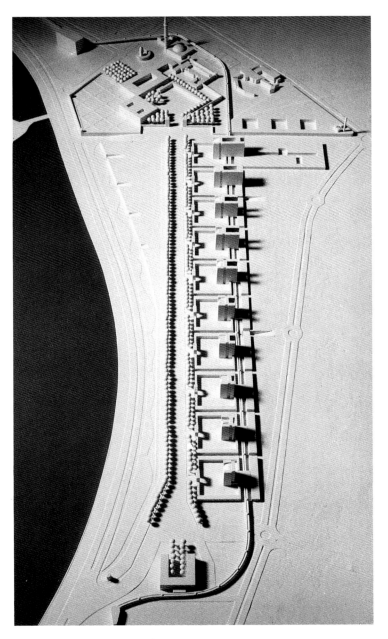

Looking along the *corniche*

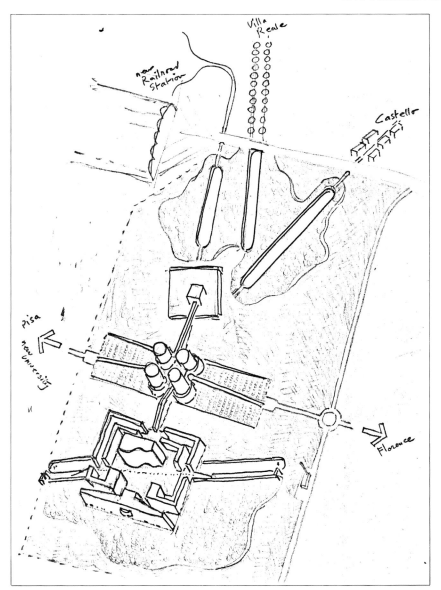

Concept doodle by JS showing new high-speed train station at the top, "sausage" connections to the station, the Villa Reale, and the town of Castello, and the tripartite scheme composed of a "stone garden", four towers, and an "island" traversed by a pedestrian promenade which is orientated on the Roman centuriation grid

View of the model from the south

Scale comparison:
Florence Cathedral and Baptistery

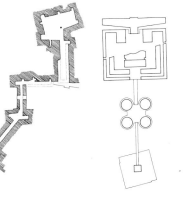

Scale comparison:
Piazza della Signoria, Ponte Vecchio,
Piazza Pitti

Location plan. Florence is off to the right

As Florence expands westward, this project was planned to relocate some functions of the historic centre: a new Regional Government building, a new Palace of Justice, an hotel, theatre, cinema, offices, commercial, residential and professional accommodation, with connections into new road, rapid transit, and railway facilities. To preserve the surrounding parkland, our design is a compact group, raised on a podium over parking and service facilities, and connected by woodland walks to the 16th century Villa Reale and a new high-speed railway station. Multi-level parking is contained under a "stone garden" orientated on the Roman grid and connected by bridge to four towers containing the hotel, offices and shops around a piazza with escalator connections to public transport and on-grade parking in four ramped "orchards". A second walkway crosses to the "island" where piazzas, shopping streets, and colonnades recall the traditional city. The Regional Government and Law Courts buildings stand among other public buildings with shops, offices and luxury apartments which overlook the surrounding parkland.

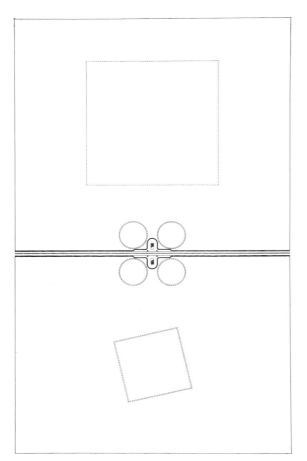

Plan at underground rapid transit level

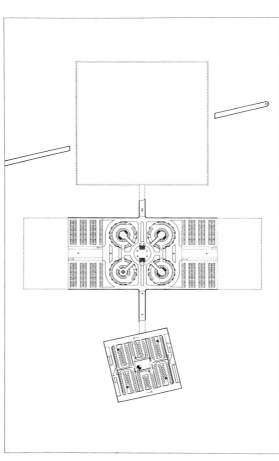

Underground parking and service access

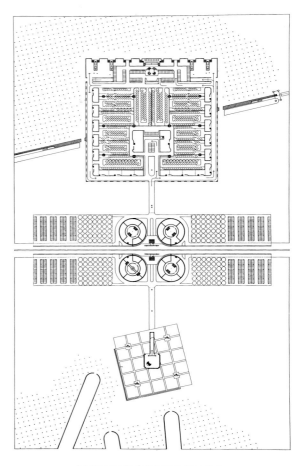

A new *autostrada* traverses the scheme

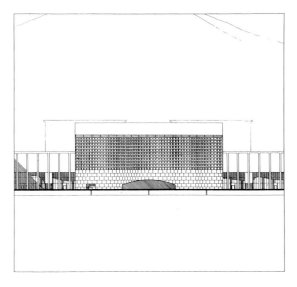

The Regional Government building

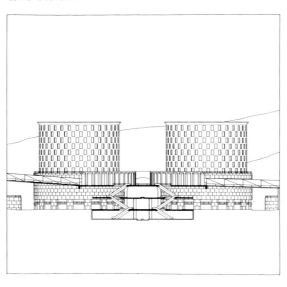

Office towers and plaza showing escalators to public transport

Multi-level parking under the stone-paved "garden"

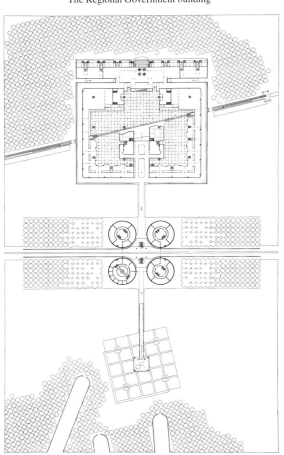

Plaza level (the Law Courts enclose the top edge)

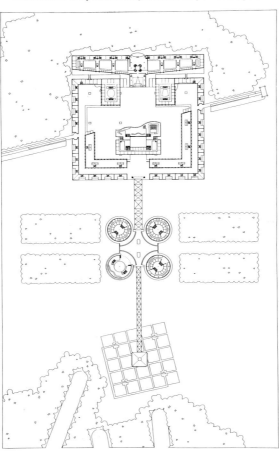

First floor plan

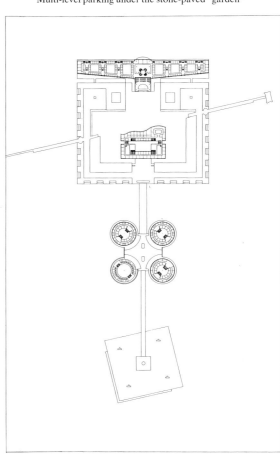

Upper part of Law Courts, Government Building, and towers

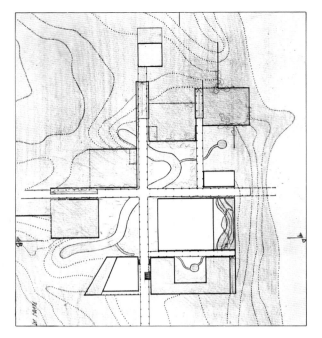

Layout based on cruciform circulation routes

These outline study schemes show four possible alternative layouts for the new United Nations Environmental Programme, which was to be located on a 100-acre site on the outskirts of Nairobi. The facilities of the centre were to include Council and conference facilities, and the programme of functions also required that the new administration buildings for the Centre "should exemplify the environmental policies of UNEP and be responsive to local conditions". In response to this requirement, these initial studies were based on low energy/low rise buildings, two and three storeys high. A windmill park and a solar lake were incorporated in the landscaping of the site.

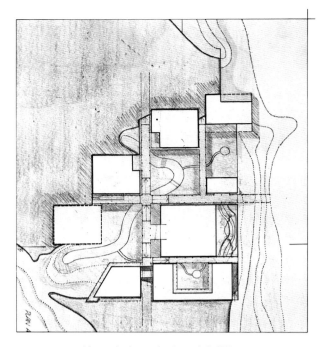

Alternative layout for the main buildings

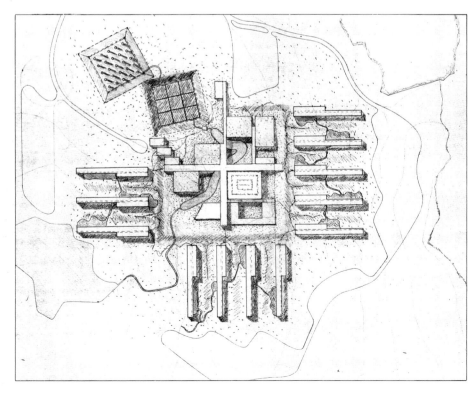

General plan with administrative buildings at the centre

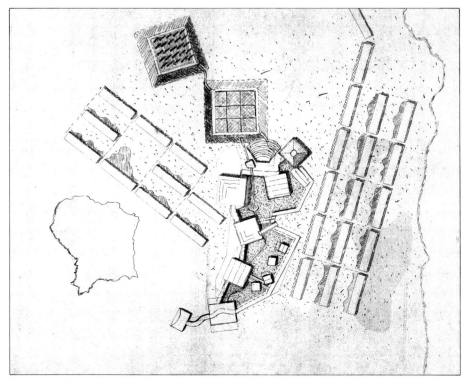

Alternative informal layout using the land contours

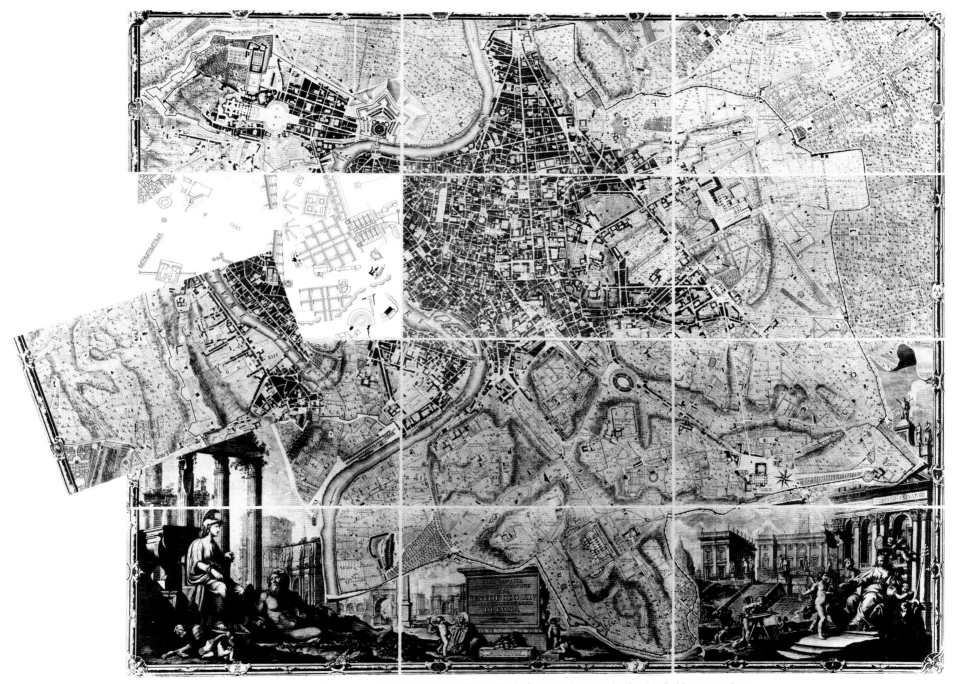

The twelve sectors of Nolli's plan of Rome of 1748. One sector is removed and replaced with our new scheme

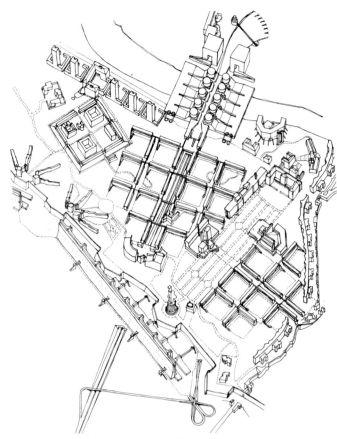

Axonometric sketch of the new scheme

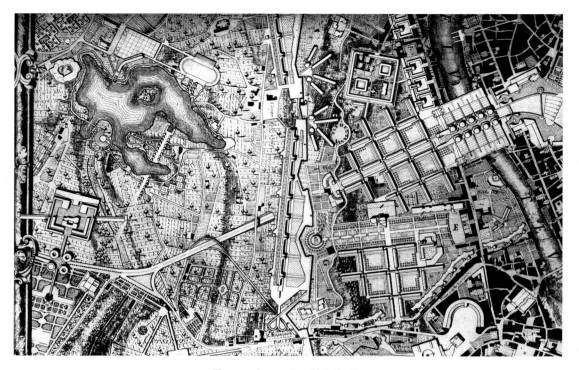

The new scheme collaged into the site

The site as recorded by Giambattista Nolli in 1748

As part of the debate on the future of the city, we were asked by the Mayor (Giulio Carlo Argan) to redesign one of the twelve segments of Giambattista Nolli's 1748 plan of Rome. We megalomaniac architects are frustrated by the projects we have designed but not built, so our initial decision was to revise Nolli's plan by incorporating all our unbuilt work into it. We ended up trying to include the entire *œuvre* and to sustain momentum a rigorous discipline was necessary. We therefore limited ourselves to projects appropriate to aspects of context and association, either to the circumstances of 1748 or to the time at which we designed them – or both. Projects were disposed in prototypical ways with "wall" buildings which reinforced or related to the Gianicolo and the Aurelian walls. Sometimes topography influenced our choice, with "hill" buildings climbing up the steep slope of the Gianicolo, and "water edge" buildings along the Tiber. Some of the projects have a parallel relationship to the context of the built form. There is also an interchange of monuments, e.g., Garibaldi replaced by the James Stirling birthday cake. A selection had to be

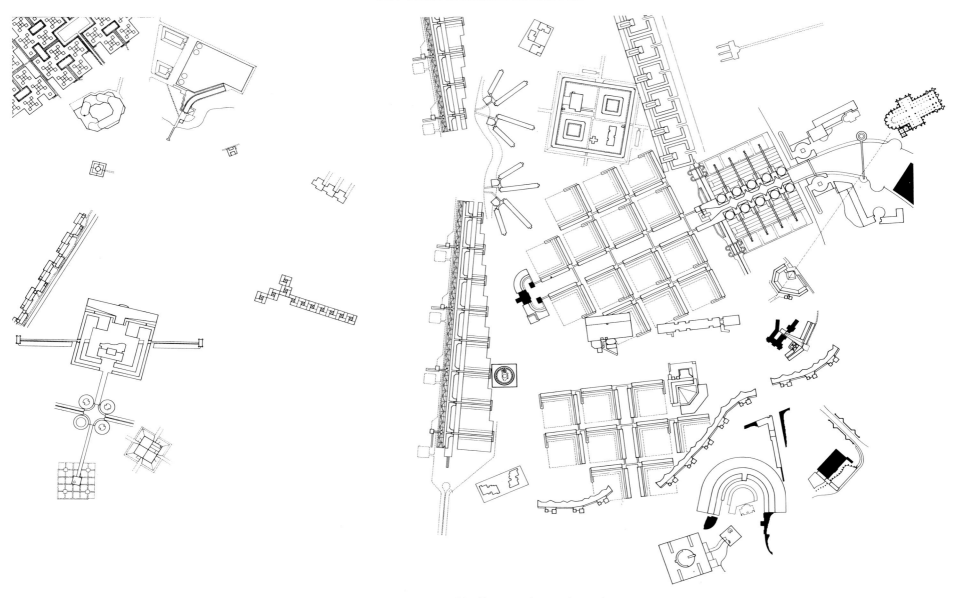

The new scheme is a reassembly of fragments of our previous projects

made of existing buildings and places essential to preserve/integrate/intensify and this, along with contextual, associational, topographical, protographical, prototypical, typological, symbolical, iconographical and archaeological considerations helped to integrate our projects. However, we had the larger objective of using our proposal to achieve a similar density to that which has been achieved via history. Thus our solution is an alternative to the buildings and surroundings now existing and would, perhaps, accommodate a not dissimilar quantity of working and living areas, institutions, and public spaces; comparison is invited. This "contextual/associational" way of planning is akin to the historical process by which the creation of built form is directly influenced by the visual setting and is a confirmation and a complement to that which exists. This may be similar to *Collage City* and the teachings of Colin Rowe, and stands against the irrationality of the postwar planning which destroyed magnificent nineteenth century cities like Liverpool, Glasgow, Newcastle in the name of "progress" by demolishing "out of date" buildings and replacing them with the lethal combination of urban motorways and "commercial" modern architecture. Expediency and commercialism corrupt the possibility of quality in urban design; irrational procedures and reversed priorities seem to be the stock-in-trade of city planners. Cities have lost their identity; townspeople are numbed by loss of memory and their children grow up in kitschplace and junkland. Before 1939 urban design was relatively well done by serious (i.e. not commercial) architects and it is preferable to return to that situation.

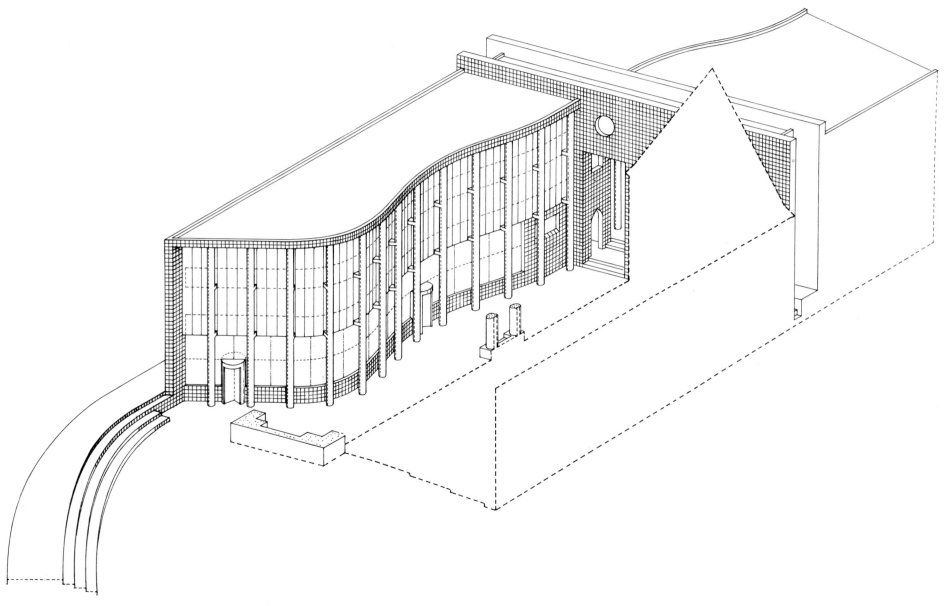

The site is defined by a freestanding gable and the heavily-rebuilt remains of an old mill overlooking the river and bridge. A flight of steps leads down into an enclosed space with a public passageway similar to many in old Marburg, and an arcade which meanders through, along the front of a new building containing a bank and offices. Pedestrians escape from the street by walking through, under an archway where two service entrances give access to the bank, the offices above, and a newspaper kiosk facing along the street. This spine-wall takes advantage of an existing kink in the street to divide the building in two, reversing the curve of the arcade and extending it beyond, where a shop and more offices overlook the street; a bus stop could be located here. A footpath and steps opposite continue the pedestrian route and lead up into the old town. The architecture of the new building responds to and enhances the context, utilizing the traditional urban language of Marburg and adding amenable public spaces to the city.

Axonometric as seen from the bridge (the existing buildings are shown dotted)

Postwar *pastiche*

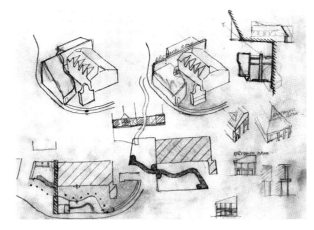

Initial studies

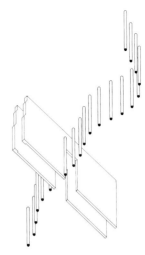

Up view of the concept

The path down from the Old Town

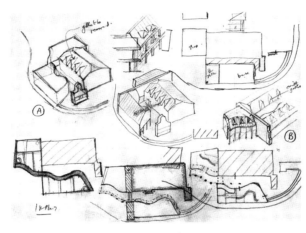

Initial studies

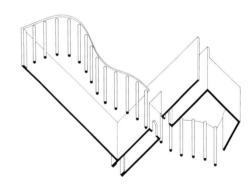

Up view of the concept

Looking along the street in the direction of the bridge

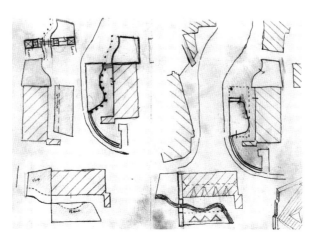

Initial studies

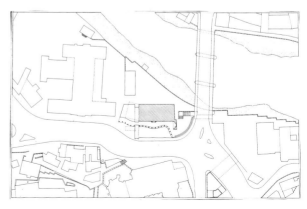

Location plan

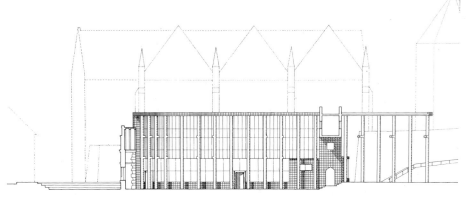

Section through the public open space showing façade and entrance to the Bank

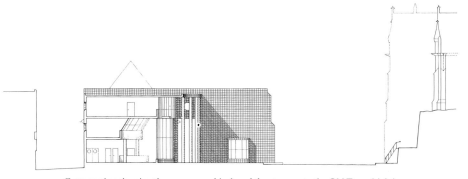

Cross section showing the newspaper kiosk and the steps up to the Old Town (right)

Down view showing the steps and path leading up to the Old Town

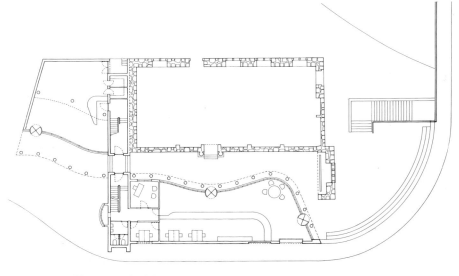

Plan at street level showing the public walkway running through the scheme

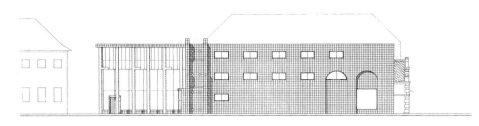

Back elevation to the noisy street

Elevation showing the grouping of old and new

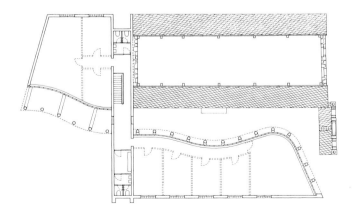

Plan at an upper level

Down view showing the newspaper kiosk

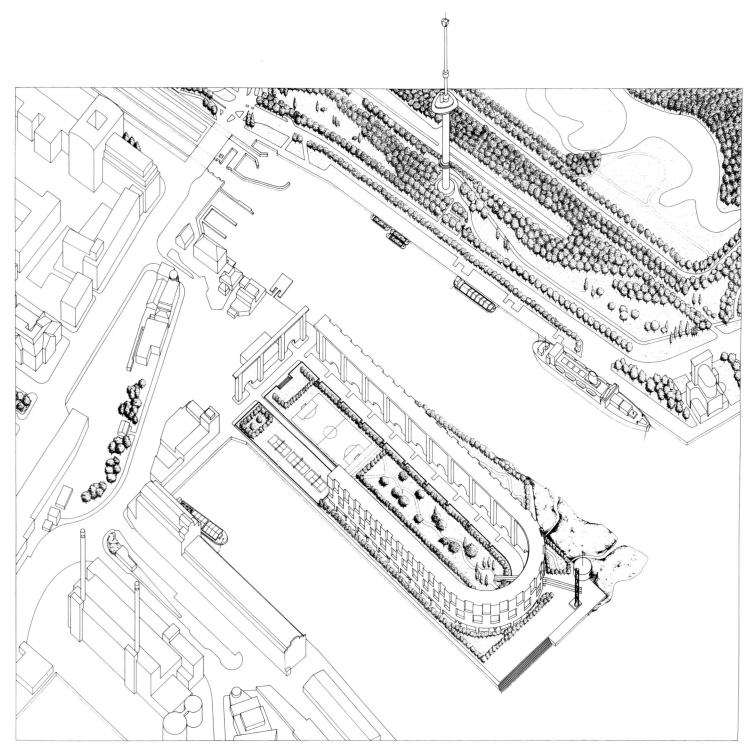

Down view

The site is surrounded by the city, close to the headquarters of important multinational companies like Shell and Unilever, and the university Faculty of Medicine. The purpose of this study was to demonstrate how new living areas could rejuvenate the harbour district of Rotterdam. The building is nine floors high and contains 800 dwellings; to create an autonomous residential quarter with good social diversity and mix, units vary in size from one-room studio flats to six-room duplex apartments. The building also contains a community centre and shops, and encloses a park with recreation facilities including squash courts, football pitches, and playgrounds. A service road running round the edge permits entry for service vehicles and gives residents access to private parking. The archways leading to each sector of the building give good views through from the inner garden towards the water. The horseshoe arrangement gives all apartments a private side overlooking the gardens, and on the outside edge, a wide prospect of the harbour scene with good views of the water and shipping. The balconies face on to a tree-lined public waterside promenade leading to a recreation area and restaurant on the promontory. This enhances sociability by inviting outsiders to come into the area and walk through it, mixing with the residents.

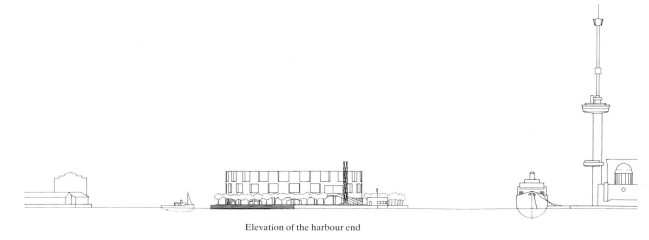

Elevation of the harbour end

Elevation of the entrance end

Side elevation showing the apartments overlooking the waterside promenade

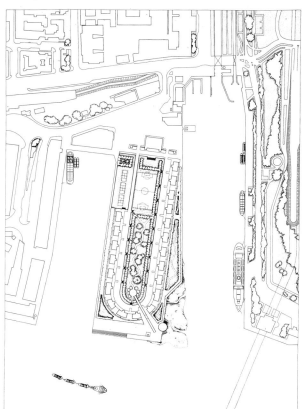

Plan

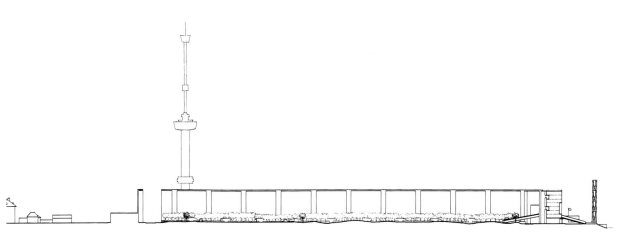

Longitudinal section through the internal garden

The gallery provides a sequence of exhibition rooms connected into the earlier Staatsgalerie, with external terraces for sculpture and a library and administration building at the back. The area's traditional character and the relationship between buildings and streets are reinforced by retaining all buildings on the side streets. A public footpath connects the hillside areas of Stuttgart to the city centre, passing through the museum, round the rotunda, and down to an ample terrace with a car park under. The gallery entrance is located here, where a ramp and steps descend to a taxi drop-off point on the busy main road. The pedestrian walk continues along the terrace past a cafeteria, and under an archway where the building projects forward to give a sense of enclosure to the terrace and to mark the Chamber Theatre. The small piano-shaped building, sited away from the noisy streets, contains a music school.

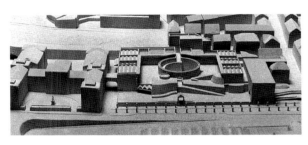

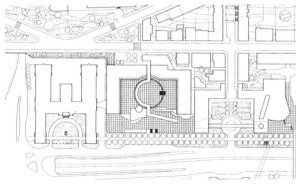

Top to bottom: model, site plan, and view of the site

55

Coved cornice to galleries

The rotunda

Rotunda and public walkway

Steps up to sculpture terraces

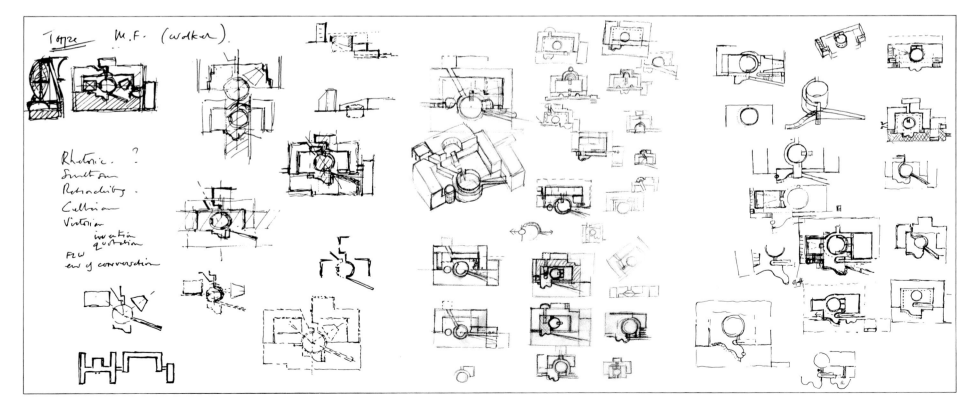

Early sketch studies

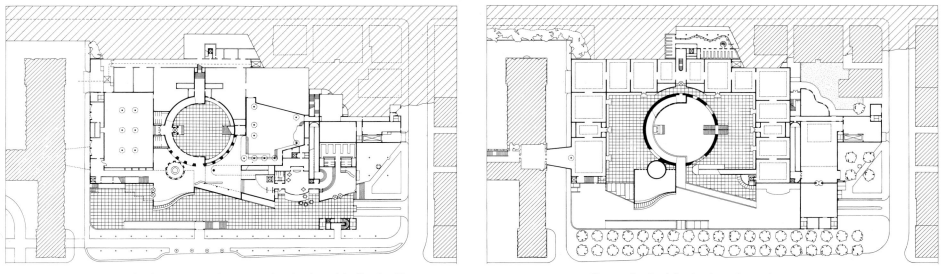

Plan at terrace level showing the entrances to the museum, the cafeteria, and the Chamber Theatre

Plan at gallery level showing the outdoor sculpture terraces

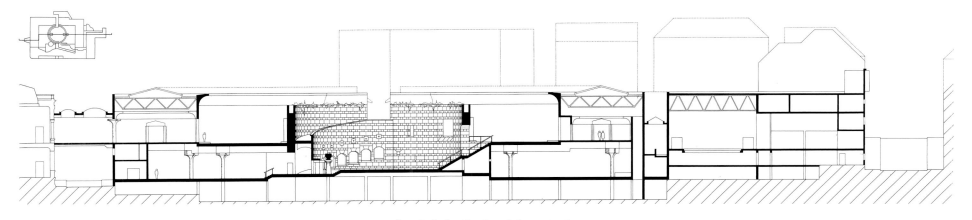

Longitudinal section through the courtyard

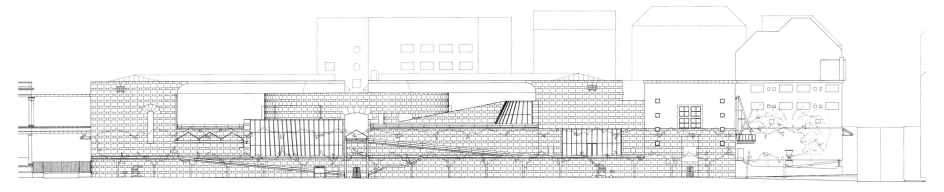

Front elevation to Konrad Adenauer Strasse

The glazed wall of the entrance hall

Interior of the entrance hall (bookshop to the right)

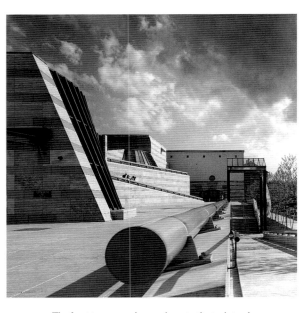

The front terrace and ramp down to the taxi stand

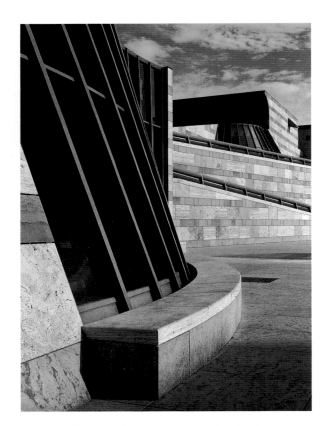

Close-up of the rainwater gutter and bench seat

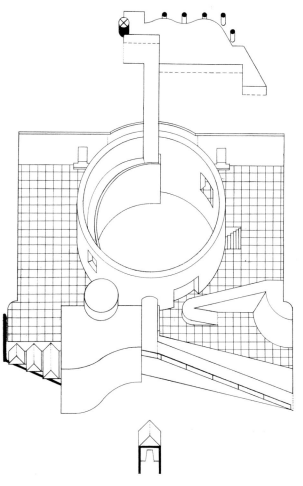

Schematic down view of the entrance hall and rotunda

The café terrace and the entrance hall beyond

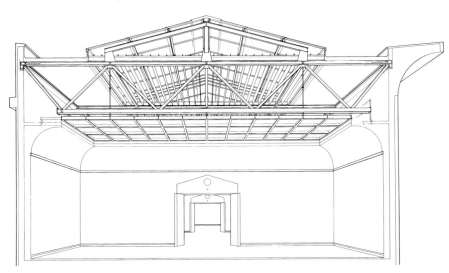

Interior of a gallery room showing roof construction and lay-light

The ceiling void above the gallery rooms

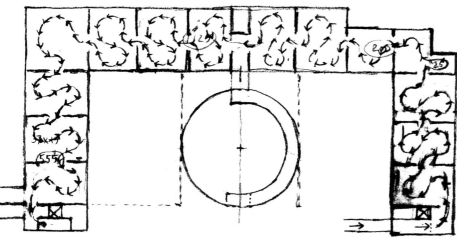

JS doodle showing how a visitor might wander through the galleries

The door which connects back to the old building

An exhibit of costumes by Oskar Schlemmer

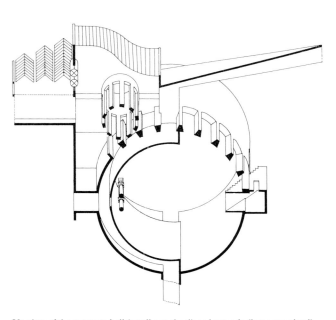

Up view of the entrance hall (small cogwheel) and rotunda (large cogwheel)

The public pedestrian route which passes down and around the rotunda

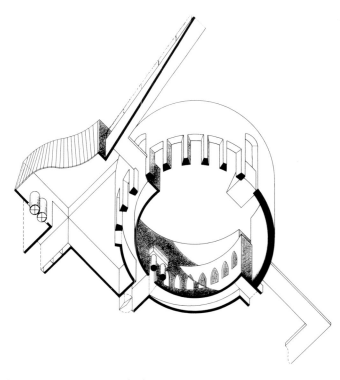

The pedestrian route passing up and around the rotunda

Looking across the rotunda towards the pedestrian route

Up view showing the entrance hall (left) and rotunda with the pedestrian route

The desert site

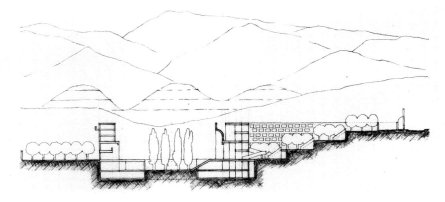

Cross section through entrance hall

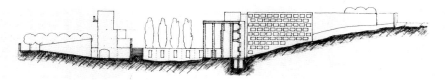

Cross section through space between buildings

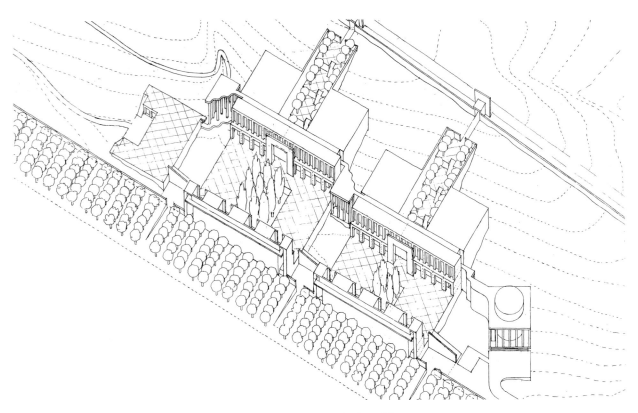

Down view of the first two faculty buildings

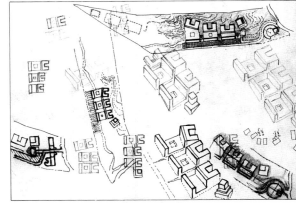

Concept sketches

This scheme is divided into three university faculty buildings overlooking central gardens; all the accommodation is arranged in parallel zones grouped across the site. The cross section of the buildings is designed as an artificial valley and the contours of the steeply-sloping desert site are used to create sequential entry. Access is from a road running along the upper edge of the slope; pedestrians descend into and through the buildings, moving down two axial distribution routes which descend by flights of steps, shaded by trees, through a series of internal courtyards.

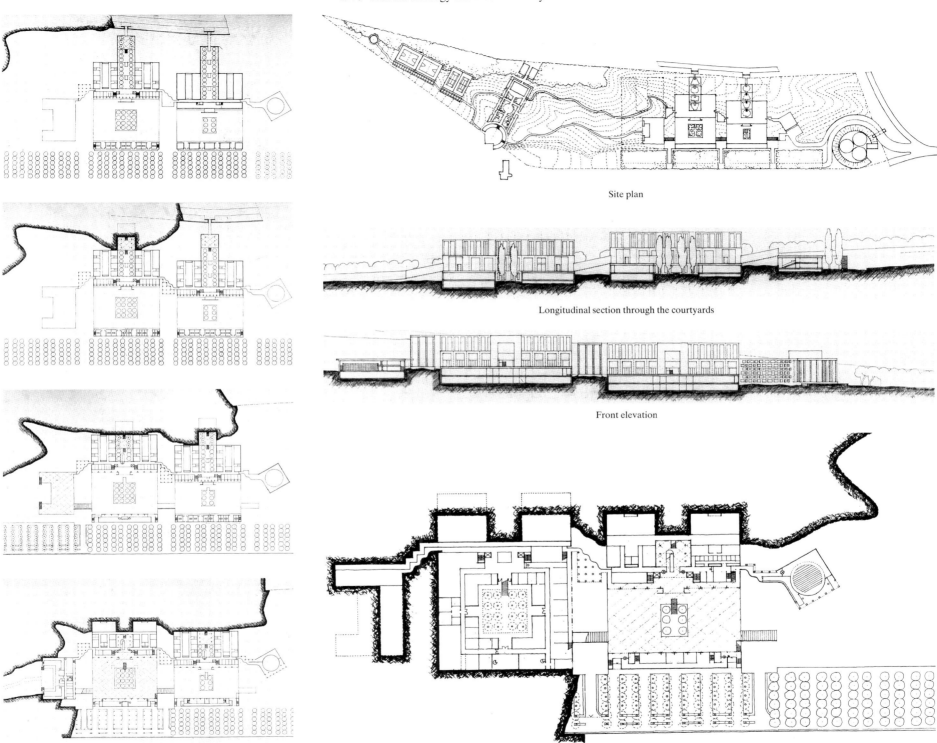

1978 Tehran: Biology and Biochemistry Institute

Site plan

Longitudinal section through the courtyards

Front elevation

Floor plans stepping up the sloping site

Plan: lower courtyard on the left; upper courtyard level on the right

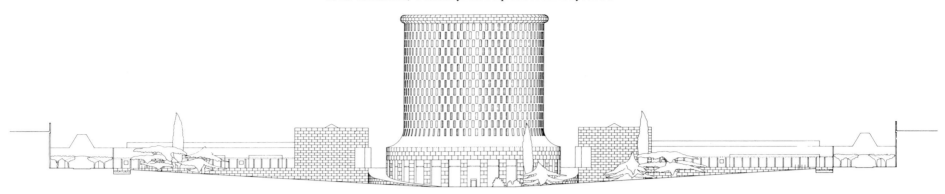

Elevation of the office tower and entrance pavilions seen from inside the park

The buildings are sited to create an arcadian building/landscape relationship similar to that of the eighteenth-century *schloss* set in picturesque surroundings. The U-shaped tower at the centre contains the administration offices and counterbalances the architectural variety of the other buildings. There is a conference centre at its base, with other central facilities in the wings which extend to either side. Entrance to the centre is past two gate lodges and through an entrance plaza into a generous landscaped park. Various laboratory complexes are disposed radially round the park, each planned as a group of buildings enclosing internal gardens; our intention was to avoid any institutional feeling in the Centre, and to achieve visual integration of the sophisticated/technical with the rustic/vernacular, so that staff using the lounges, arcaded corridors, and internal gardens might feel that what they were experiencing was more akin to a sequence of Florentine courtyards and gardens, rather than the purely functional environment of an anonymous laboratory complex.

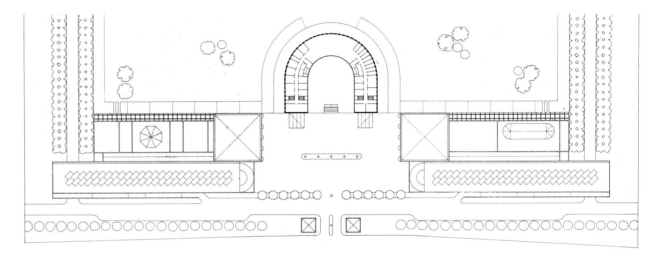

Upper floor plan of the office tower

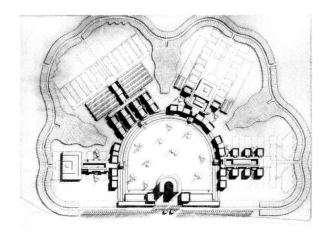

Site plan with shadows

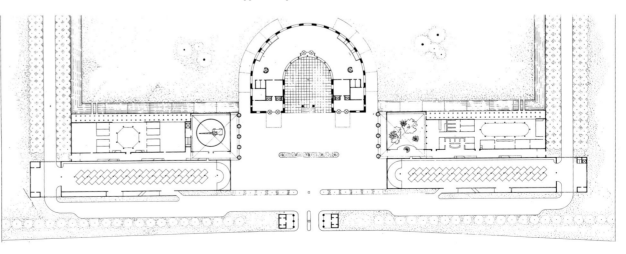

Plan at street level showing the entrances

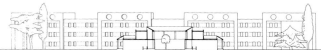

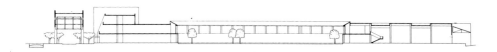

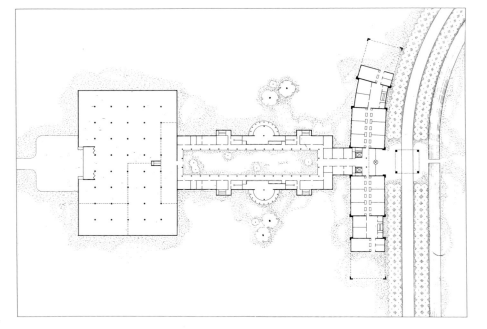

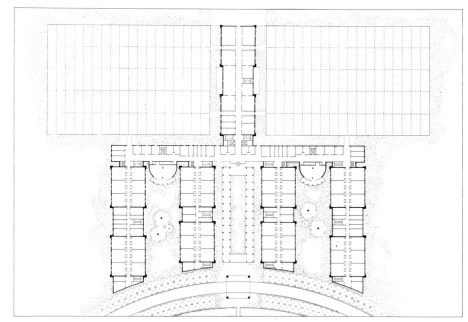

The central services complex

The Bio-1 complex with its experimental greenhouses

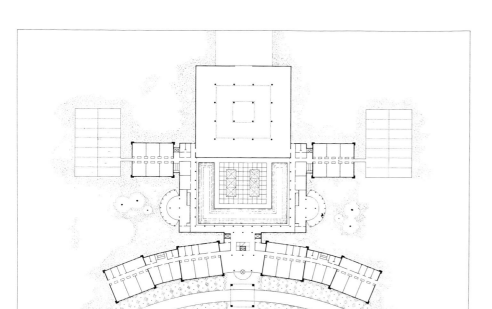

The Bio-2 complex

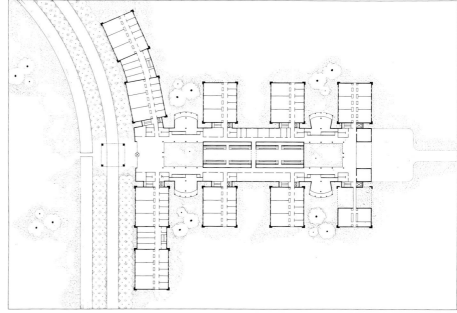

The chemistry complex

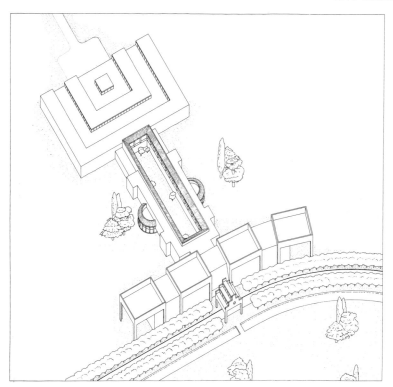

Down view of the central services complex

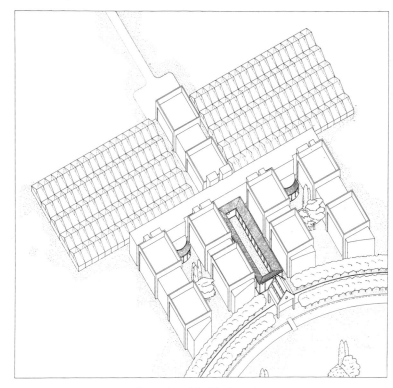

Down view of the Bio-1 complex

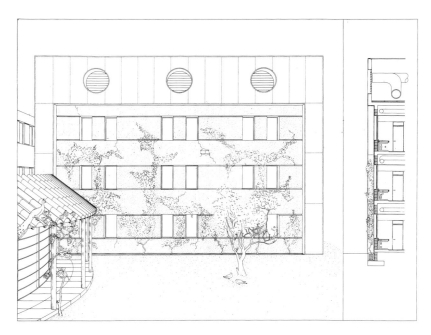

Perspective and section showing part of a typical laboratory cluster

Front view of the model

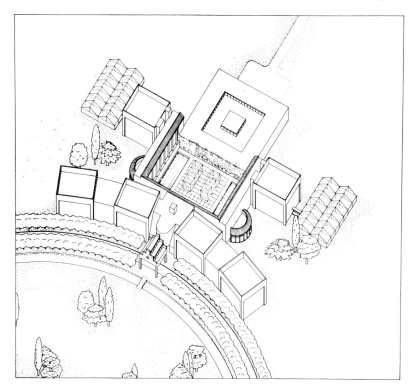

Down view of the Bio-2 complex

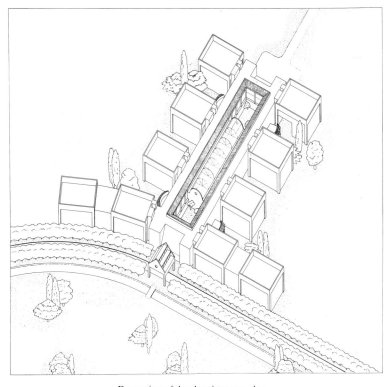

Down view of the chemistry complex

Side view of the model

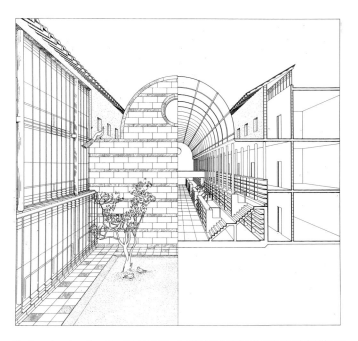

Sectioned perspective showing inner court of the chemistry complex and the library

JS sketch of the street frontage

The client was an architect/developer who asked for 11 luxury townhouses and apartments five storeys high, to be built over an existing underground garage. The garage roof structure had been built as a series of beams on 18-foot centres intended to take the party walls of a terrace above. Our new houses would have had a concrete or steel frame with brickwork cladding, and we used the 18 ft. dimension to plan an 18 ft. (thin man) single house which alternated with a 36 ft. (fat man) building containing a 3-floor house at the lower levels and a 2-floor apartment above it. This gave three different types of unit in the terrace. The client asked for luxurious, wealthy dwellings with lavish provision of bathrooms and private elevators, and the 36 ft. dimension allowed us to plan for generous rooms in the 3-storey house and 2-level apartments. The 18 ft. dwelling benefits from the independence and luxury of being a complete house; its circulation core is offset into the 36 ft. units, allowing for large and regularly-shaped rooms. The in-and-out movement of the street façade expresses the different dwelling types, and the most important interior rooms are marked by bay windows, studio-type glazing, balconies, etc., to echo the surface projections of the traditional New York town houses and brownstones which exist all around the site and which give this area of the Upper East Side its particular quality. The small front gardens set behind railings are also similar to sidewalk and basement areas in this part of New York.

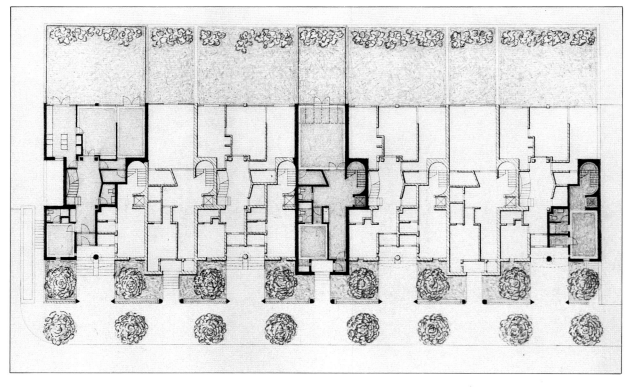

Plan at street level

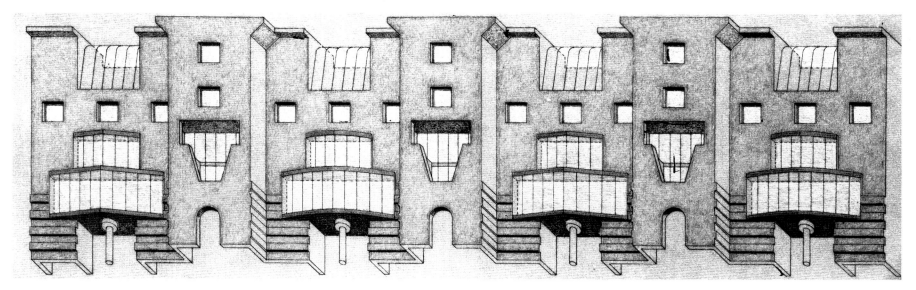

Up axonometric of the street frontage

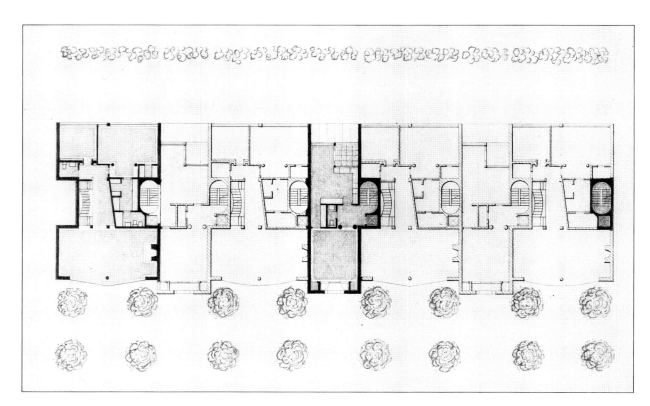

Plan at upper level

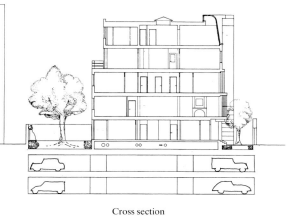

Cross section

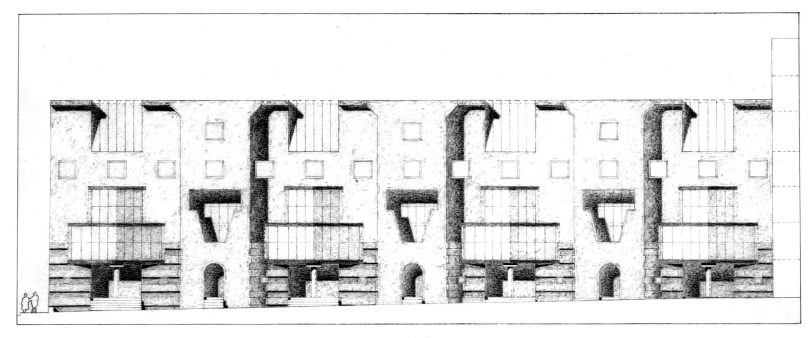

Street elevation

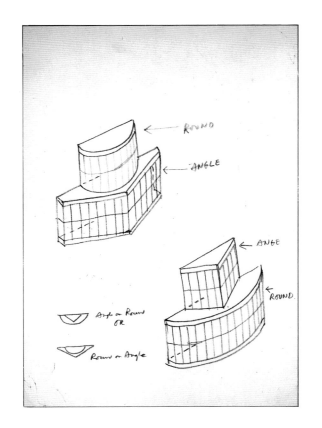

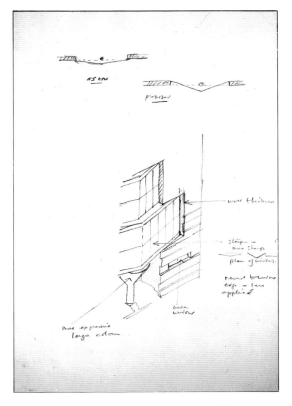

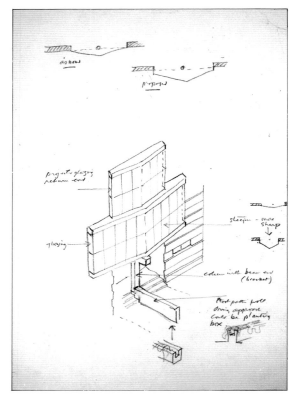

Three doodles by JS showing possible alternative bay window arrangements

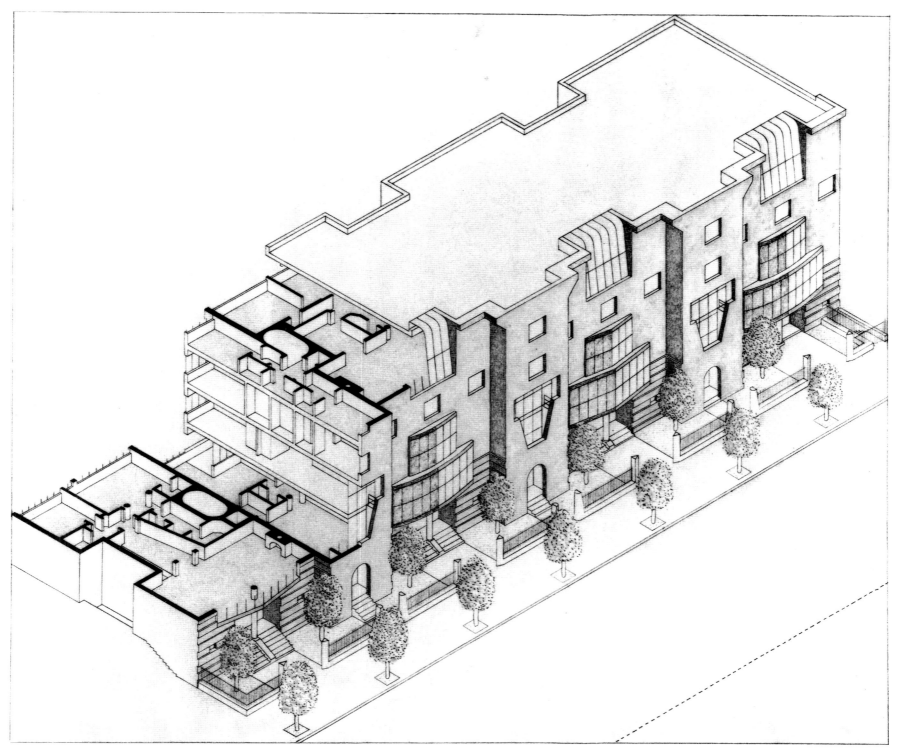

Cutaway down axonometric

The new L-shaped addition interlocks with the existing building to form a courtyard. The ground is finished in stone and brick interspersed with box hedges, flowering shrubs, and stone seats, and the existing trees are retained to give shade. The new façades respond to the campus style; materials are matched to the existing, and eaves and cornice lines carried through. A platform and steps at the entrance form a focal point for the garden, acting as an informal stage and seating area and leading to a spacious double-height circulation gallery and exhibition/jury space. This integrates the new wing with the existing building and serves as the focus for the life of the school. Two staircases connect the entrance hall to a mezzanine, which bridges the main exhibition and jury space and stops at two semicircular ends, giving overlooks from the balcony to the space below and allowing light from two roof lanterns to spill down through the full height of the hall. All internal circulation within the building takes place through this central gallery, maximising contact between students, faculty, and visitors and encouraging a sense of community. As an exhibition and jury space, it can be adapted for various activities by means of moveable interlocking screens, and also serves as the school's information centre, with pin-up boards and posters. Students can use it for impromptu crits and juries. Enclosed exhibitions, juries, and lectures for a seated audience of 200 can take place simultaneously, and the whole area can be adapted to accommodate exhibitions, receptions, parties, or large lectures for about 300 people. In fine weather, it can be extended for receptions and ceremonies by leaving open the glazed doors to the courtyard garden. The faculty room, administration offices and washrooms are located adjacent to the exhibition space. The existing building was replanned to accommodate design studios, seminar rooms, and classrooms.

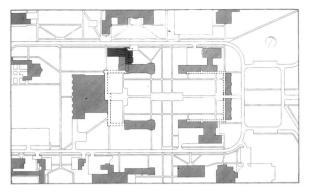

Campus location plan showing the new building

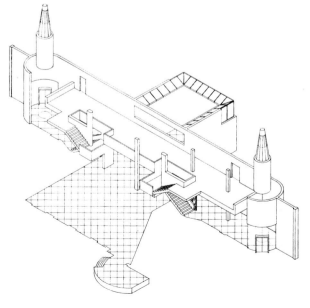

Down view

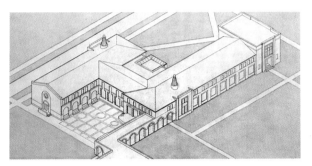

View of the quadrangle

Gallery, crit space, and entrance hall

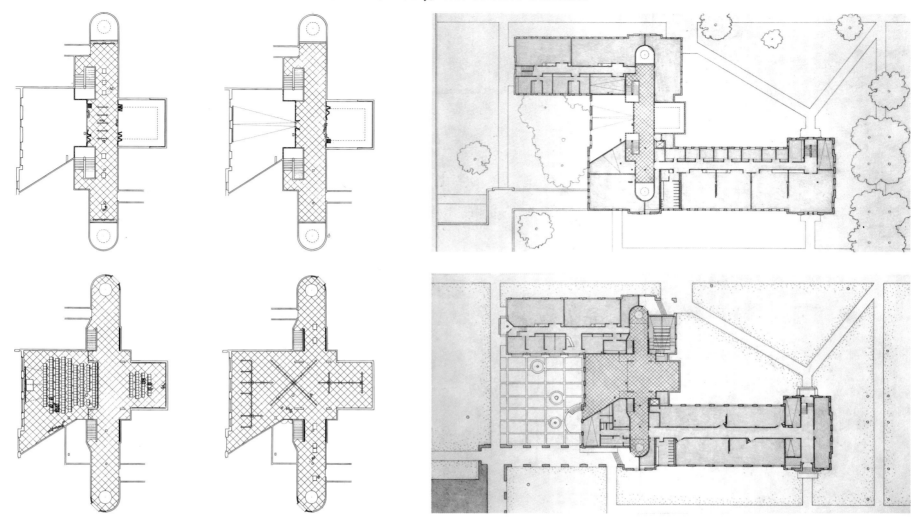

Alternative arrangements of the gallery and crit space

Ground floor plan and first floor plan

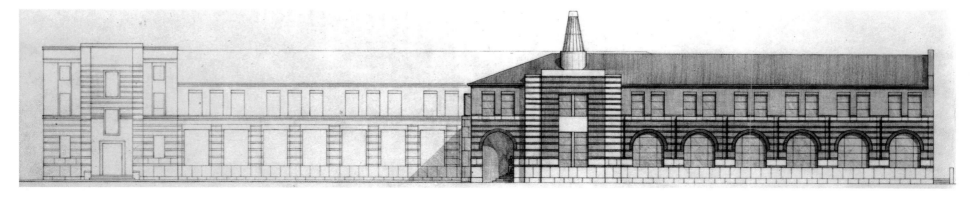

Side elevation

The Wissenschaftszentrum is a sociological research institute. The old *Beaux-Arts* building somehow survived the war and we converted it into secretariat and conference facilities with a new opening into a colonnade behind so that visitors can walk into the garden. The garden loggia has each column tuned like an organ pipe so that in really depressing wet weather the rainwater makes a metaphysical sound rather like Japanese music. The new buildings contain many small offices and to avoid banal repetition we grouped them in five shapes juggled together with the old one, giving each department an identifying form and linking them as a single organism. Walls and windows are applied ironically like wrap-around wallpaper. From inside, projecting stone architraves create the illusion of being in a building with thick walls, which gives a cosier feeling in the offices. The outsides are stuccoed, though not in the usual Berlin Grey; our colours were probably influenced by neoclassical Helsinki and St. Petersburg and some Italian buildings. The plasterers wouldn't stop working accurately and consistently so we had to bring in two old restorers from the Charlottenburg Palace who taught them how not to be so perfect.

View from across the canal

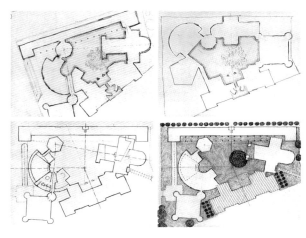

Studies of alternative layouts and alignments

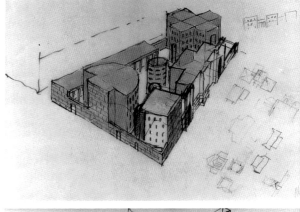

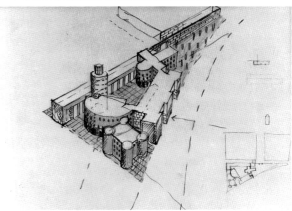

Alternative massing studies

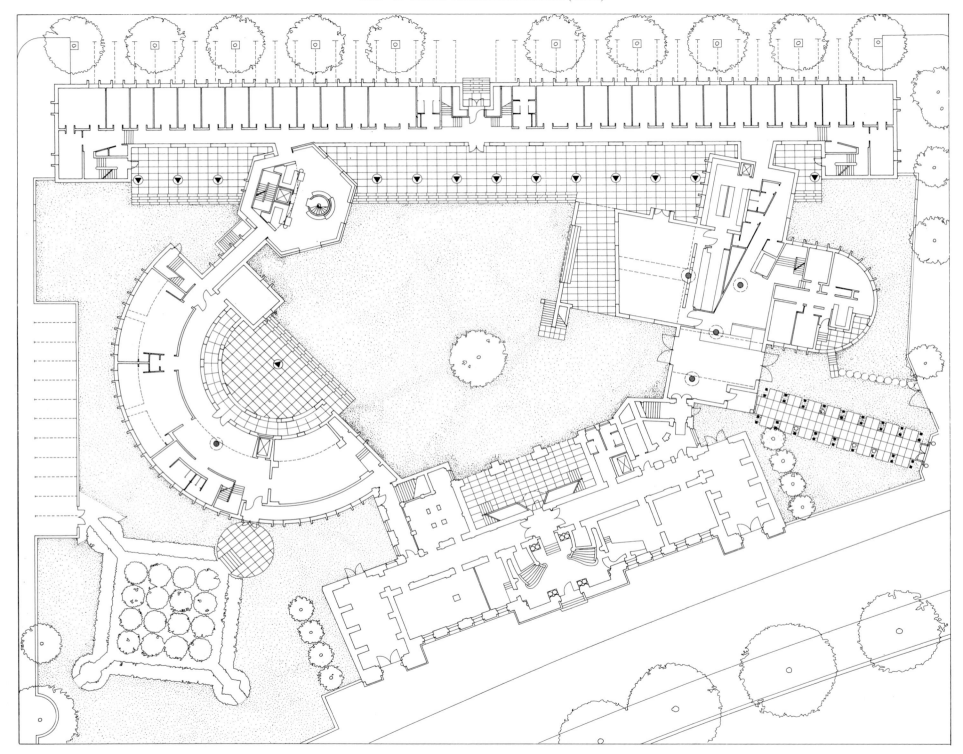

Plan at ground floor level

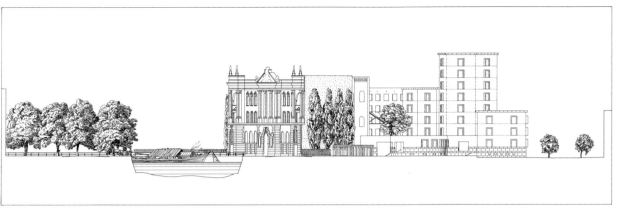

Elevation showing the old *Beaux-Arts* building (now the new Secretariat)

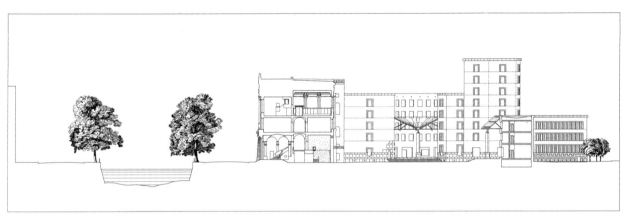

Cross section through the old *Beaux-Arts* building, the courtyard, and the Loggia

Elevation

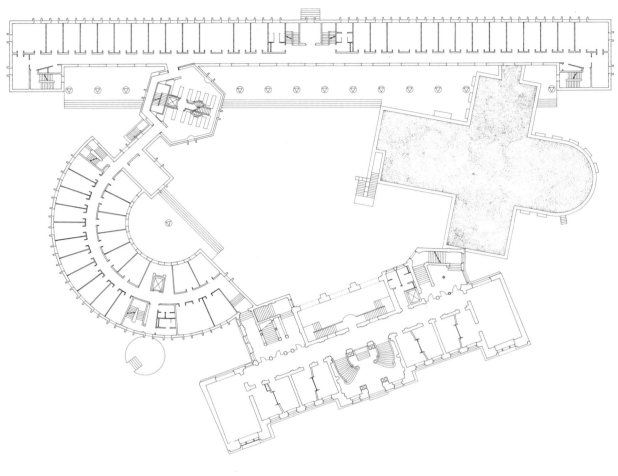

First floor plan. The hexagonal building contains the Library

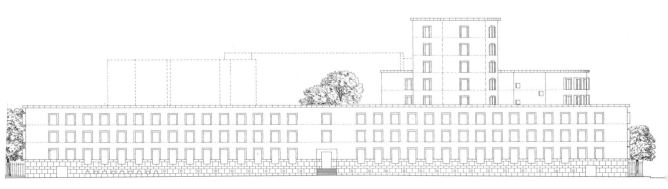

Elevation

1979–87 Berlin: Wissenschaftszentrum (WZB)

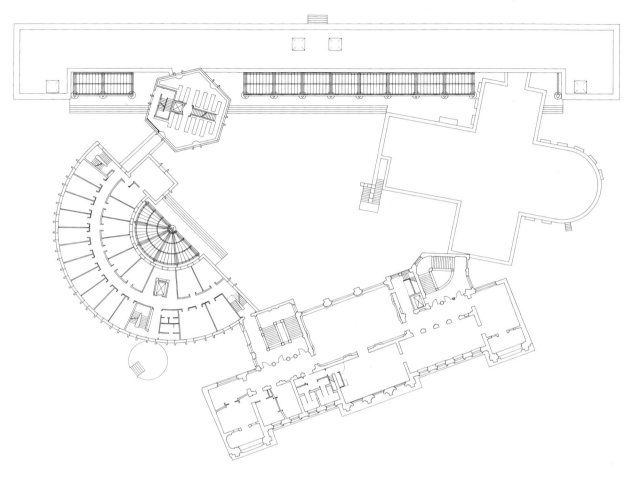

Upper level of offices and library

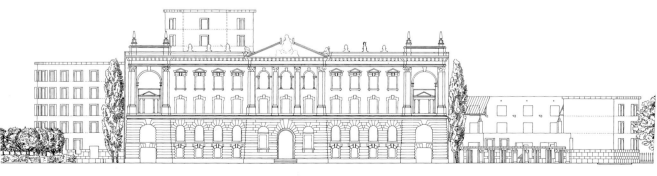

Front elevation showing the old *Beaux-Arts* building

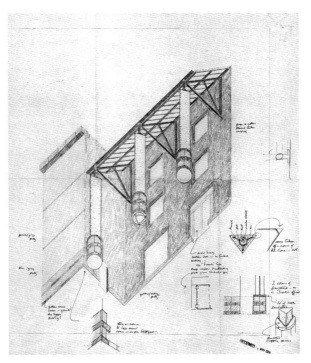

Detail studies for the loggia annotated by JS

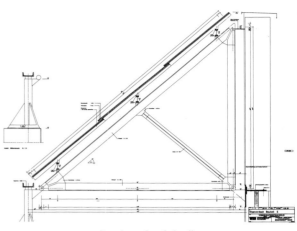

Loggia steelwork details

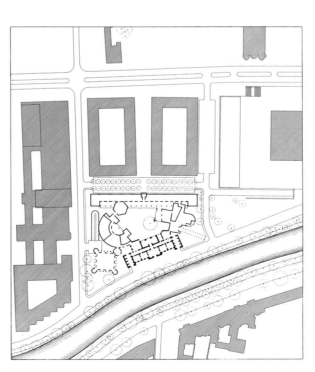

Location plan

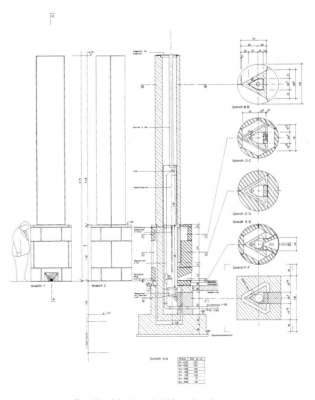

Details of the "musical" Loggia columns

The main entrance flanked by pylons to support the future bridge

The rounded end of the building

The museum occupies a L-shaped site on the Harvard campus opposite the Fogg Museum. It houses oriental, ancient, and islamic art and provides space for special exhibitions, curatorial departments, library collections, teaching rooms, and offices. The principal façade stands on a sunken forecourt. The main entrance is flanked by two "monumental" columns which will carry a future bridge linking the museums. A vehicle passage through the building keeps service invisible from the street. The curving façade responds to the polychrome brick of an adjoining building; its "random" windows result from being centrally placed in different-sized rooms. The vestibule leads into a lobby with a gallery for temporary exhibitions. A grand staircase, lit by a rooflight, rises straight ahead. Its polychromed walls harmonise the interior of the building with the exterior. Halfway up, a doorway on the left opens into five office levels and a door on the right leads to the second level of exhibition rooms. At the head of the stair, a glazed door opens into top-level galleries, with ceiling scoops to allow indirect daylighting of the exhibits.

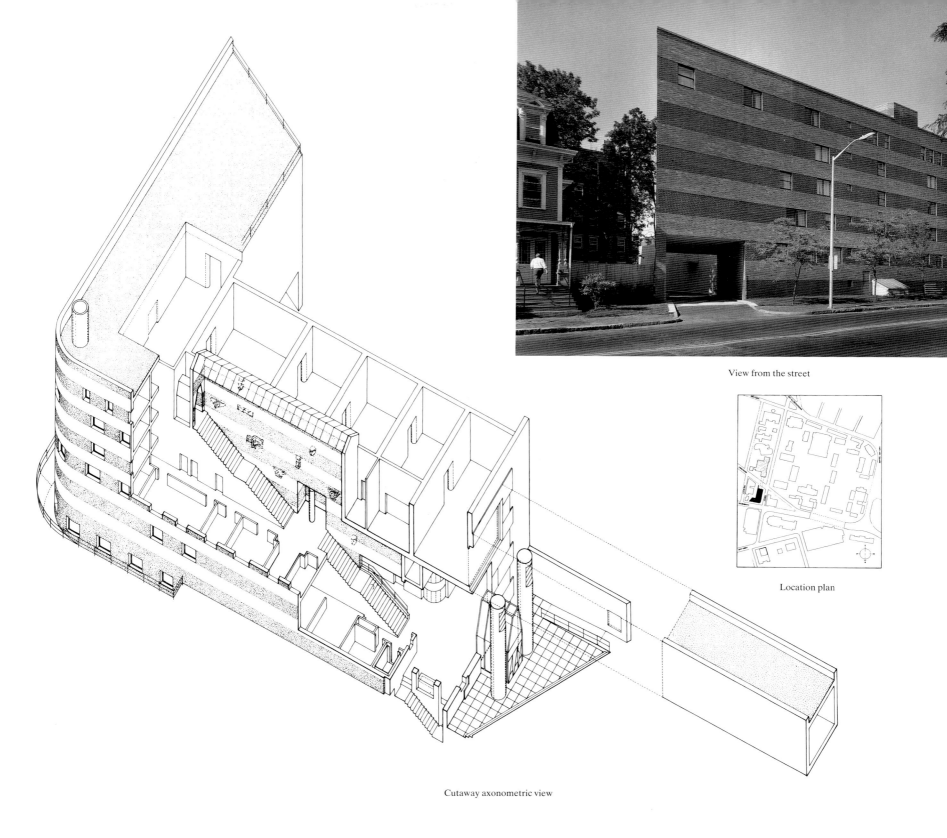

View from the street

Location plan

Cutaway axonometric view

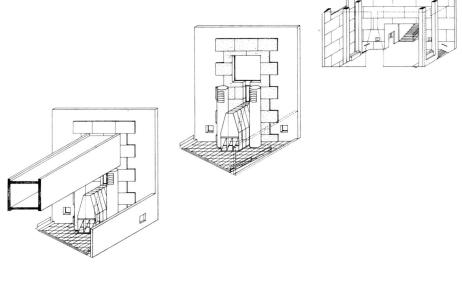

The future bridge and the entrance

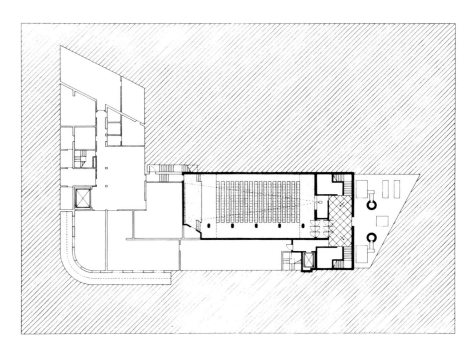

Basement plan with lecture theatre

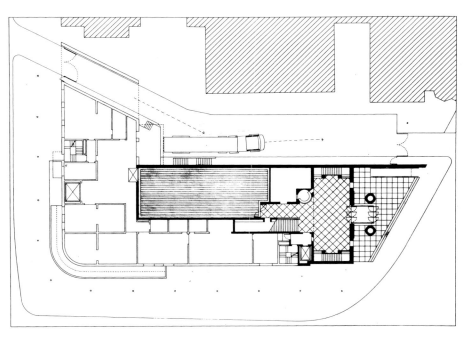

Entrance level plan with ground floor gallery

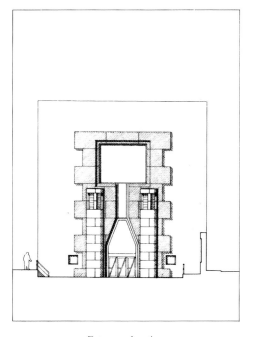

Entrance elevation

Perspective of the future bridge

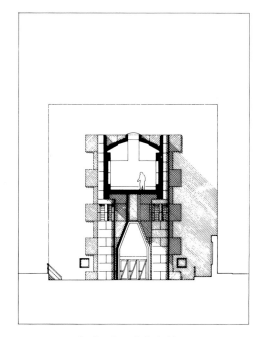

Section through the bridge

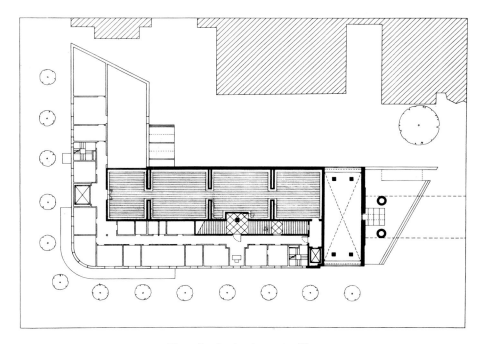

First gallery level and access to offices

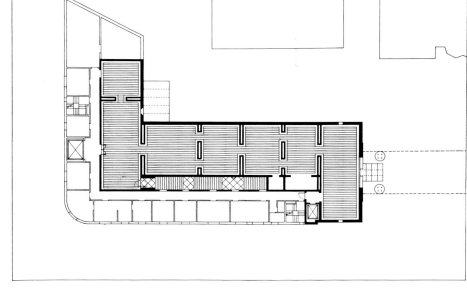

Second gallery level

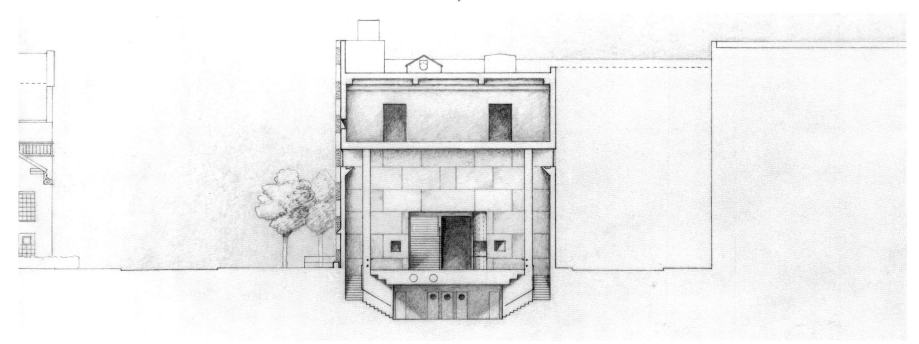

Cross section through the entrance hall

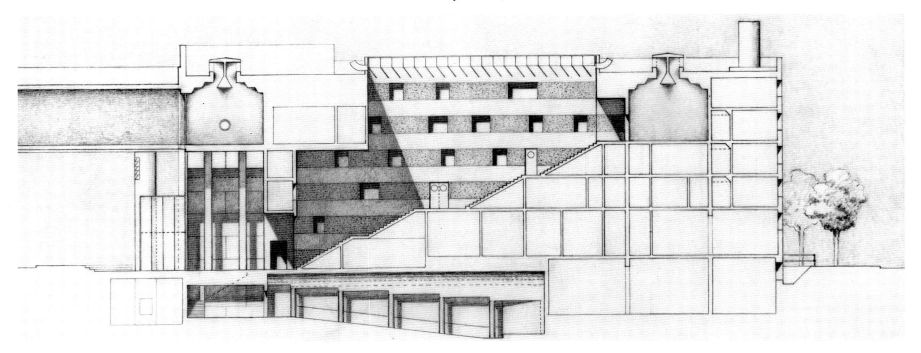

Longitudinal section through the entrance hall and central staircase

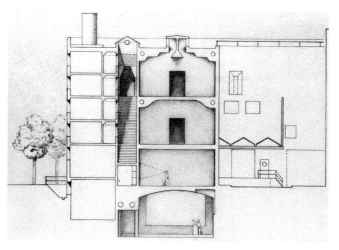

Cross section showing the offices, the central staircase,
the three levels of galleries, and the basement lecture theatre

Interior of a top-lit gallery room

Looking down the central staircase towards the entrance hall

The view from Broadway

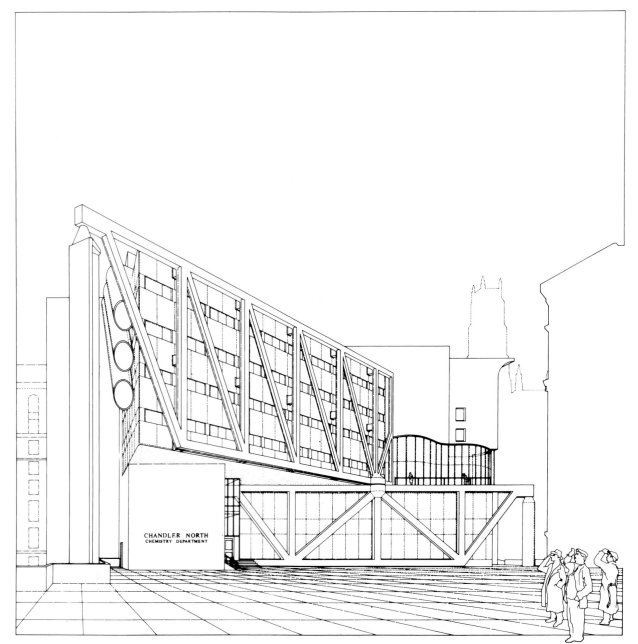

The steel structure and the reading room beyond

CHANDLER NORTH
CHEMISTRY DEPARTMENT

The new department maintains the alignments and rhythms of existing buildings on Broadway. The lower floors have a steel structure which vaults over an existing gymnasium and shelters the main entrance; above, the building splits into two diverging wings of chemistry laboratories. To encourage sociability, monotonous corridors are avoided by arranging circulation through the laboratories themselves and by focusing on a spacious lobby at the core of the building, where informal discussions could take place. Receptions and special events are held at the sixth floor, in a reading and meeting room with an external balcony overlooking Broadway.

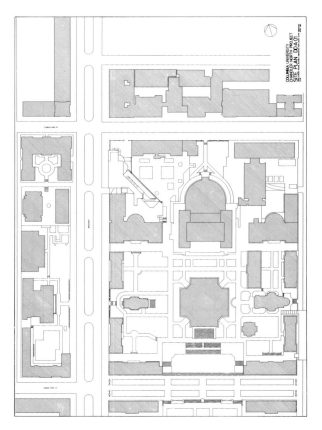

Location plan

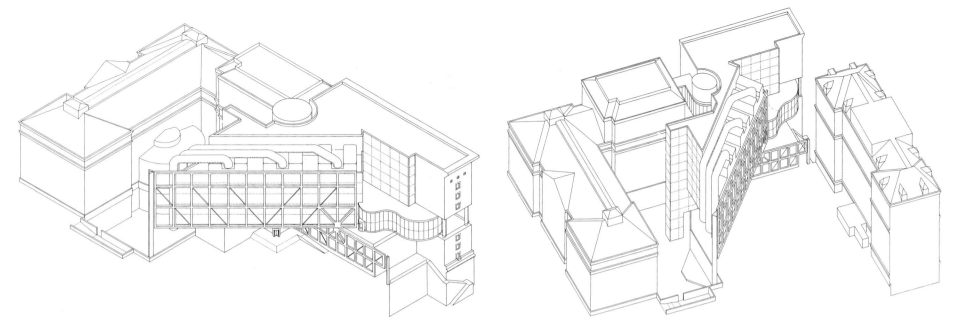

Down axonometrics of an earlier scheme

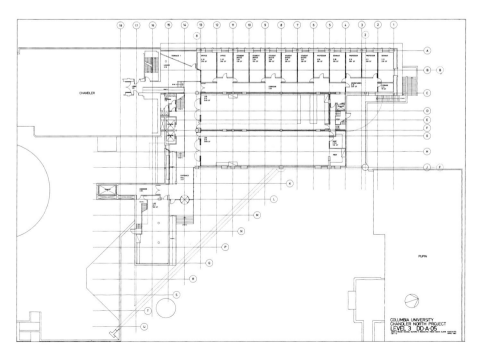

Plan at entrance level

Plan at reading room level

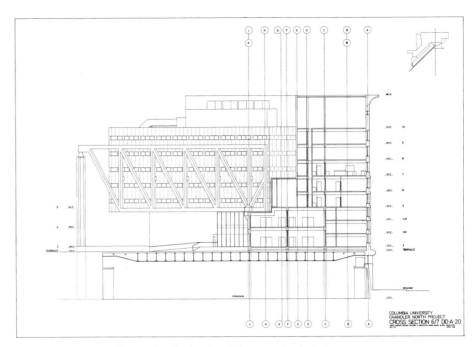

Cross section showing the existing gymnasium in the basement

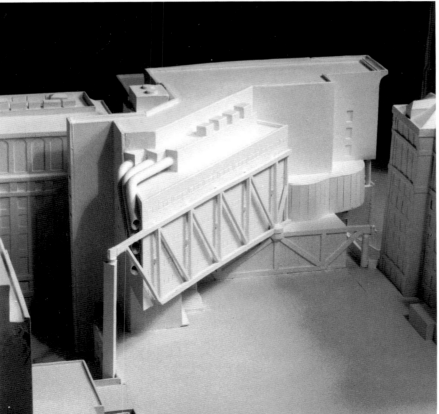

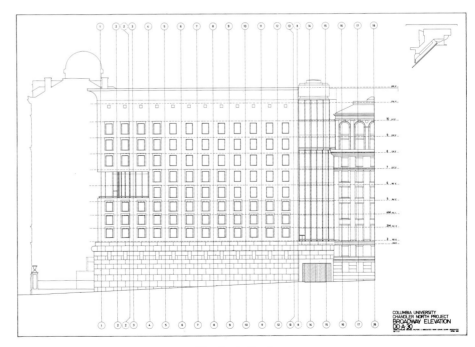

Elevation to Broadway

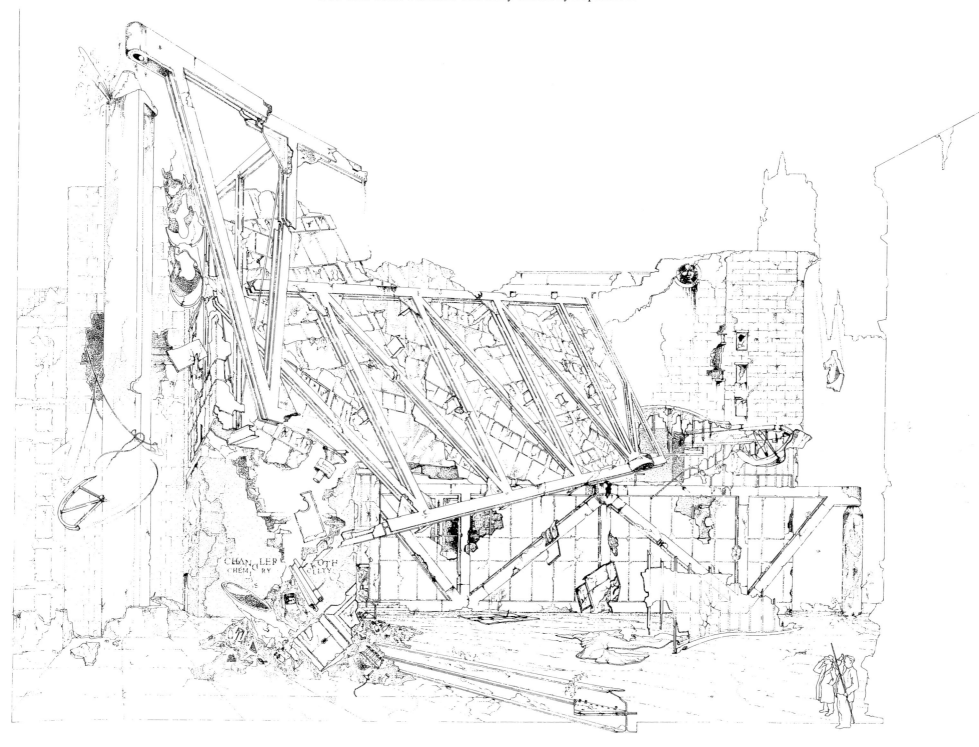

The project was cancelled due to departmental reorganisation

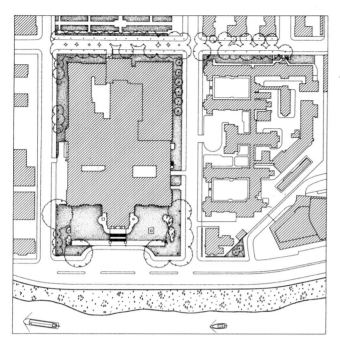

Plan of the Tate Gallery in 1980

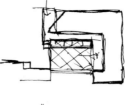

Initial studies

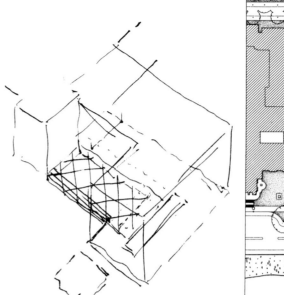

Early sketch

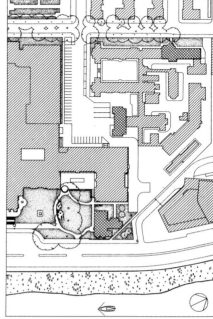

Plan with Clore Gallery added

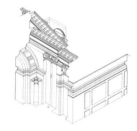

Architecturally, the Clore mediates between the existing Tate Gallery and Lodge. It maintains the existing cornice line but sets back to leave the symmetrical front of the Tate undisturbed; by bringing the new entrance wing forward and making it higher to echo the corner pavilion of the existing building, a sense of enclosure is given to the garden. The new gallery is linked internally to the older building, but also offers an alternative approach through the garden, along a sunken terrace with a pergola, a pool, and benches. Visitors arrive in a "monumental" entrance and lobby, and mix informally in the brightly-coloured double-height entrance hall. Public facilities include a ticket and bookshop counter, cloakrooms, a lecture theatre, and a periodicals reading room with a bay window seat which looks out across the garden towards the river Thames. Non-public areas at this level include a paper conservation department, staff rooms, and a private room for the Turner Society which also overlooks the garden. The main staircase is naturally lit from a skylight above, and leads to the more formal atmosphere of the Turner exhibition galleries at the upper level. These are planned as a promenade through a sequence of rooms, each related to the scale or groupings of the works on show; the main galleries are lit from above by natural daylight through specially-profiled ceiling scoops, fitted with computerised louvres which adjust automatically to compensate for variations in the intensity of the sunlight. A bay window with seats allows visitors to rest and enjoy the garden.

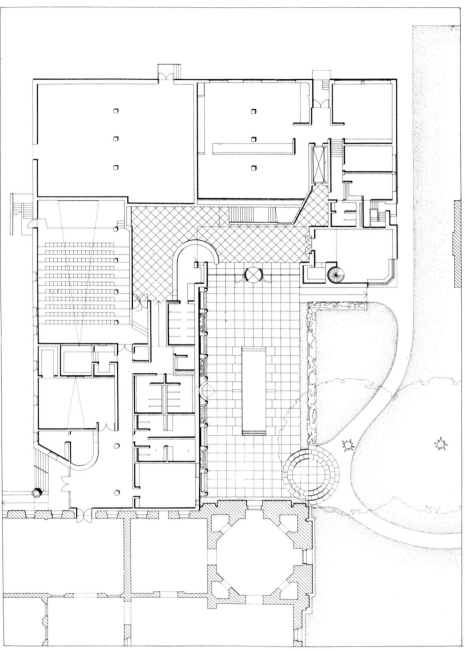

Ground floor plan

1980–86 London: Clore Gallery (Tate Gallery)

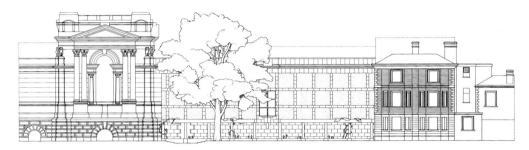

Elevation to Millbank and the River Thames

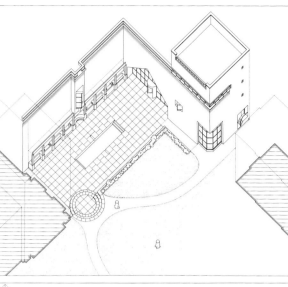

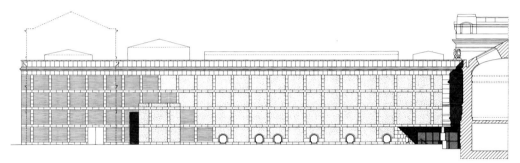

Back elevation

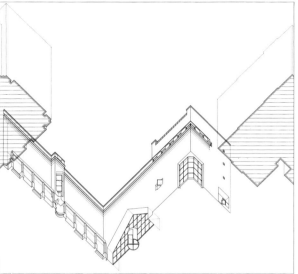

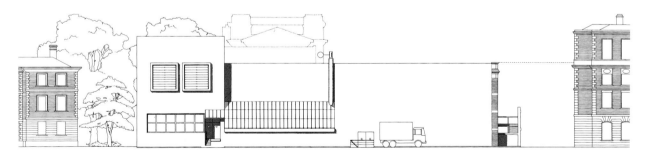

Side elevation to the service yard

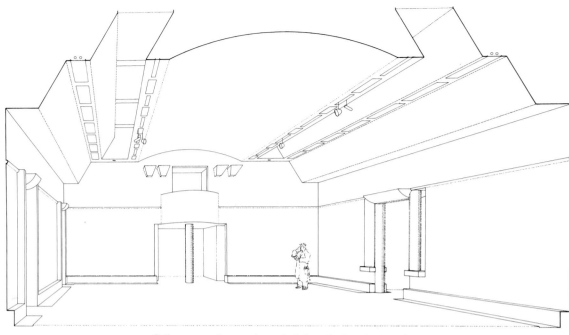

Gallery perspective; opening under balcony leads to the upper foyer

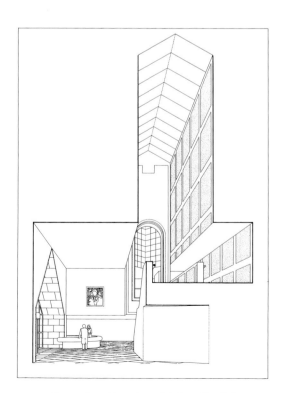

Perspective of foyer towards information desk

Foyer and main staircase

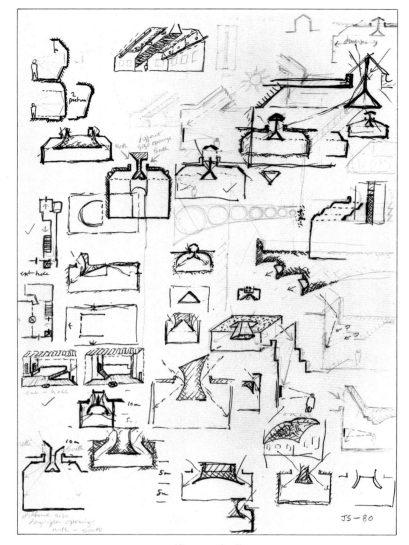

JS concept doodles

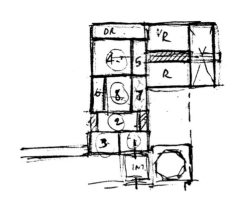

Early sketch of gallery layout

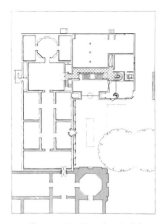

Octagonal gallery (not built)

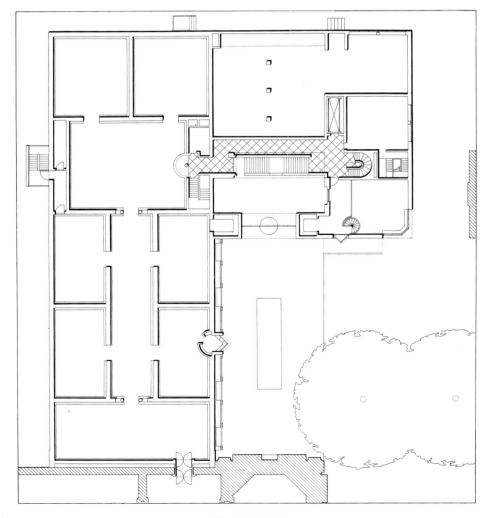

Plan at gallery level

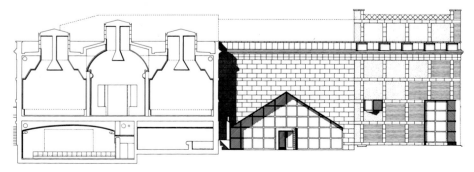

Cross section showing top-lit galleries

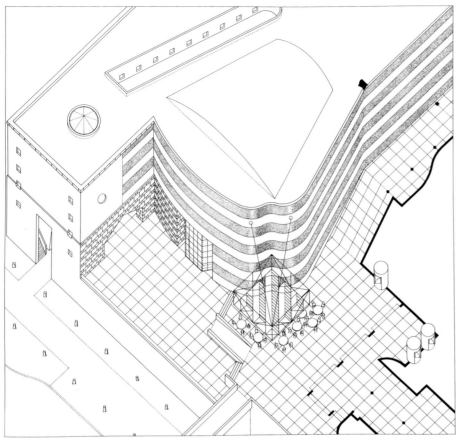

Down axonometric

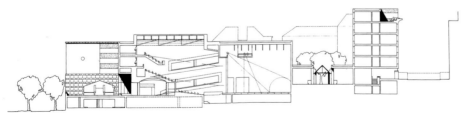

Longitudinal section

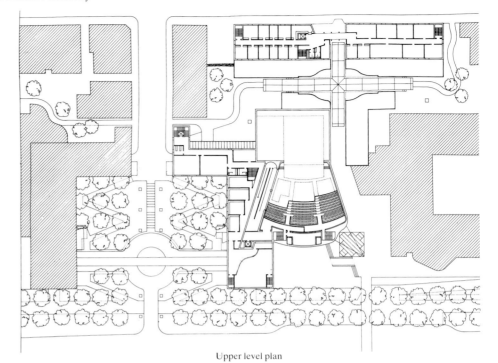

Upper level plan

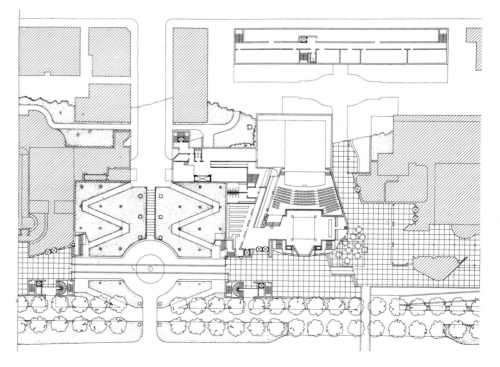

Plan at entrance level

This was an early study scheme for a group of buildings which included the Ministry of Sports and Culture, a concert hall, a school of acting and opera, and a multifunctional zone with shops and art galleries. It was designed as a continuation of our Neue Staatsgalerie and Chamber Theatre (1977) and occupies the same site as our later project for the Music School and Theatre Academy (1987). The acting and opera school overlooks a new public garden created by repeating the projecting wing of the Chamber Theatre, and an existing pedestrian walk-through from the back of the Staatsgalerie is extended to form a garden arcade flanked by shops and restaurants. The rectangular Ministry building is at the rear and contains five floors of administrative offices, with a continuous arcade of commercial art galleries at ground level along the street.

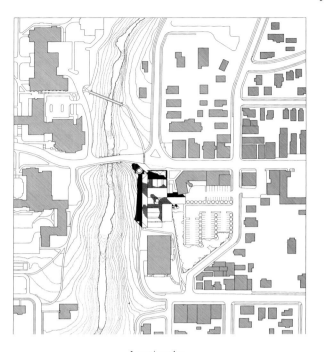

Location plan

Cornell campus in 1983; Cascadilla Gorge is at the left. The site is beside the Gorge

The building's position, beside a bridge over Cascadilla Gorge, is marked by an octagonal pavilion denoting the gateway to the Cornell campus and attracting outsiders to theatrical events; it serves as a bus shelter and houses the campus information centre. The sidewalk extends round it into a plaza, with a pergola and seats where students can meet. Entry is by steps or ramp down from the plaza to a loggia, which connects the various parts of the building as a promenade overlooking the gorge, looking out towards Lake Cayuga. During intermissions, the public can use the loggia as an extension of the foyer, encouraging interaction between performers, guest artists, students, and faculty. Midway along, a three-storey entrance hall gives access to the various departments and serves as foyer to both the Proscenium and the Flexible Theatre. The upper balconies are connected by a stair and elevator (marked by a campanile). Underneath is a film forum for 100 people. The 450-seat Proscenium Theatre is horseshoe-shaped with a forestage which is adaptable as a thrust stage or orchestra pit; under it is a dance performance studio with removable seating for up to 132 people. The Flexible Theatre allows arena, thrust, or proscenium seating for up to 175 people, and under it is a laboratory/black box studio for a total of 100 people. In all, the building contains a total of 10 auditoria or studios, as well as a reading room, green rooms, administration and faculty offices, acting and dance studios, scenery rooms, props rooms, and costume shops.

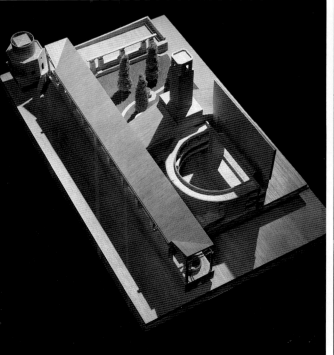

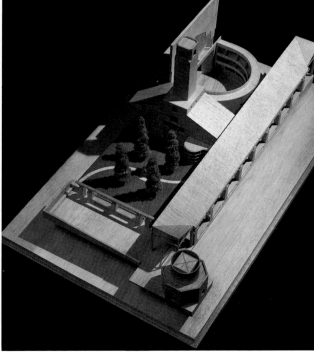

Model showing Phase 1 of the project

109

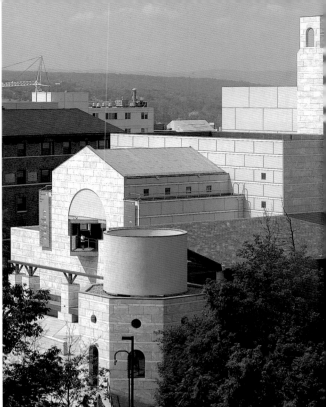

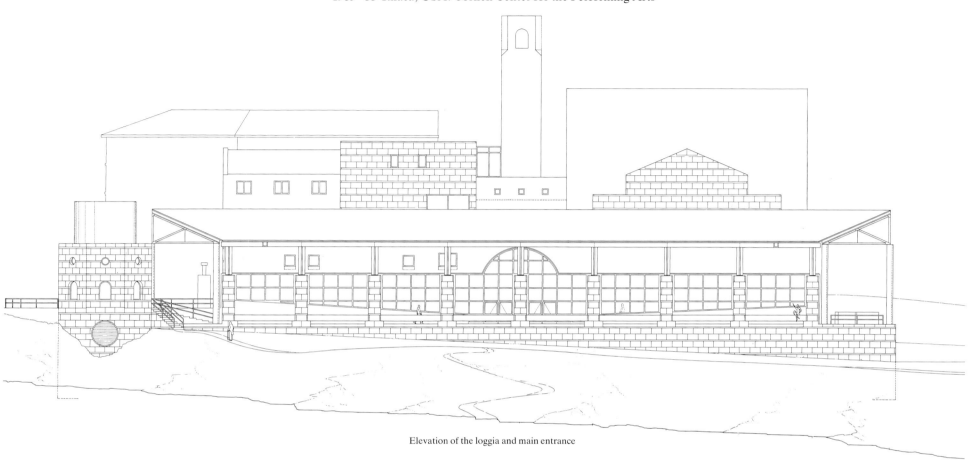

Elevation of the loggia and main entrance

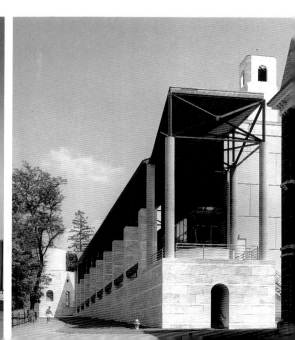

Forecourt and loggia

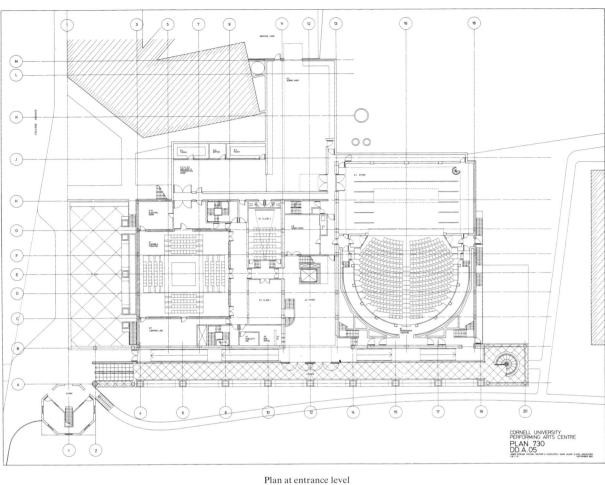

Plan at entrance level

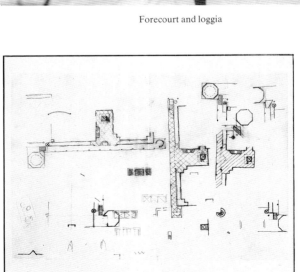

Concept sketches

The foyer

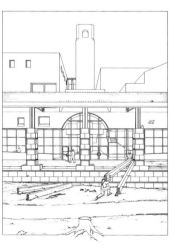

The main entrance

Interior of the foyer

112

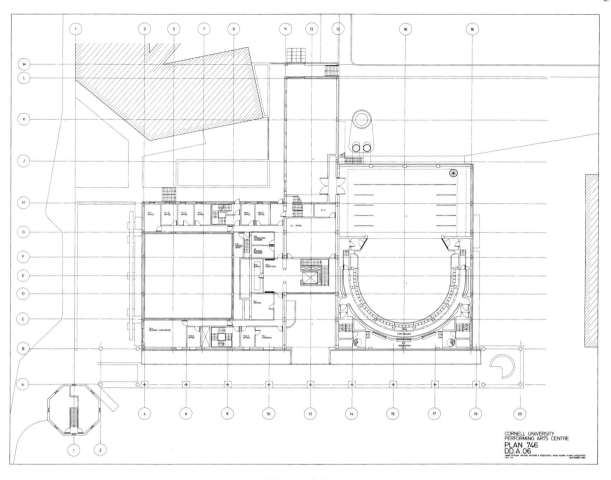

Upper level plan

Flexible theatre

Sectioned perspective of the foyer

Flexible theatre

1983–88 Ithaca, USA: Cornell Center for the Performing Arts

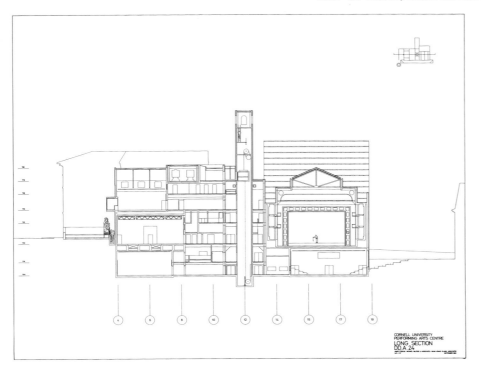

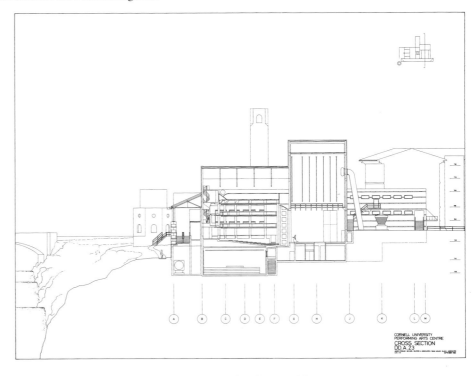

Section through flexible theatre and proscenium theatre

Section through proscenium theatre and fly tower

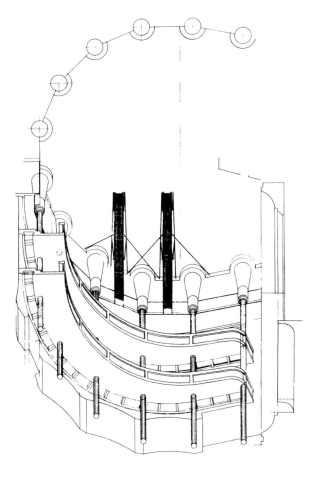

Up axonometric of the proscenium theatre

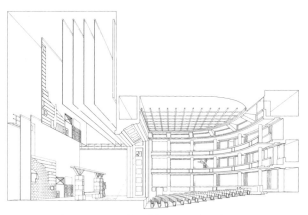

Cutaway perspective of the proscenium theatre

View from the street

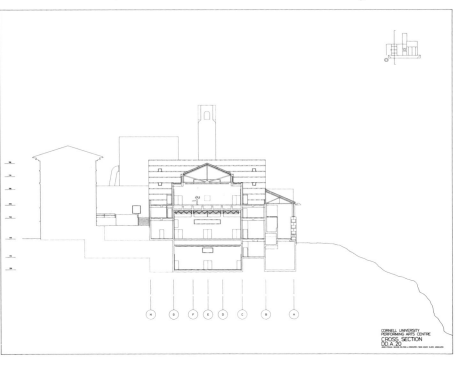

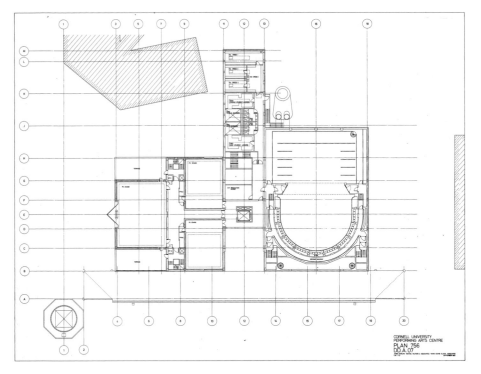

Upper level plan

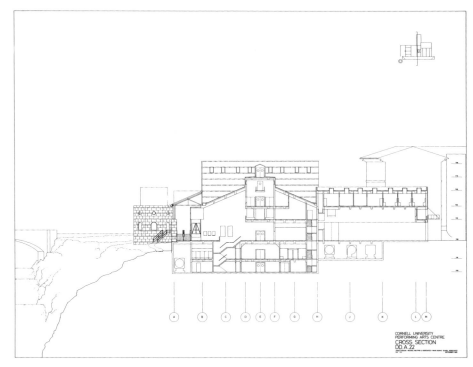

Cross section through entrance hall

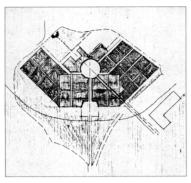

Sketch scheme

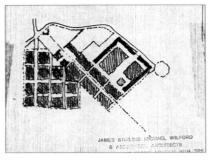

Sketch scheme

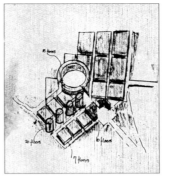

Sketch scheme

This was our uncompleted scheme for the development of a green-field site in the south-western suburbs of Bologna, designated to act as a new centre for the surrounding town of Casalecchio, with a new town hall, school, housing for 10,000 inhabitants, and shops and small offices. Because of its location beside the junction of three national motorways, the client also required the provision of a hypermarket, a trade centre, large headquarters offices for international companies, and a national alternative energy research centre, with easy drive-in access for all functions and direct connection into the motorway system. The quantity of accommodation required meant that the density of the scheme would be very high, and the regulations required enormous amounts of car parking. The area was surrounded by motorways, feeder roads, railway stations and shunting yards, as well as Casalecchio cemetery, all protected by statutory zones where no building was allowed. All regulations on street widths and setbacks had to be respected. These constraints made it impossible to achieve physical connection of the new centre into the existing urban context of the town, pushing all the buildings away from the edges of the site into the middle. The schemes were based on a triangular piazza at the centre, surrounded by offices and shops, with three multistorey cylindrical towers containing offices and a hotel. The research centre was placed to the north, near the motorways, and the other large functions attracting motorway traffic were located around the edges of the scheme, with car parking spreading out to occupy most of the green areas where building was not permitted. The residential and small business functions would have been placed at the centre in courtyard blocks on arcaded streets, in the traditional local manner.

Plan study

Plan study

Plan study

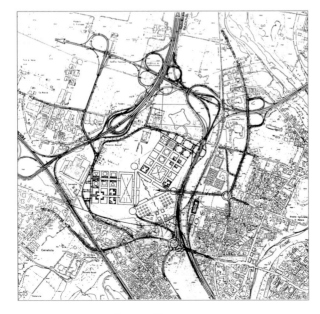

Layout with motorways

Study layout

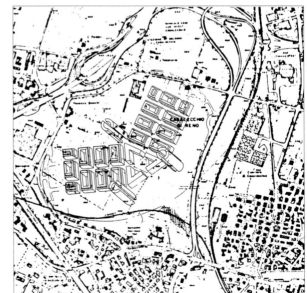

Volumetric study

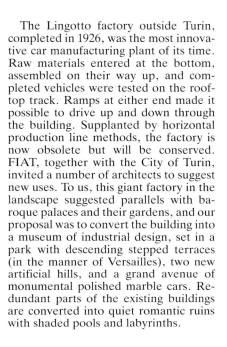

The Lingotto factory outside Turin, completed in 1926, was the most innovative car manufacturing plant of its time. Raw materials entered at the bottom, assembled on their way up, and completed vehicles were tested on the rooftop track. Ramps at either end made it possible to drive up and down through the building. Supplanted by horizontal production line methods, the factory is now obsolete but will be conserved. FIAT, together with the City of Turin, invited a number of architects to suggest new uses. To us, this giant factory in the landscape suggested parallels with baroque palaces and their gardens, and our proposal was to convert the building into a museum of industrial design, set in a park with descending stepped terraces (in the manner of Versailles), two new artificial hills, and a grand avenue of monumental polished marble cars. Redundant parts of the existing buildings are converted into quiet romantic ruins with shaded pools and labyrinths.

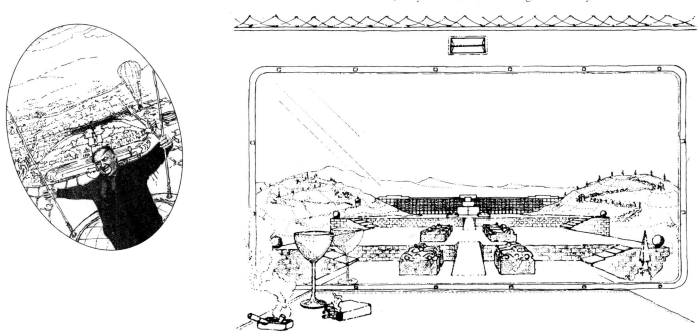

The view from the train

Elevation from the railway showing the two new artificial hills

Lingotto in 1983

Typical interior in 1983

Design museum interior

119

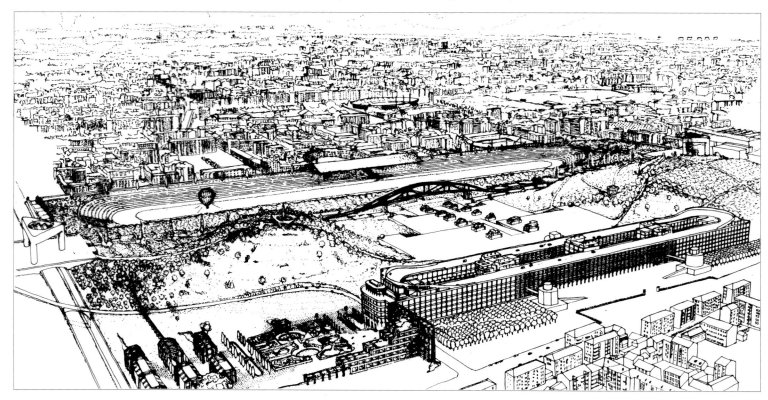

Aerial view

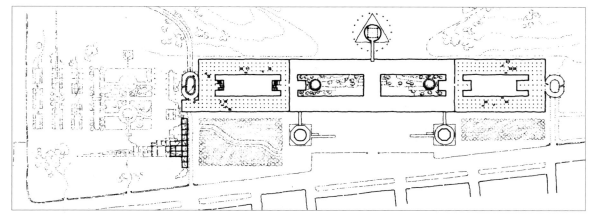

Plan at upper floors

Cross section showing the grand Circus (left), the Avenue of Cars, and the Museum (right)

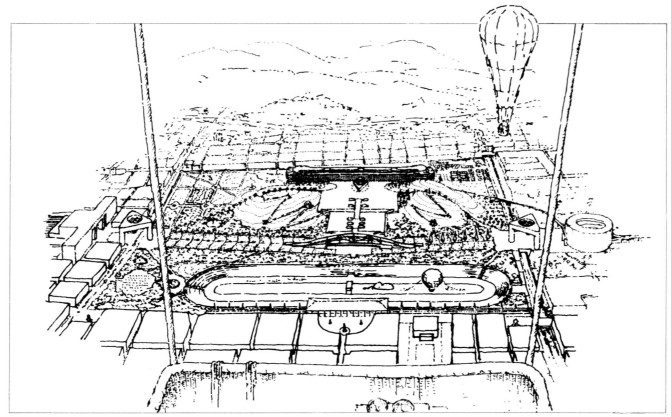

View as seen from the balloon

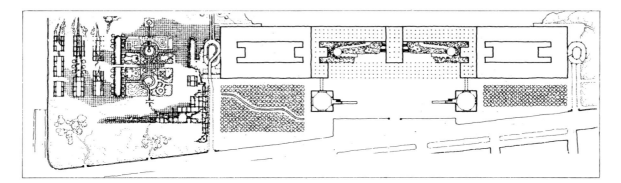

Plan at lower level

Front elevation

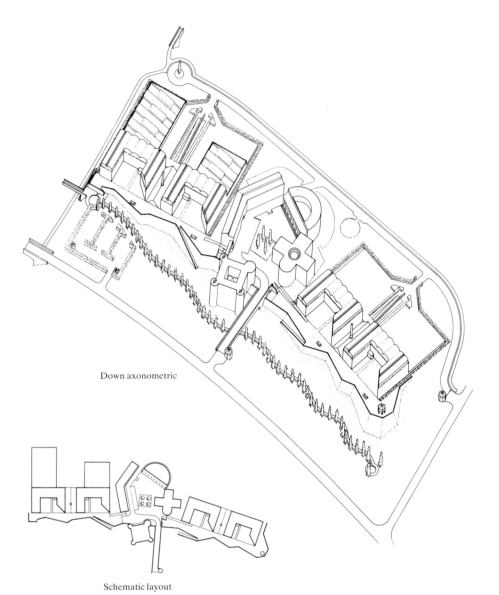

Down axonometric

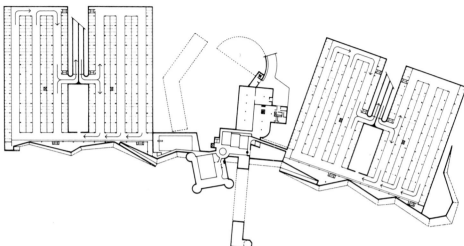

Lower level plan with underground parking

Schematic layout

Model

Front elevation sectioned through the "castle"

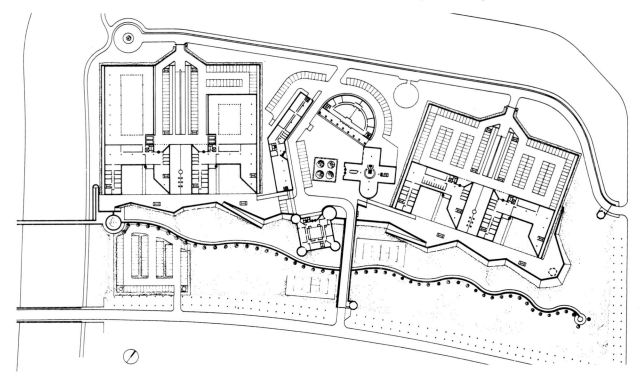

Entry level plan

This headquarters for a newly-privatised national tele-communications company avoids monotony by creating an informal grouping of buildings set on an artificial plateau, in a "campus" arrangement of departmental buildings enclosing open courtyards, with special buildings clustered around a plaza at the centre. The different shapes ensure that the headquarters avoids an "institutional" feel and that users can orientate themselves easily. By planning the various facilities as pavilions placed along a promenade, a considered relationship between architecture and landscape is achieved. The largest departmental buildings are placed at the back and look south towards the main boulevard, enjoying panoramic views over the open landscape. The foreground is designed as a park with tennis courts, terraces, lawns, fountains, and a tree-lined walk which runs alongside an artificial "moat". Large areas of unsightly car parking are concealed by locating them in an undercroft behind the retaining "fortress" wall along the front of the site. The two large U-shaped buildings contain various office and service departments, splayed to reflect the grid layout of central Milton Keynes and the alignments of the surrounding roads. The buildings grouped round the plaza comprise: a cranked shape containing the Directorate and Reception, linked by a footbridge to the adjoining departmental building; a cruciform block with three levels of restaurants and private dining rooms all arranged so that they enjoy good views to the outside; and a semicircular building which contains a conference centre. The "castle"-shaped building at the front extends the "rampart" theme established by the retaining wall and is a floor higher than the other buildings to enable its four towers to support satellite dishes.

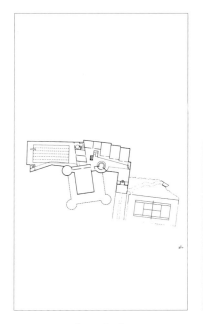

Lower level

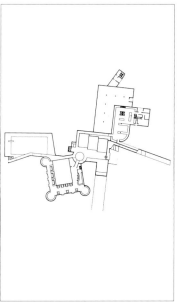

Intermediate level

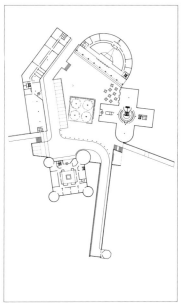

Entrance level

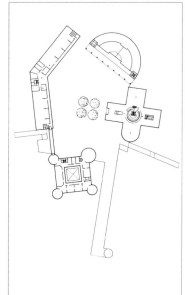

First floor

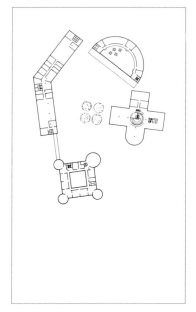

Typical upper floor

The model showing existing 1930s garage, garden, and new library

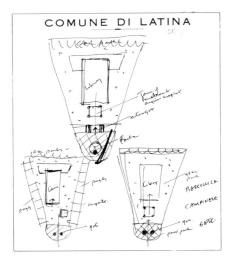

JS doodles

Latina was built in the 1930s in the swamps south of Rome: a city without a history. The new library was to fill this cultural gap by providing space for over 200,000 books and accommodation for up to 500 people at any given time. The building connects two streets along one edge of a triangular site, facing a new public garden which incorporates two existing 1930s buildings. At garden level the building contains a children's library, bar, lecture theatre, and general hall. From a public loggia at the main level above, the entrance hall gives access to two reading rooms: lending library on the left (with a ziggurat) and reference on the right (with reading balconies). The glazed roofs incorporate control systems which optimize reading light. The extremities of the building contain bookstacks and informal reading rooms with windows overlooking the street. Administration offices, clubrooms, meeting rooms etc. are located at the non-public upper floors.

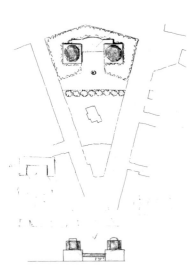

Concept sketch annotated by JS

124

1983 Latina, Italy: Municipal Library

The site in 1983

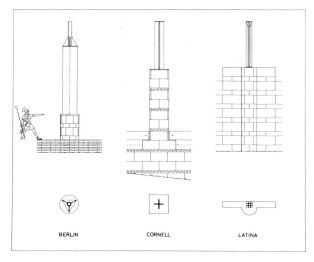

Comparative column studies:
Berlin 1979 – Cornell 1983 – Latina 1983

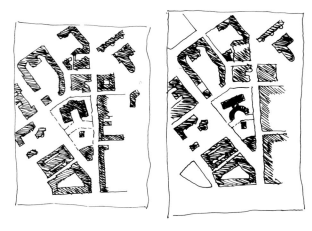

Alternative block studies

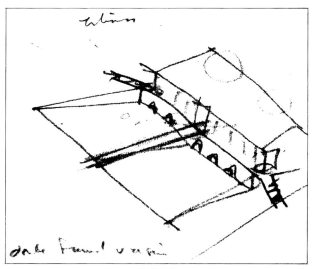

JS doodle

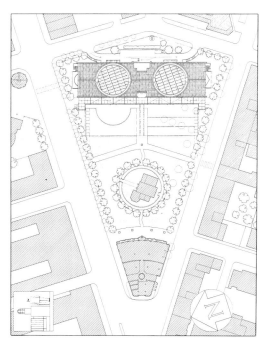

Site plan

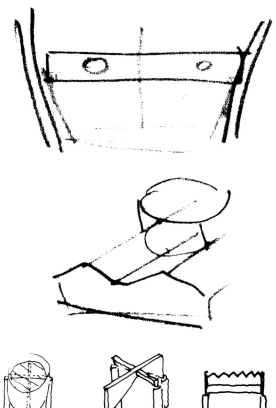

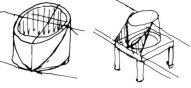

Sketch studies of the daylighting drums and roof

View of model showing public loggia and ramp down to the garden

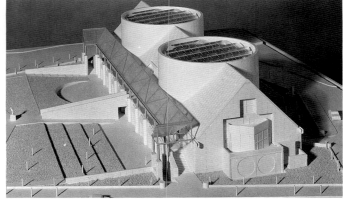

View of the model showing roof-top glazing

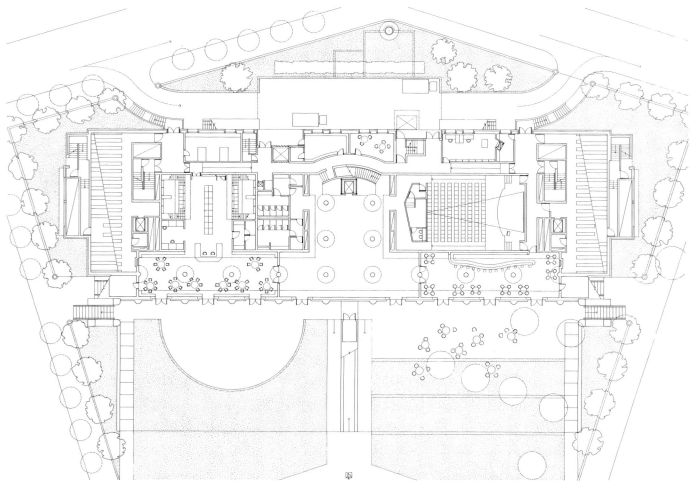

Garden level with children's library, cafeteria, service access at rear

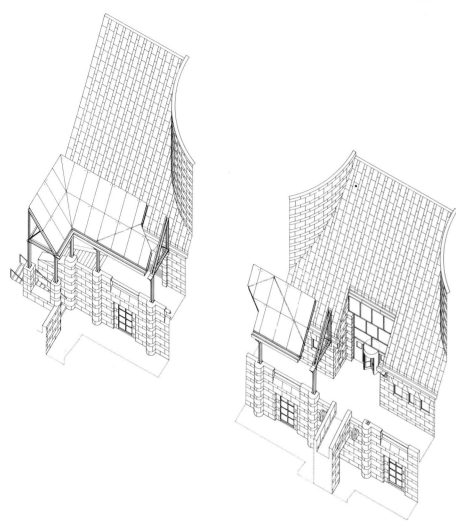

Down view of part of the main front (the loggia is cut away to show the entrance door)

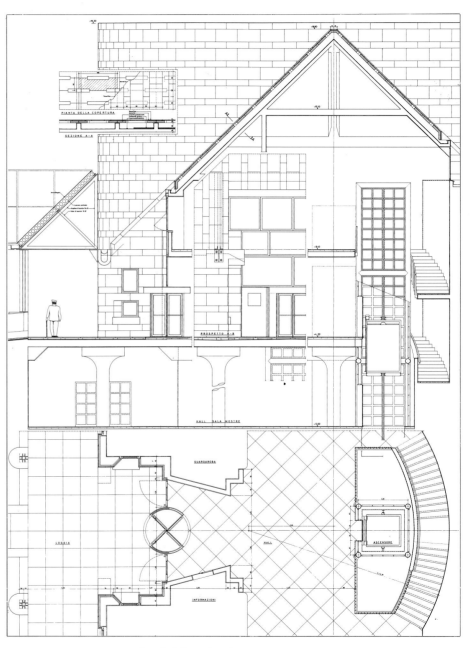

Detailed plan and section of the entrance hall

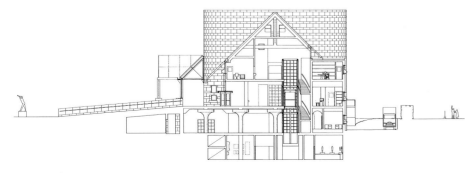

Cross section through the garden ramp and entrance hall

Model with the roof removed

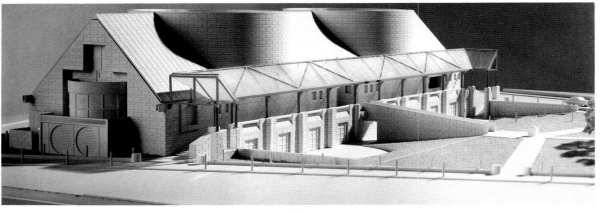

View of the model

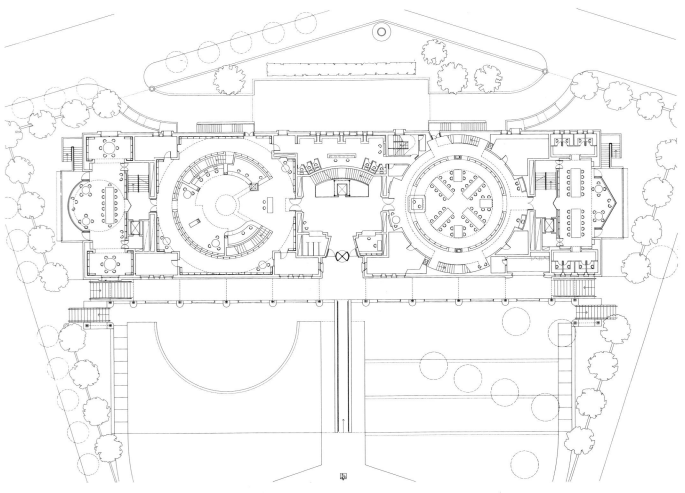

Plan at main entrance level with lending library (left), reference library (right)

1983 Latina, Italy: Municipal Library

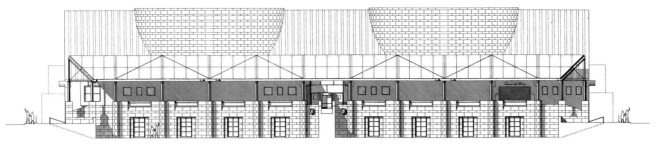

Front elevation seen from the garden

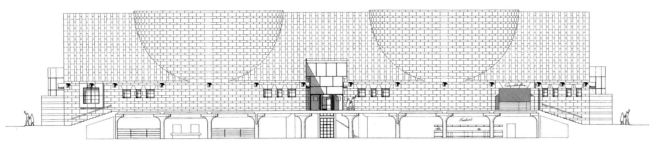

Longitudinal section through the loggia overlooking the garden

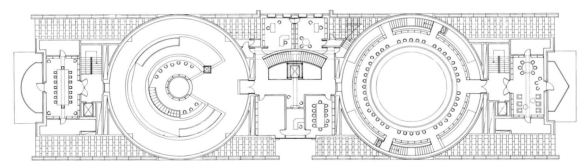

Plan at upper level of the libraries

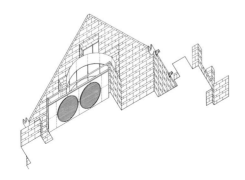

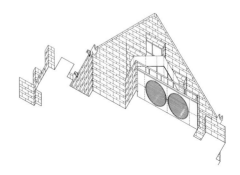

Up axonometrics of the two ends of the building

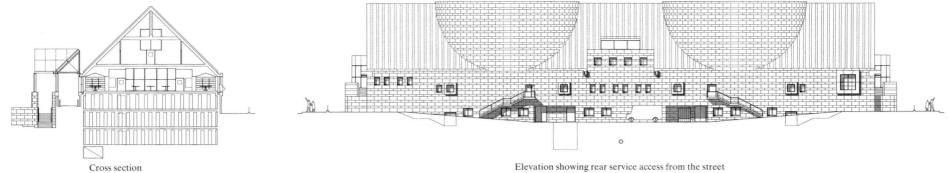

Cross section

Elevation showing rear service access from the street

Model (glazed roofs removed to show lending and library, bottom, and reference library, top)

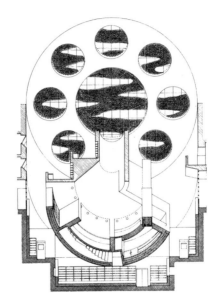

Up axonometric of the lending library

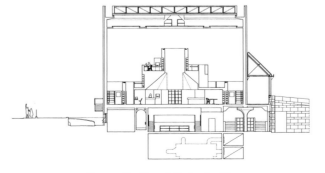

Cross section through the lending library

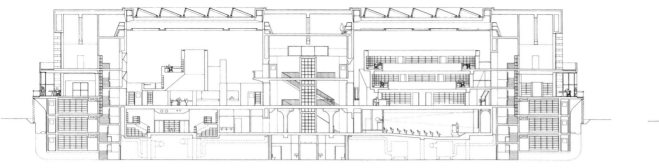

Longitudinal section through lending library (left), and reference library (right)

Cross section

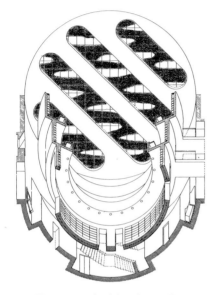

Up axonometric of the reference library

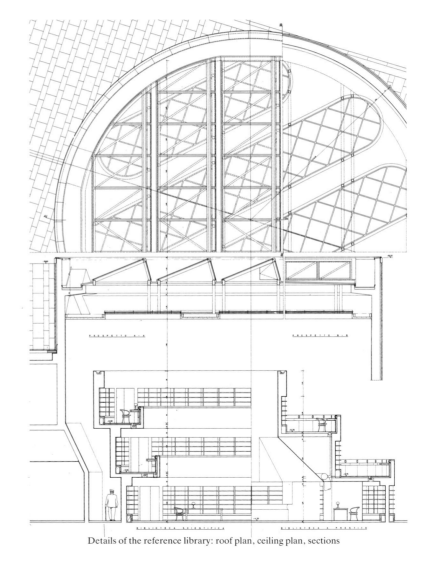

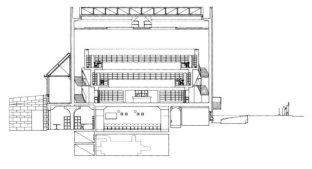

Cross section through the reference library

Details of the reference library: roof plan, ceiling plan, sections

The Tate Gallery occupies one end of Jesse Hartley's 1846 warehouses, on seven floors with a mezzanine at ground floor and a basement. The layout was initially determined by the position of an existing stair at one end, which was retained. Keeping alterations to a minimum, the parts where internal height was greatest were modified, to provide a sequence of galleries with a large entrance hall and new technical services to international standard. Other spaces where the ceiling height was lower were adapted for administration and curatorial offices, a videothèque, educational facilities, and a reading room. The main entrance to the museum is under an arch in the colonnade where ships were once unloaded by crane. This marks the middle of a generous public lobby which extends across four bays of the building and is enclosed by a new external wall with "porthole" windows and "nautical" colours which identify the museum from across the dock. Part of the mezzanine was removed to create a double-height lobby and a balcony for the coffee shop and bookshop. Visitors walk directly into ground floor galleries which can be used separately or together. A new stair and lifts give access to the galleries at the upper floors. A handling and transit area at the third floor is served by a new picture hoist which uses an existing opening at the ground floor. The most important alteration is the addition of a central spine for vertical services distribution, stairs, and lifts. At roof level this contains cooling towers, lift motor rooms, and the tank room. Air handling units are installed at the third floor and make use of existing openings for intake and exhaust. Because the building has low ceiling, new air and power ducting are distributed horizontally around the perimeter in a cavity created by constructing an inner wall alongside the original walls. The new wall provides the hanging surface in the gallery rooms. To ensure good distribution of temperature and humidity in the galleries, air had to be delivered from the centre of each room; to achieve this, a duct system was designed to carry all services, located at high level in the centre of each gallery and supplied from both ends to reduce their overall size. They are supported on brackets which leave the vaults undisturbed.

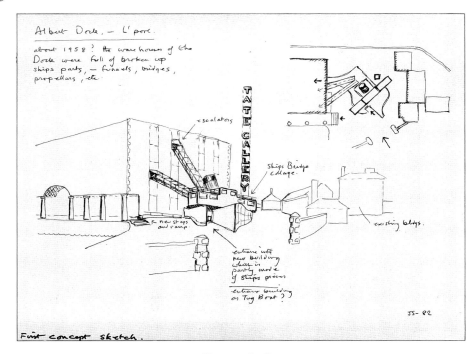

JS concept doodle

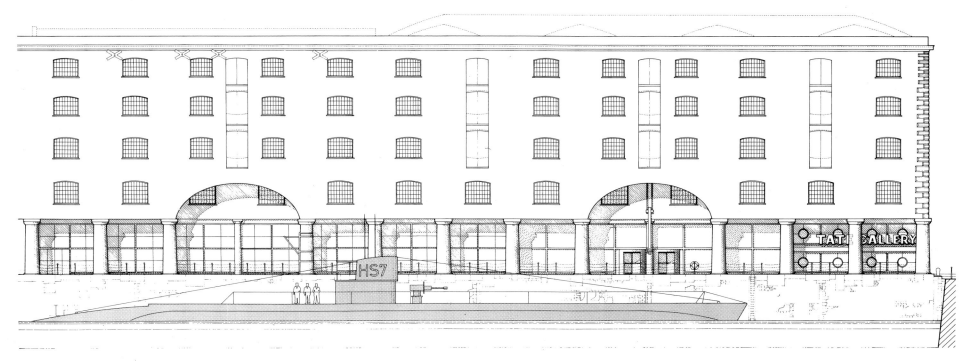

Elevation seen from the Albert Dock

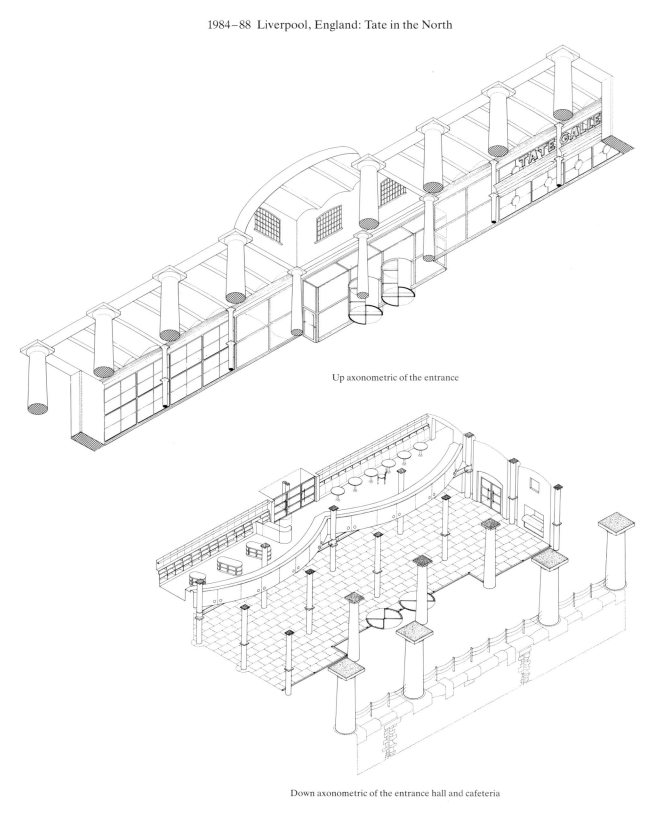

Up axonometric of the entrance

Down axonometric of the entrance hall and cafeteria

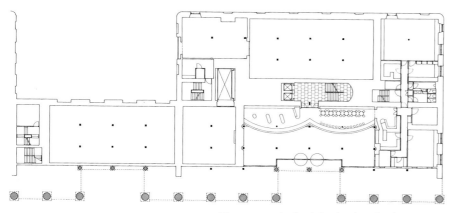

Plan at mezzanine level showing the cafeteria

Plan before refurbishment

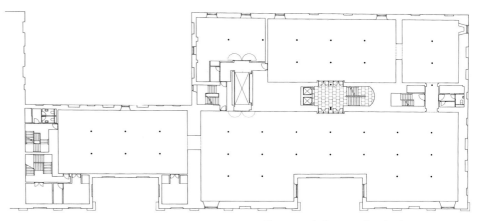

Plan at a typical upper gallery level

Plan before refurbishment

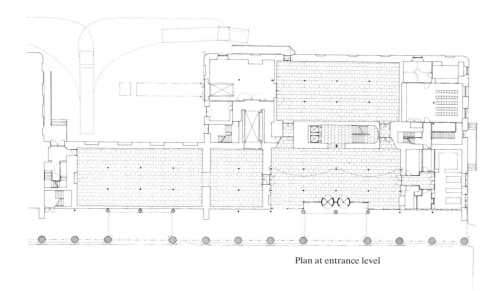

Plan at entrance level

Plan before refurbishment

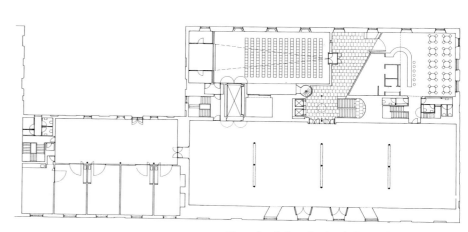

Plan at fourth floor showing the lecture theatre

Plan before refurbishment

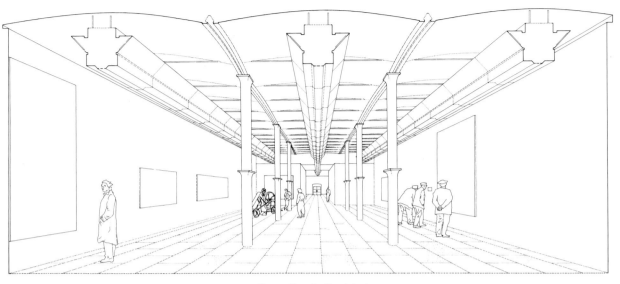

Perspective of gallery interior

Gallery interior

Visitors walk along the cross-axis of the main Tate building, coming out of the galleries into a bow-fronted glazed concourse. Here they can pause to view sculptures arranged in a courtyard below, which is enclosed on one side by the Clore Gallery (Stirling Wilford & Associates, 1980–86). The symmetrical planning of terraces and ramps allows an existing Edwardian building to be incorporated into the layout. People arriving from a street at the back enter through a walled court into a double-height foyer, daylit from a conical lantern above. Paired columns running along this foyer mark the junction between phases 1 and 2 and direct visitors by stairs or lift to the lowest level basement gallery, high enough to accommodate large contemporary works. From the ground floor galleries on the inner side of the building, visitors can go out into the sculpture court or to a cafeteria in the bow-fronted concourse; adjacent to the cafeteria, stairs and lift connect to the upper galleries. The upper floor is occupied by exhibition rooms, all with natural daylighting from above. On the courtyard side, a series of top-lit sculpture rooms leads directly back into the Tate without changing floor level.

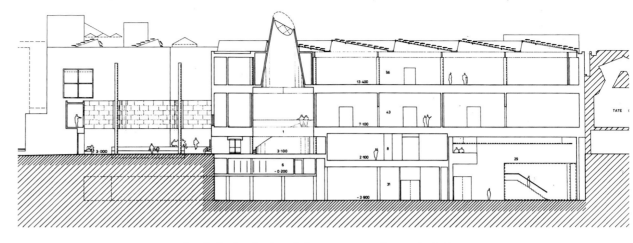

Longitudinal section through the entrance court, foyer, and galleries

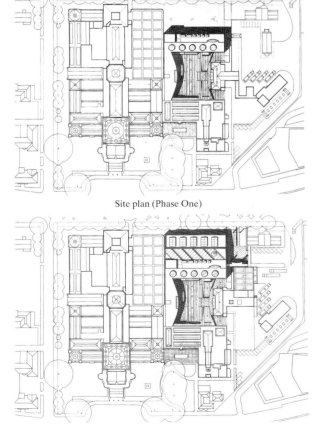

Site plan (Phase One)

Site plan (Phase Two)

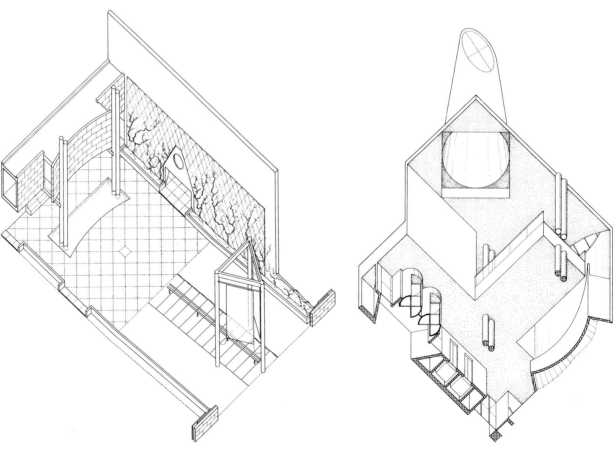

Down axonometric of the entrance court

Up axonometric inside the foyer

139

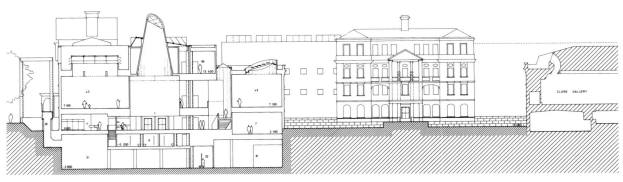

Cross section through the foyer

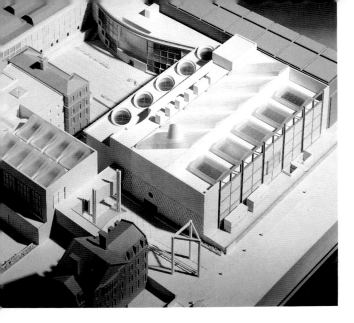

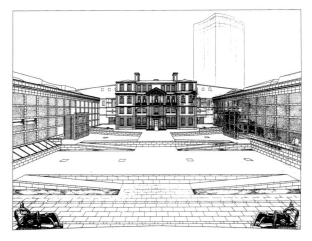

The sculpture courtyard

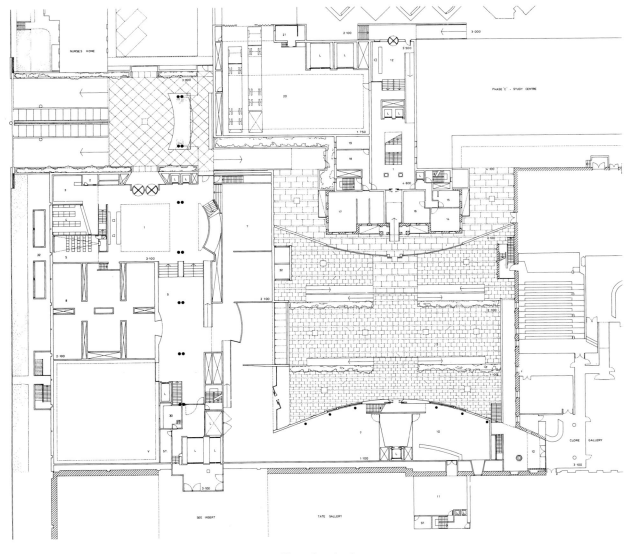

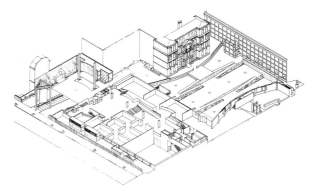

Cutaway plan of museum and courtyard

Plan at foyer level

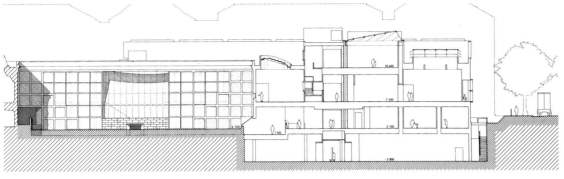

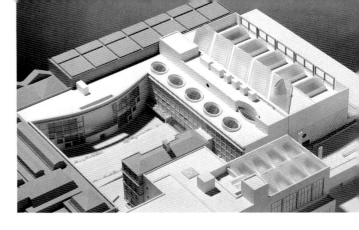

Cross section

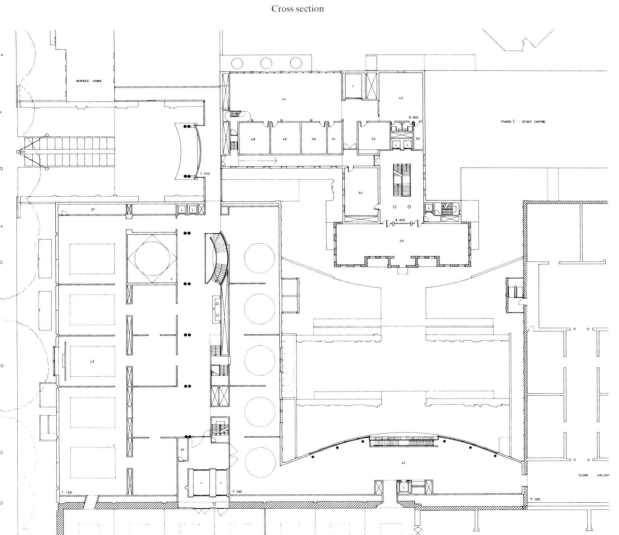

Plan at first floor level

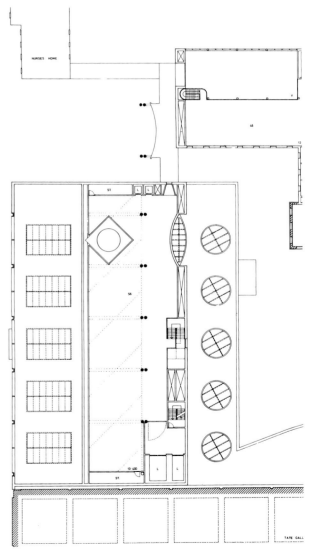

Plan at upper gallery level

This scheme was our first version of a project to integrate the city's transport services into a single interchange. Local and national train services connect into the metro system and link with a new suburban and national bus station. An existing station for commuter and suburban trains is replicated with a second vaulted shed to serve long distance and airport express trains; the two stations are joined by a concourse and have escalator connections to the metro. At the other end of a central plaza, suburban and intercity bus services are combined in a single terminal. Intercity ticketing and check-in are handled in a fan-shaped booking hall, where eighteen separate long-haul bus companies each have their own

facilites. Escalators and lifts connect the hall to departure and arrival levels above. The concourse for suburban buses is in a large rectangular hall with a central information display board and a circular bar/lounge area daylit from a roof lantern above. Waiting areas are adjacent to the twelve departure/arrival gates. The escalators also connect to the intercity bus departure lounge, where there is a second information display and a waiting area with seats. A bar and newspaper shop are located on either side of a central window, with a balcony overlooking the plaza. Passengers walk through glazed doors to board or get off their bus at the twelve arrival/departure bays. Handling docks for baggage and parcels

are located on a central island and are connected by goods lift to the check-in points below. Further bus parking bays are provided adjacent to the entry/exit ramps at the far end, with facilities for cleaning and emergency maintenance; a tower above contains a drivers' cafeteria and dormitory. The heart of the project is the arcaded plaza surrounded by shops, bars, restaurants, and leisure facilities, with offices and hotels above and 400 underground parking spaces below. It is crossed by pedestrian routes which connect the old and new parts of the town and provides a new focus for the central business and shopping district of the city.

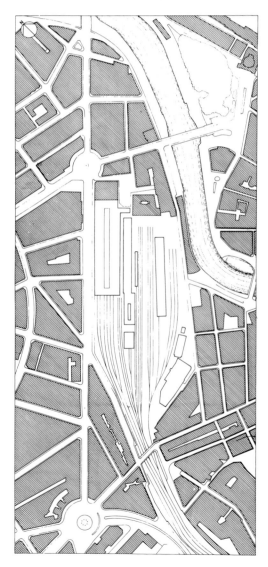

Existing site plan

View of the site in 1985

Location plan (new interchange at centre right)

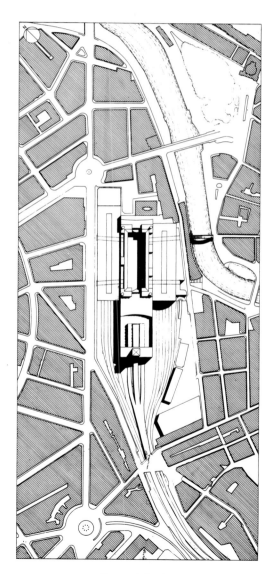

Proposed site plan

1985–   Bilbao: Abando Transport Interchange

Front elevation of the bus station

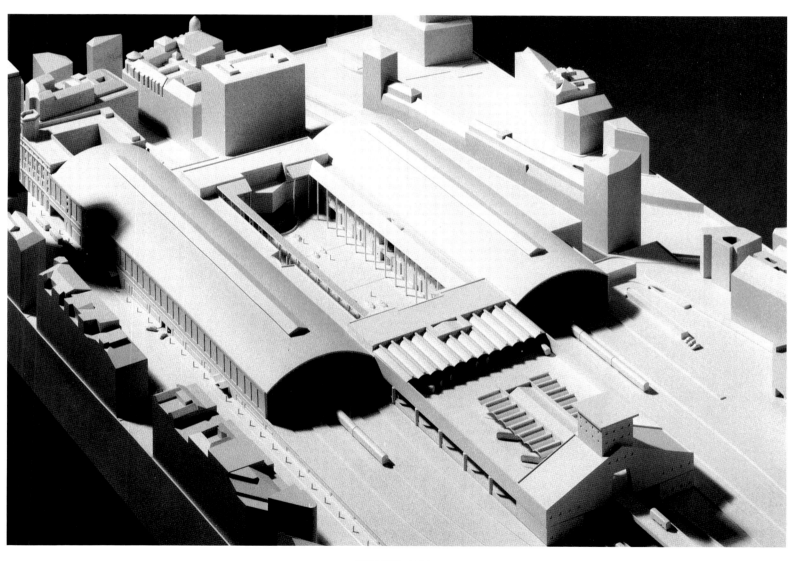

View of the model

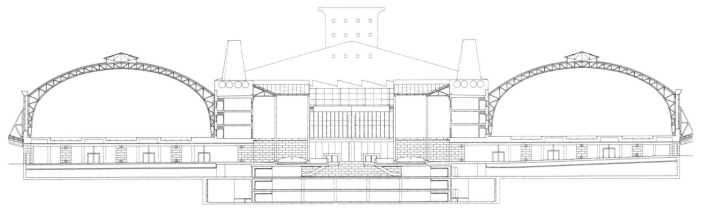

Cross section through the station concourse showing escalator connections to the metro

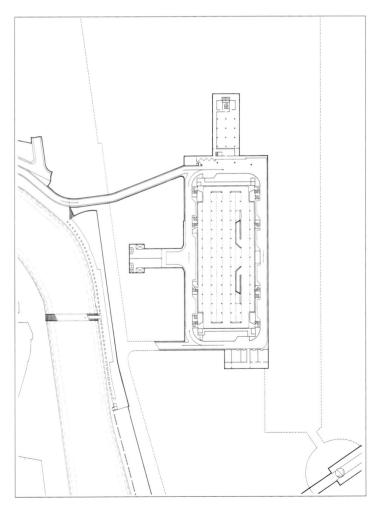

Plan at underground parking level

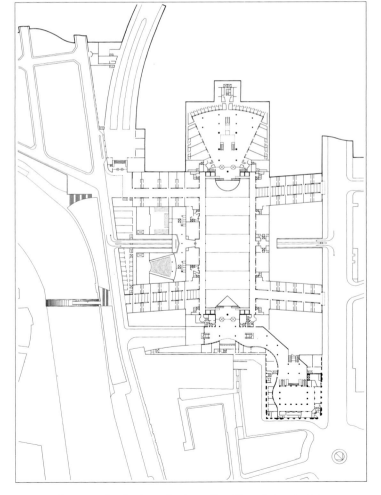

Basement plan showing pedestrian malls and intercity bus check-in

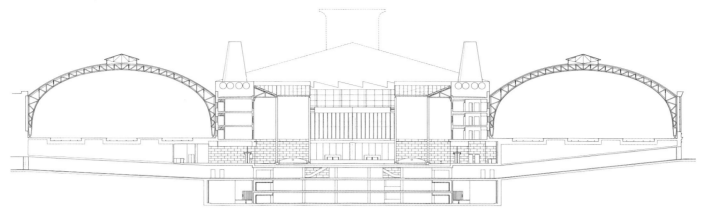

Cross section showing the public pedestrian route under the plaza

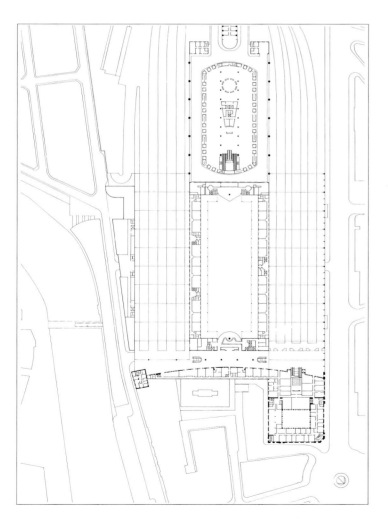

Plan at station concourse level showing intercity bus terminus

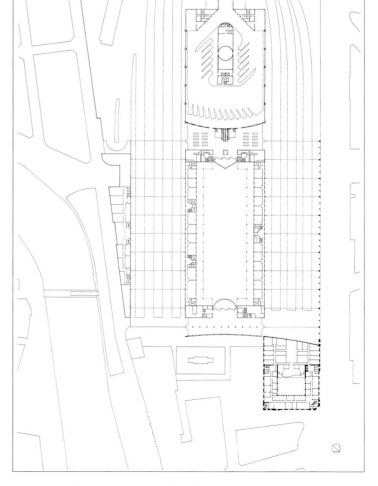

Plan at upper plaza level showing suburban bus terminus

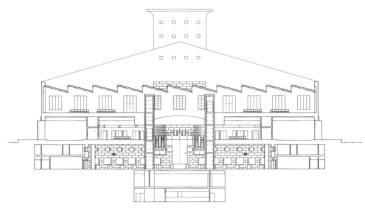

Cross section through bus station booking hall

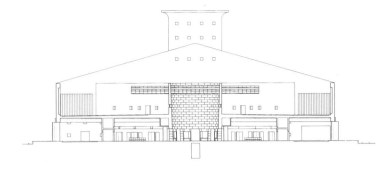

Cross section through bus station

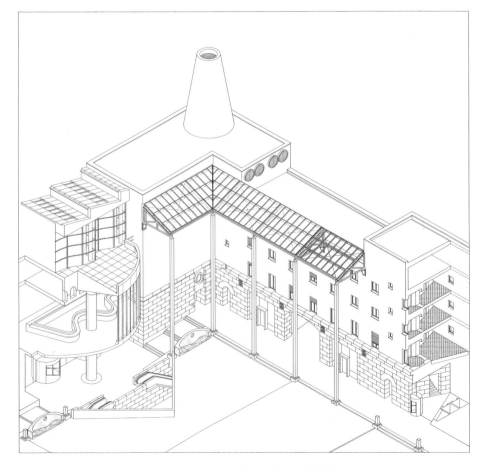

Corner of the plaza (bus station on the left)

View of the plaza towards the bus station

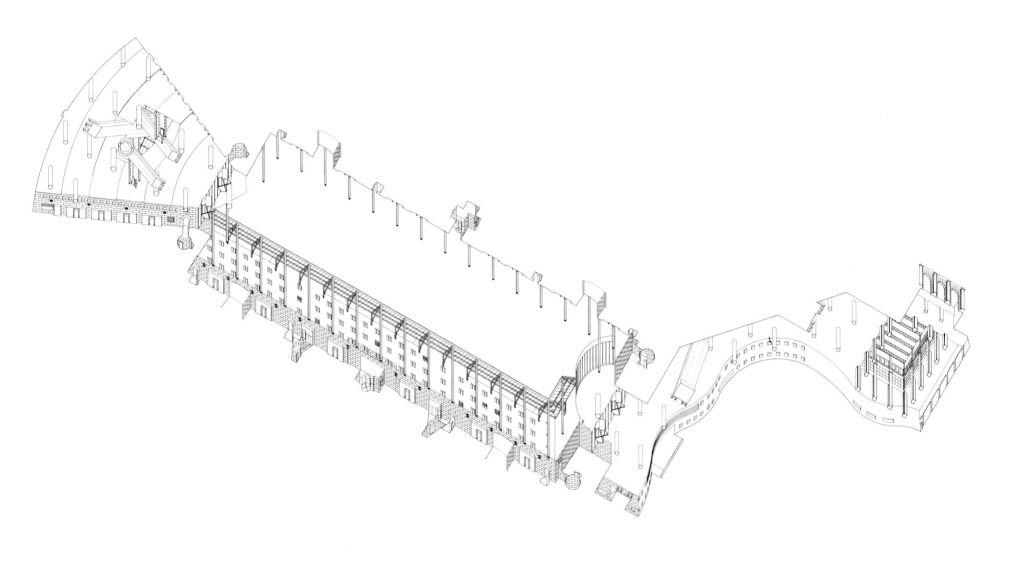

Up view of the plaza (bus station on the left)

Perspective view from Trafalgar Square

This was a competition project for a new building on the corner of Trafalgar Square, linked by a bridge to William Wilkins' original National Gallery of 1834–38. It was to contain galleries to house the Northern European and Early Renaissance collections, including Van Eyck's Arnolfini Marriage, Uccello's Battle of San Romano, and the Baptism by Piero della Francesca. The brief asked for a stone building which would not compete with the existing gallery and for top-lit exhibition rooms of "substantial" character. Trafalgar Square is defined by the colonnades of Wilkins' building and the baroque portico of St. Martin's-in-the-Fields, which projects forward to face the square obliquely. Our new building projects forward to complete this composition, echoing in a limited way some elements of the National Gallery by lining through with its plinth and cornice; but like St. Martin's, it stands as an autonomous building. To the square, it presents a grand stone-dressed pavilion or *palazzo* with a tympanum, cornice, and rooftop rotunda which echo architectural elements of the existing buildings. To the rear, the back elevations, which overlook very workaday streets, are finished in simple plaster rendering with stone bands. Visitors approach either from the main gallery by way of the connecting bridge, or from the square. Circular steps at the entrance create a small plaza with a halfway landing where people can meet or linger. Inside, the entrance hall is faced with stone and has a large window overlooking the square, and a circular opening at the centre which overlooks the bookshop below, recalling the shape of the rooftop drum. The bookshop has its own independent entrance from the street and is connected by stairs back to the entrance hall. The bar/restaurant is reached from the upper level of the foyer, approached by a gently sloping ramp; a monumental staircase leads up to the main floor of toplit galleries, designed as regular, calm, dignified rooms. The basement contains two lecture theatres, cloakrooms, and a large room for changing exhibitions.

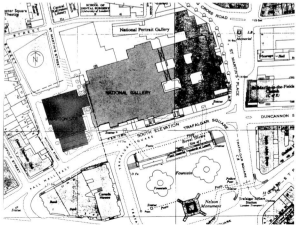

Location plan

The National Gallery in 1986

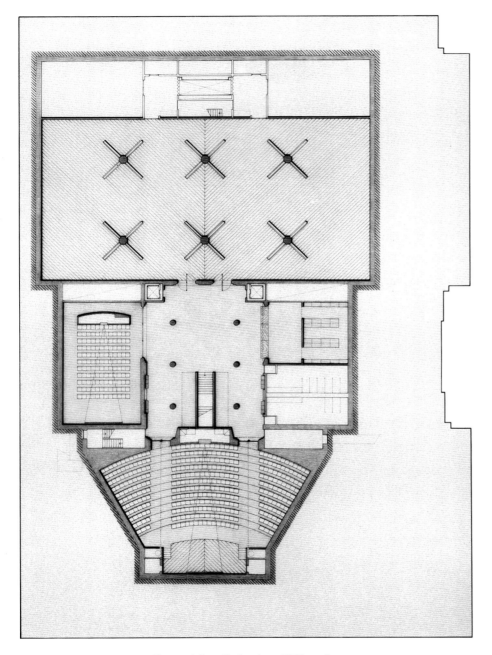

Basement plan with changing exhibition gallery

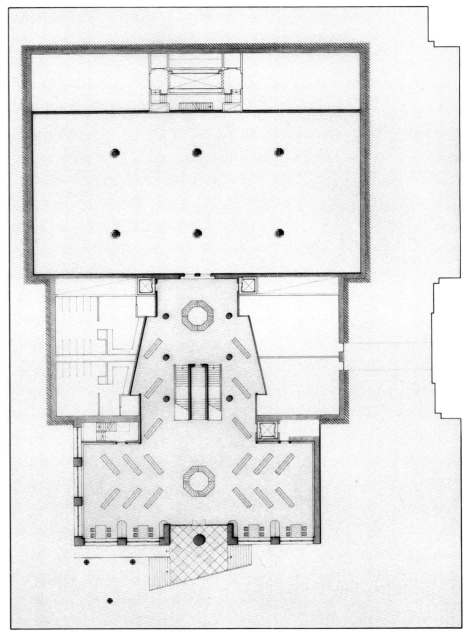

Plan at lower entrance level with bookshop

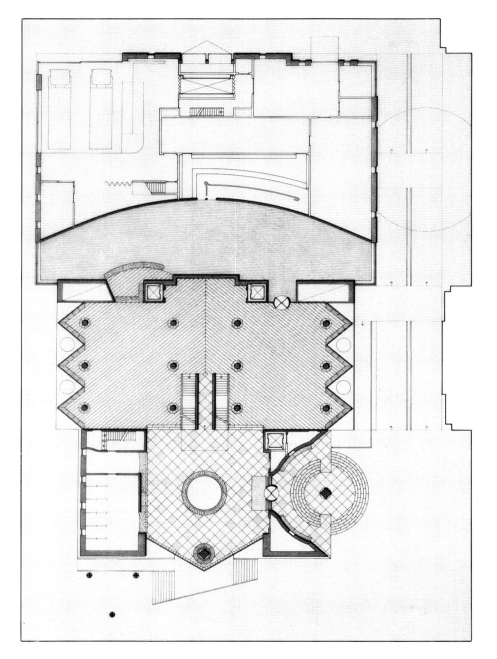

Plan of main entrance and self-service restaurant

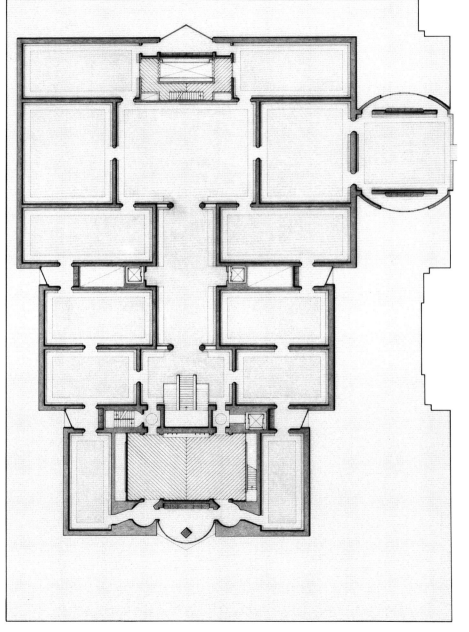

Plan of the galleries and bridge link

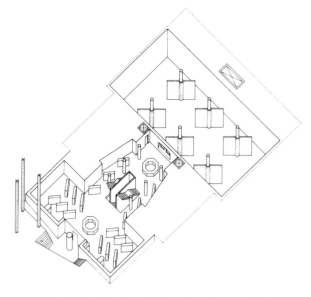

Down view of bookshop and changing exhibition gallery

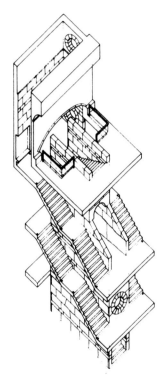

Down view of the central staircase

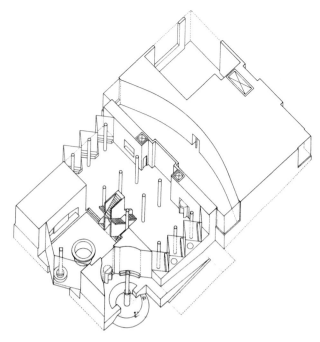

Down view of the main entrance hall and restaurant

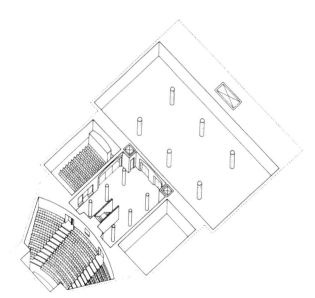

Down view of basement lecture theatres and changing exhibition gallery

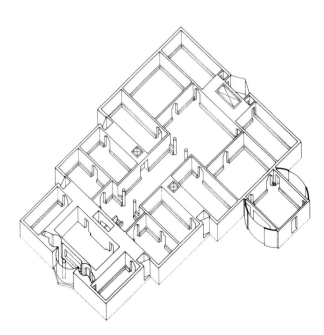

Down view of the galleries and bridge link

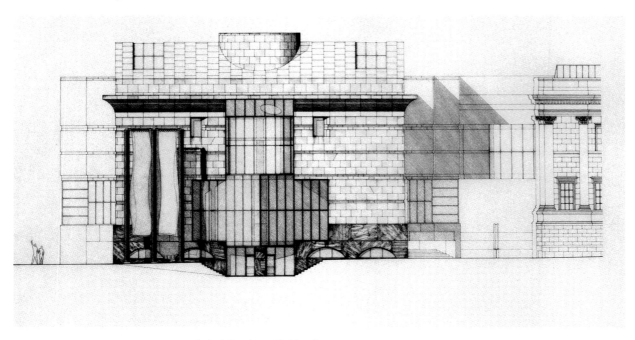

Principal elevation to Trafalgar Square

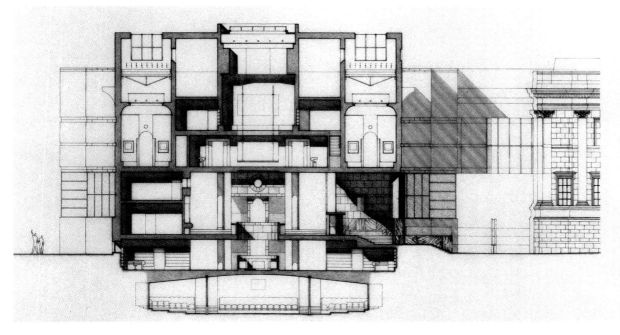

Cross section

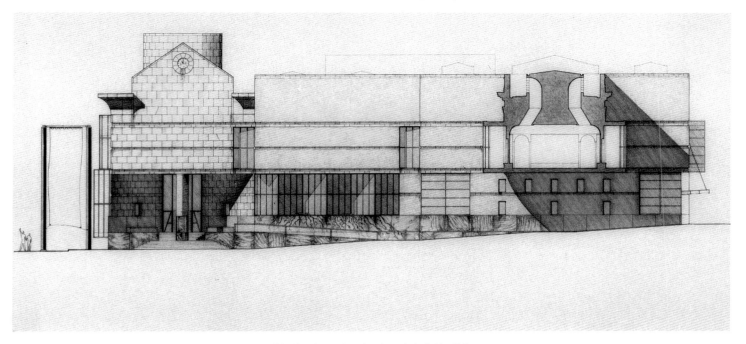

Side elevation and section through the bridge link

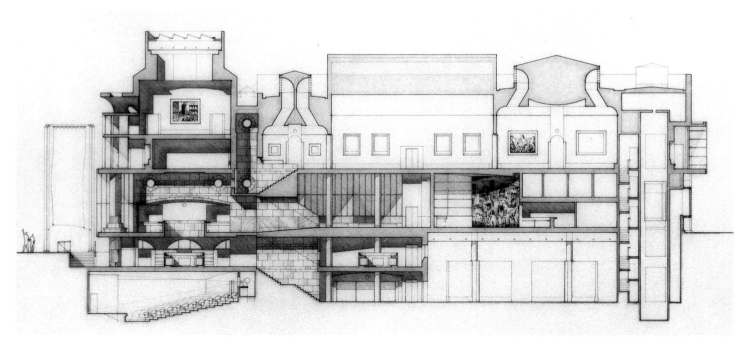

Longitudinal section

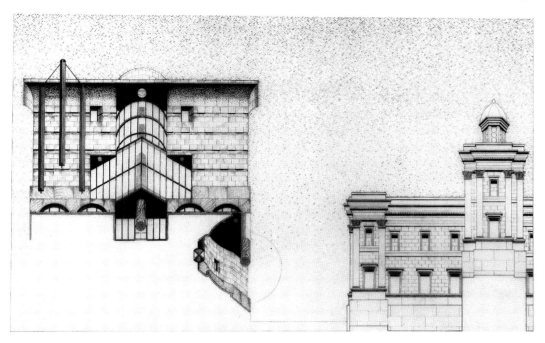

Up view from Trafalgar Square

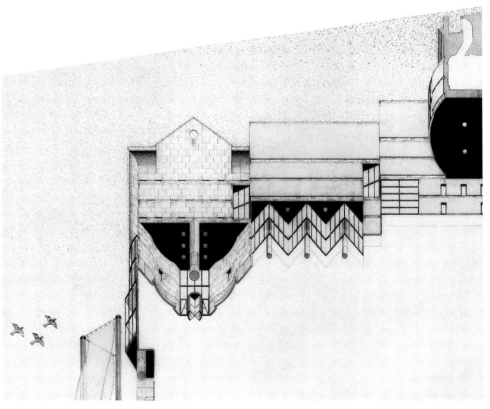

Up view of the entrance hall

The design for No. 1 Poultry refers to existing urban patterns around the junction of city streets at Bank underground station, and to buildings by important architects which overlook the site: Soane's Bank of England, the Midland Bank by Lutyens, and the church of St. Mary Woolnoth by Hawskmoor. The symmetrical planning of these buildings contrasts with the informality of the mediaeval street pattern, and we responded to this by arranging No. 1 Poultry around a central axis, with the same façades to Queen Victoria Street and Poultry. The building's height and the vertical divisions of its elevations echo those of its distinguished neighbours. It contains commercial accommodation at the basement and street levels, with offices at the upper floors and a restaurant and garden on the roof. At pavement level there are shopping arcades to Poultry and Queen Victoria Street, with a public footway linking two central archways through into a central court, where the public entrances are located, with escalators down to the Underground and basement shopping. The courtyard changes from round to triangular at the upper levels, and permits daylight to penetrate into the offices in the middle of the building. On the point of the building there is a separate entrance and lobby for VIPs, with a grand staircase which leads up to a landing overlooking the courtyard. The rooftop restaurant has an enclosed circular garden, offering sanctuary from the hustle and bustle, with good views over the neighbouring buildings.

The model in its context

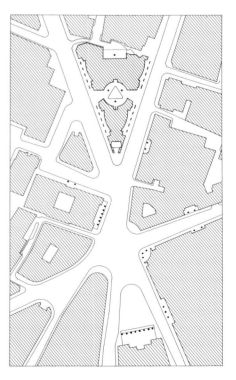

Site plan

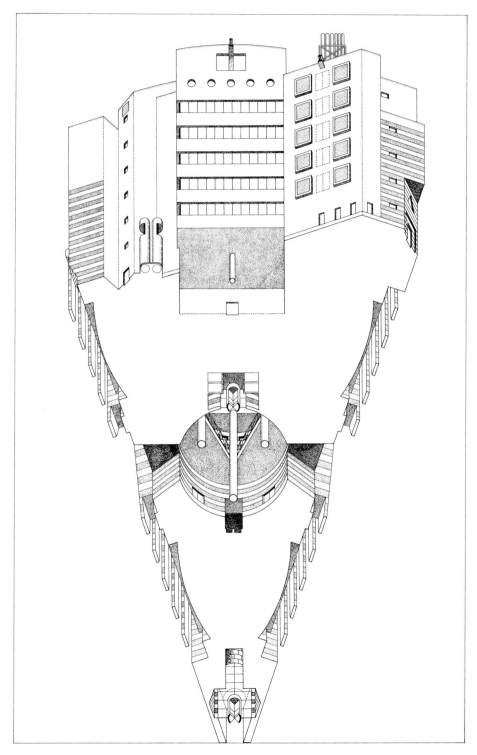

Up view of the west elevation

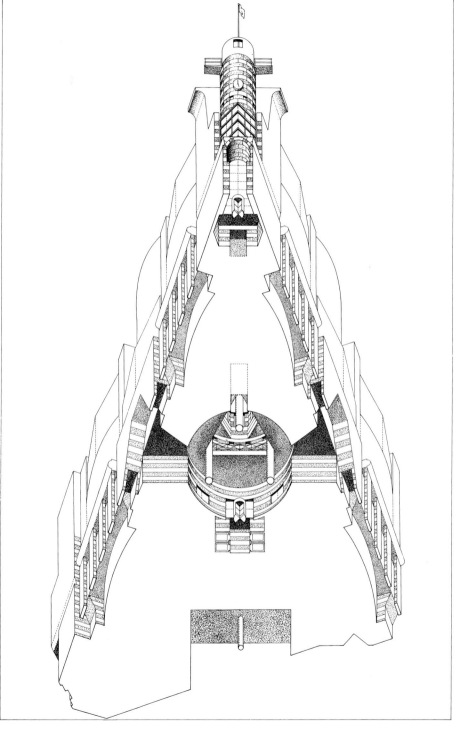

Up view of the corner entrance

The existing buildings in 1986

Mies Van Der Rohe's original project (1969)

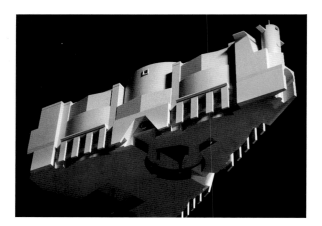

Up view of the model

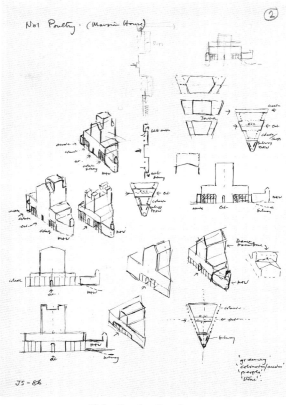

JS doodles of earlier scheme
retaining the existing Victorian building

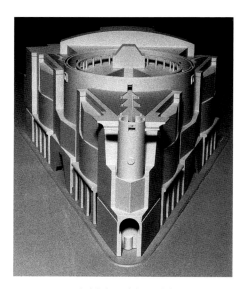

Axial view of the model

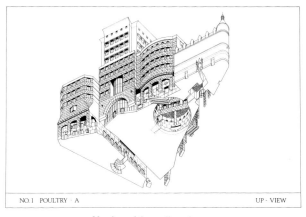

Up view of the earlier scheme

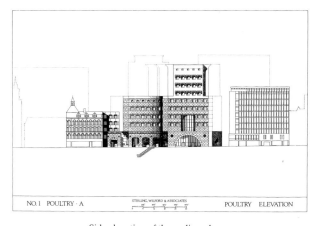

Side elevation of the earlier scheme

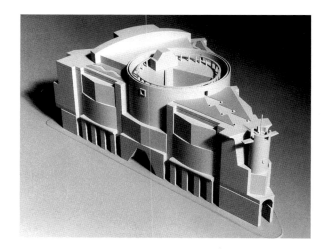

Down view of the model

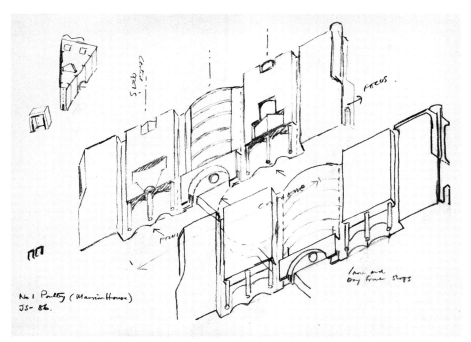

JS doodles for alternative elevations

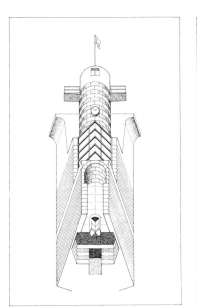

Up view of the entrance

Street view

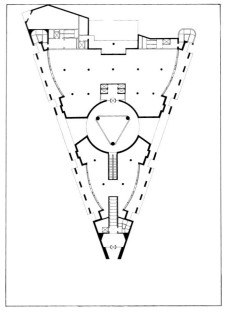

Ground floor plan

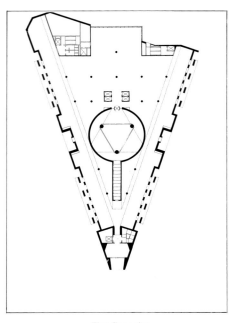

First floor plan

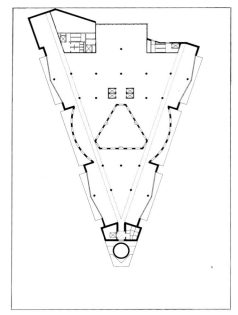

Plan of a typical office floor

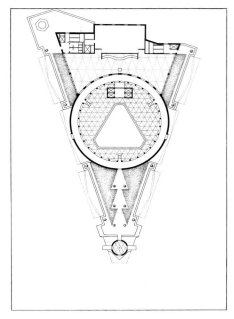

Plan at roof level

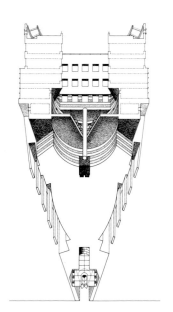

Up view sectioned through the courtyard

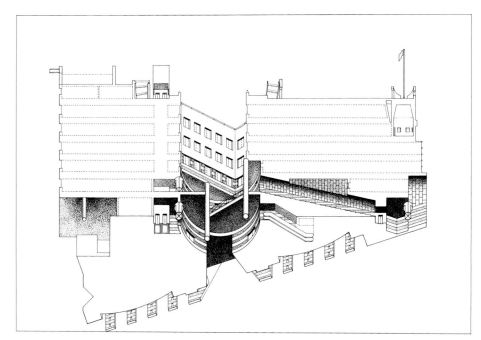

Up view sectioned through the courtyard

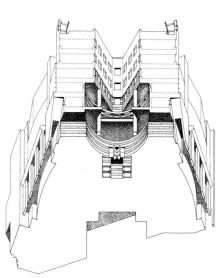

Up view sectioned through the courtyard

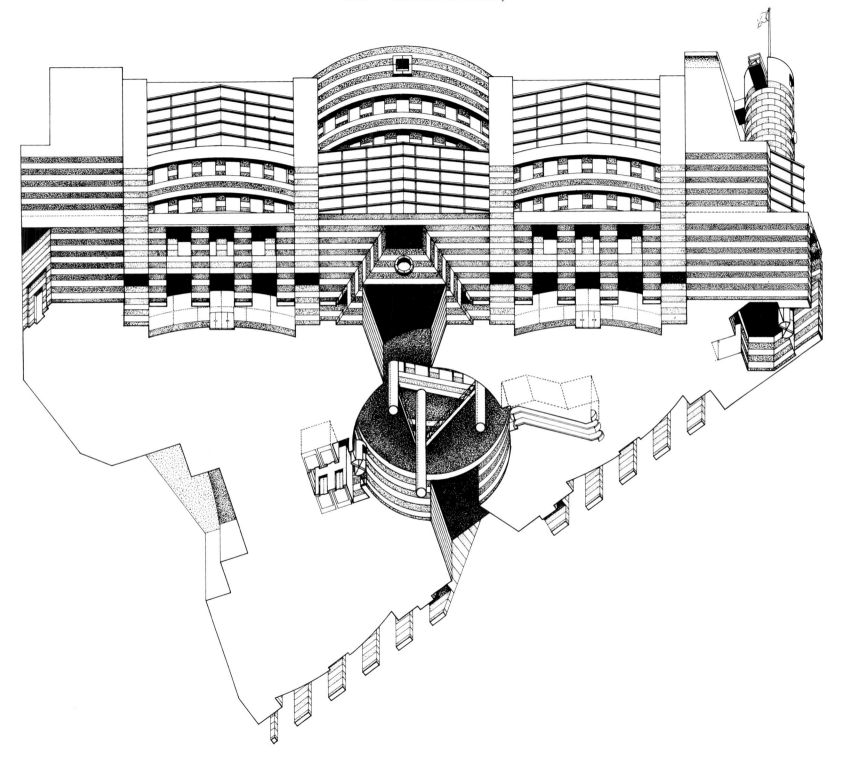

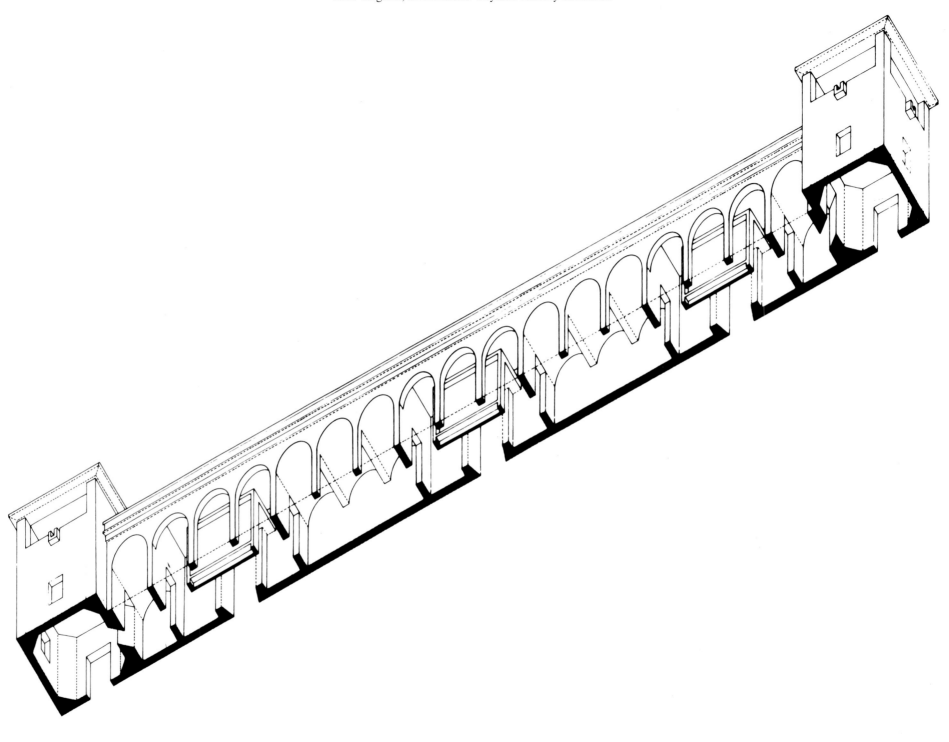

The new building responds to its setting by adding a second gallery wing to the existing museum, placing the villa at the centre of a symmetrical composition, and incorporating an existing pergola into the project. Visitors walk along a path parallel to the pergola and enter a circular foyer containing the ticket office, bookshop, and cloakrooms, with an adjacent audiovisual room and a café-restaurant overlooking the garden. From a new "monumental" staircase there are connections through to the existing gallery and to administration spaces at mezzanine level, with a private door into the Villa and an access to the exhibition rooms above. A picture hoist links the exhibition floors with a delivery area in the basement. The galleries which occupy the top floor are arranged around a large top-lit central space which can be organised for temporary exhibitions, with a number of smaller galleries around the perimeter. Visitors circulating from one gallery to another come out into a long loggia where they can rest on benches and admire the view over Lake Lugano to the mountains beyond.

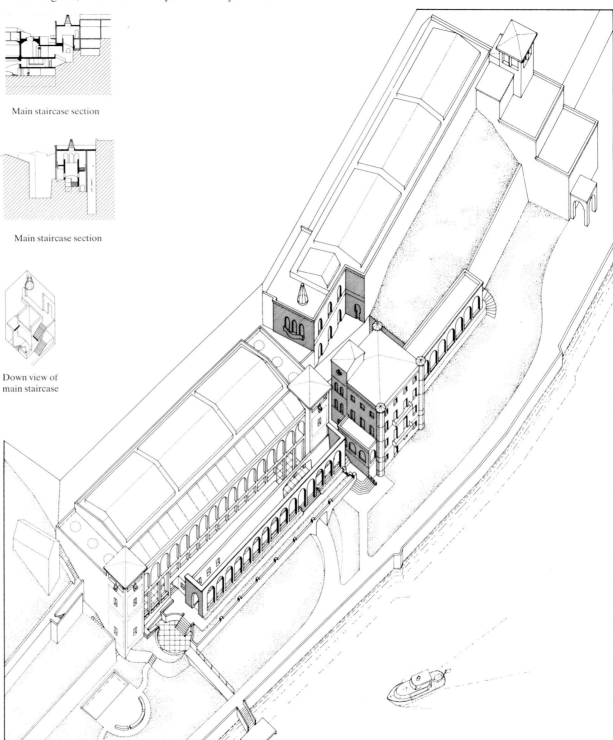

Main staircase section

Main staircase section

Down view of main staircase

Down axonometric of the new gallery added to the existing buildings

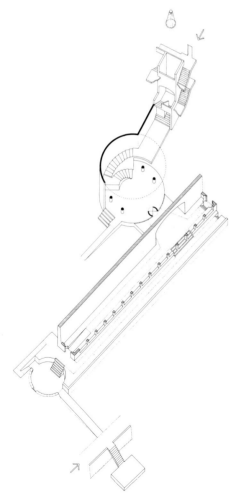

Part axonometric of the entry sequence

163

Views of Lake Lugano, the villa, the gardens, and the existing arcade

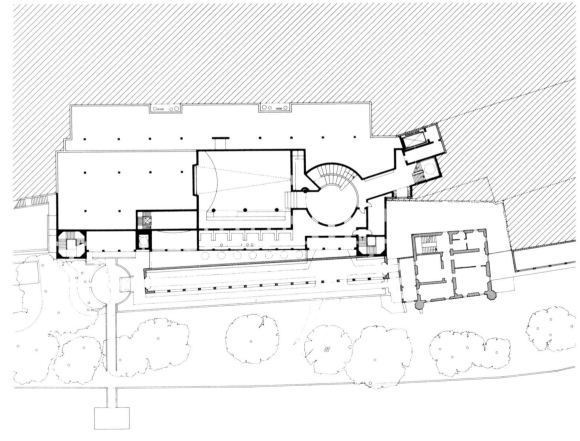

Plan showing entrance promenade along the existing arcade

1986 Lugano, Switzerland: Thyssen Gallery extension

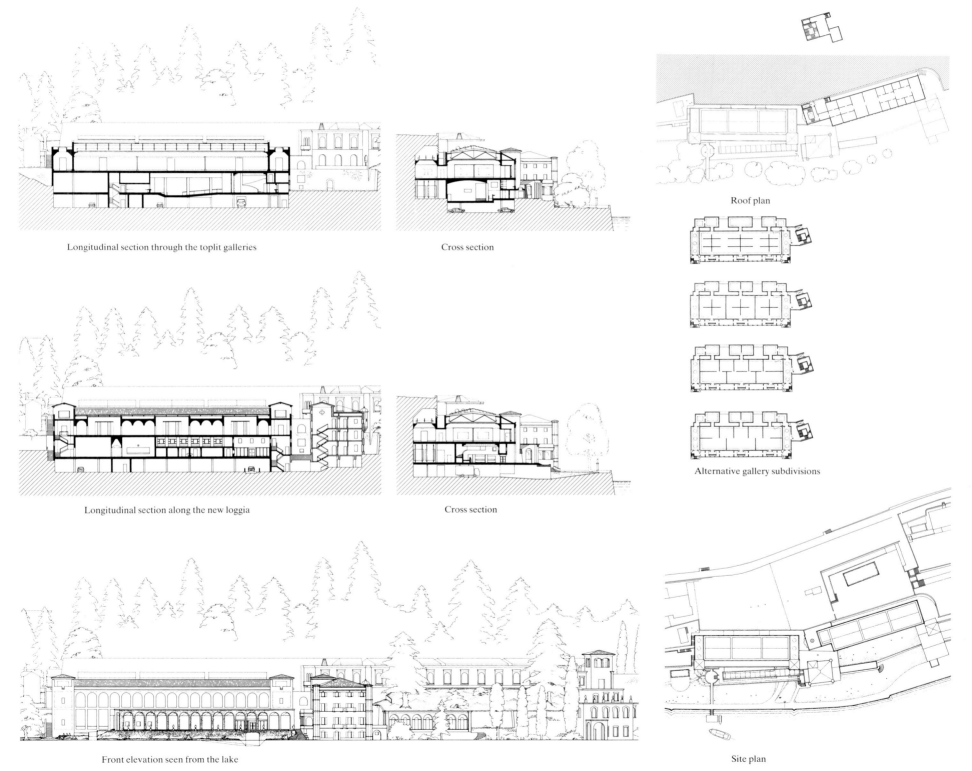

Longitudinal section through the toplit galleries

Cross section

Roof plan

Alternative gallery subdivisions

Longitudinal section along the new loggia

Cross section

Front elevation seen from the lake

Site plan

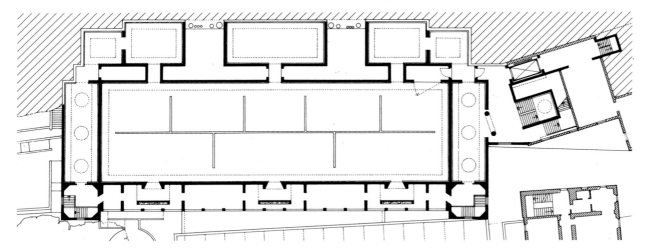

Plan of the top gallery level

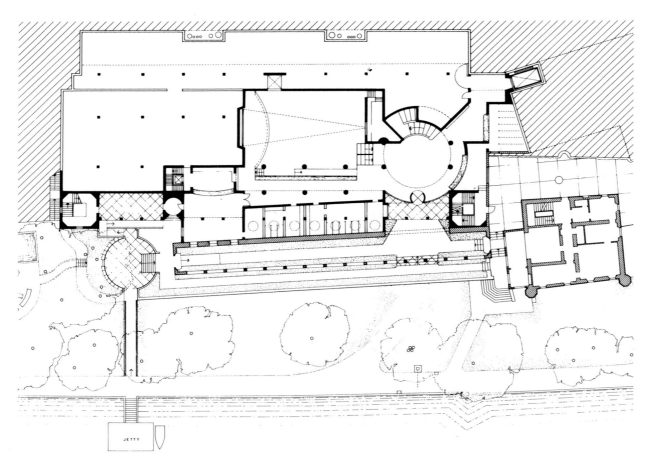

Plan at entry level

View along the loggia

View of the entrance hall

1986 Lugano, Switzerland: Thyssen Gallery extension

Gallery interior

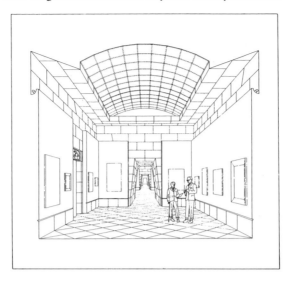

Gallery interior

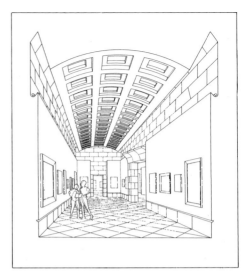

Gallery interior

View from the loggia over Lake Lugano

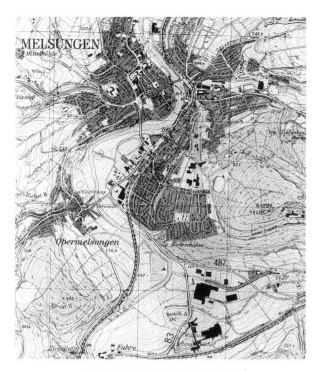

Location plan (Braun HQ at bottom centre)

View from the east

This factory for medical plastic products expresses the oscillation between functionalism and historic association characteristic of our work. It recalls the man-made objects in the landscape of the Roman *campagna:* viaducts, bridges, canals, and embankments. The site is in rolling hills outside Melsungen, two hours north-east of Frankfurt. At the front is a garden with a tree-lined canal, a water, and a lake. In the middle, a multi-storey car park is linked by a long walkway to the staff canteen at one end and the administration building at the other. This sits on a small hill and contains offices with computer facilities in the base. Production takes place in a central building and finished goods are dispatched at the rear. The large lozenge-shaped building is a general distribution centre for all goods produced in Braun's German factories.

View from the west

169

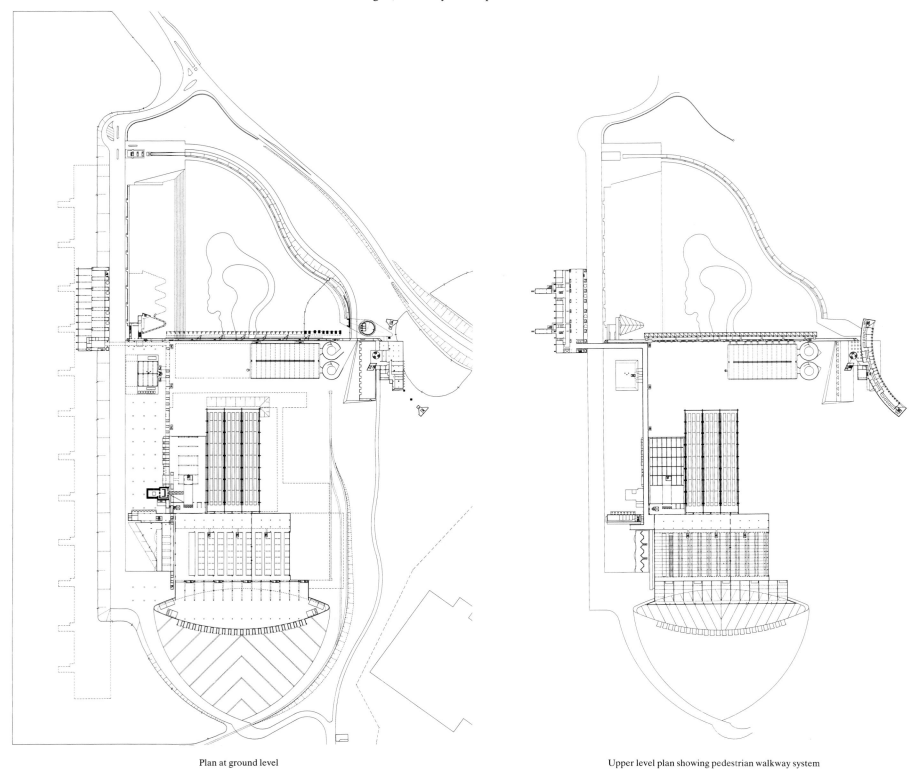

Plan at ground level

Upper level plan showing pedestrian walkway system

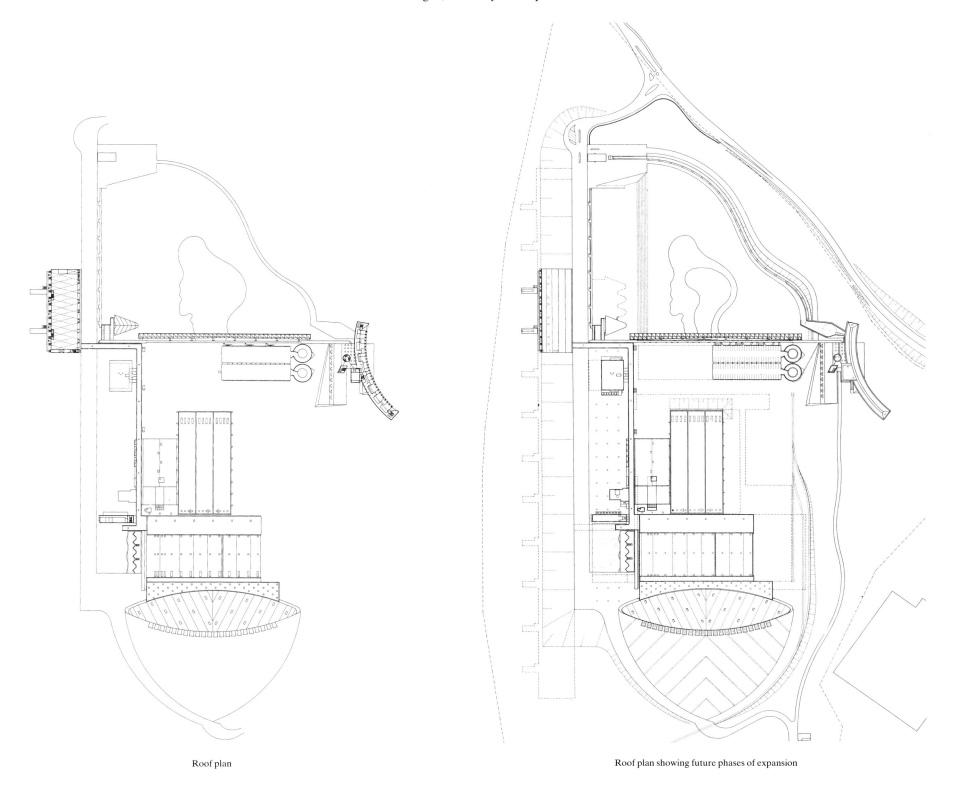

Roof plan

Roof plan showing future phases of expansion

Administration Building

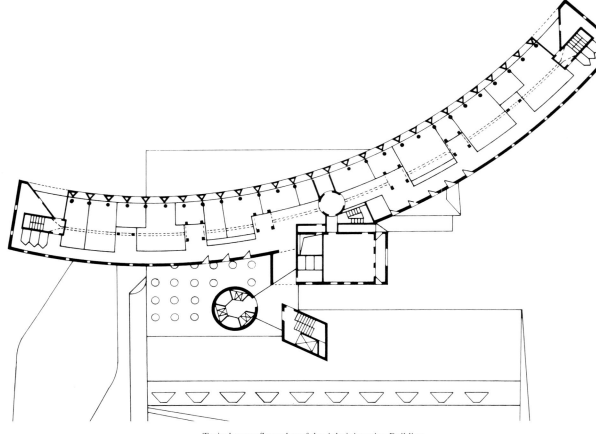

Typical upper floor plan of the Administration Building

Goods distribution and dispatch building

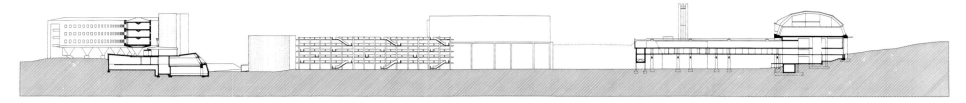

Longitudinal section

Production building on the left, Goods Distribution Office Building on the right

Goods Distribution Office Building on the left, Dispatch Building on the right

Goods Distribution Office Building

173

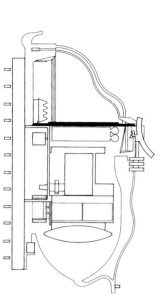

Schematic plan

Pedestrian walkway, garden, lake

Pedestrian walkway leading to the canteen and the production building

The administration building

The administration building

Konrad Adenauer Strasse is a multi-lane urban highway which splits the city in two. Future plans envisage sinking this road underground and using the free space to create a linear park, known as the Cultural Mile, which would be surrounded by important civic buildings including the State Theatre, the Landtag, the Neue Staatsgalerie, and the Music School and Theatre Academy. In the context of these future provisions it was considered that the existing 1960s scenery workshop, annexed to the State Theatre, will be inappropriate and will require improvement. The city organised a competition to extend it along Konrad Adenauer Strasse with new accommodation 8–10 metres thick and a new façade to the future park. Our project counterbalances the overbearing effect of the existing building, which looms outwards at the upper floors, by screening it off with an arcade projecting forward at ground level. The entry and exit ramps for scenery trucks are marked by two end pavilions which frame this arcade; inclined panels on the front of the pavilions would be used to display information about events in the State Theatre. The frontal, symmetrical, deliberately "representational" arrangement of the new arcade counteracts the asymmetrical, discontinuous frontage of the Staatsgalerie opposite and relates the building to its context by using alternated bands of local stone and stucco, which echo the materials of the Staatsgalerie. The dropped cornice aligns with the parapet of the State Theatre. The invited architects were also asked to make proposals for the park, which we have laid out with trees, watercourses, kiosks and pavilions which could contain cafés, information booths, and small exhibitions.

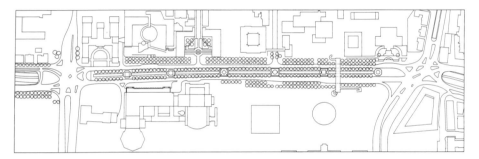

Plan of the proposed "Cultural Mile" (State Theatre Workshop centre left)

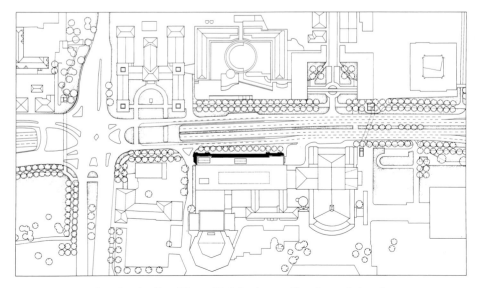

Location plan (State Theatre Workshop bottom, Neue Staatsgalerie top)

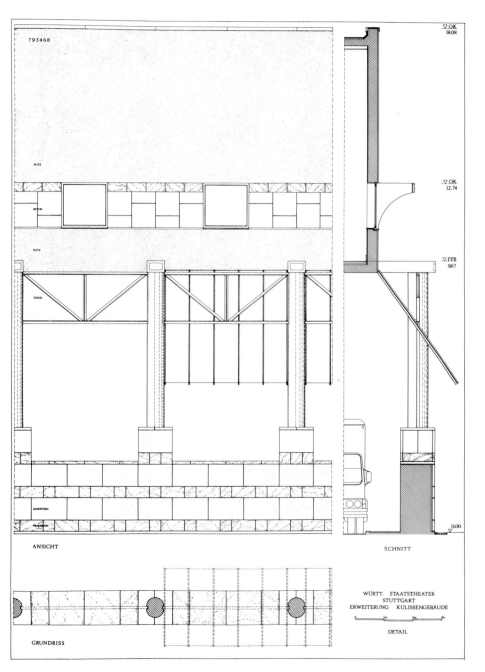

Detailed plan/elevation/section of the new façade

176

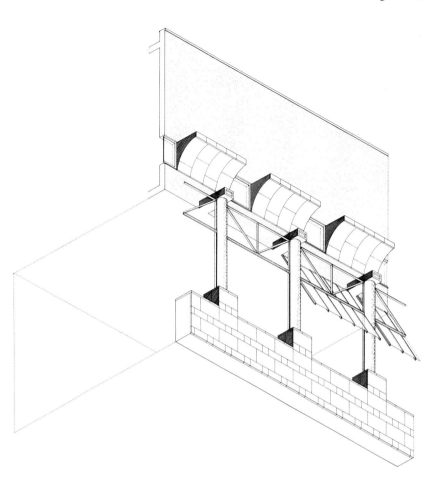

Up view of the new colonnade

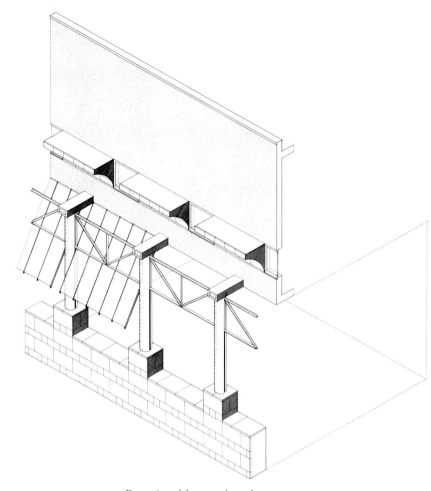

Down view of the new colonnade

The State Theatre Workshop in 1986

Proposed alterations

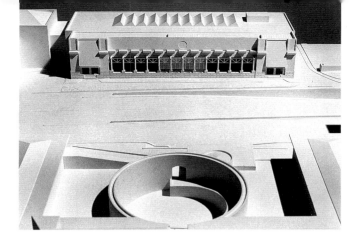

The Neue Staatsgalerie and the State Theatre Workshop opposite

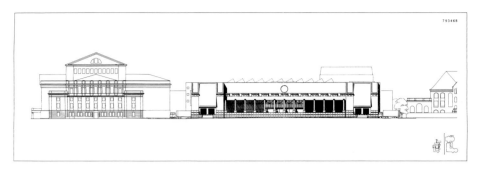

Front elevation

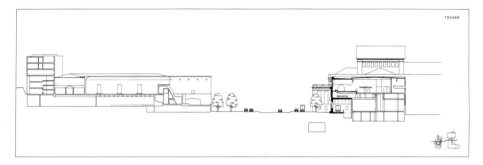

Cross section (Staatsgalerie is on the left)

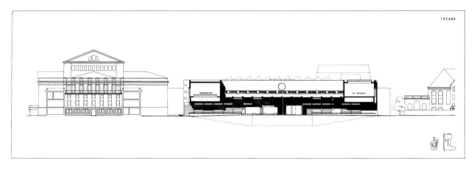

Front elevation (sectioned)

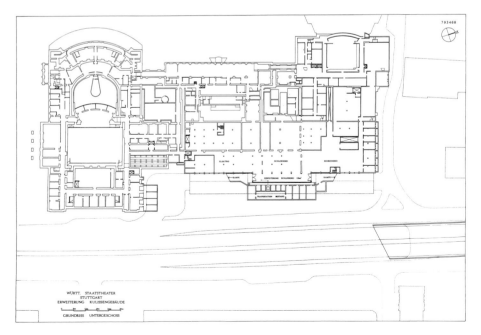

Basement plan with delivery ramps

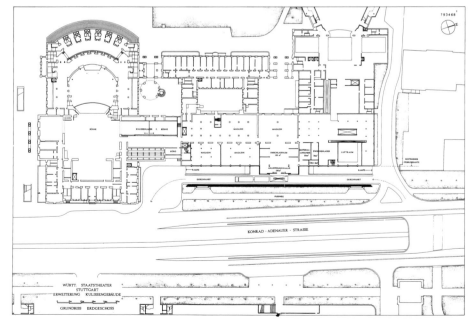

Ground floor plan with vehicle access

View of the model

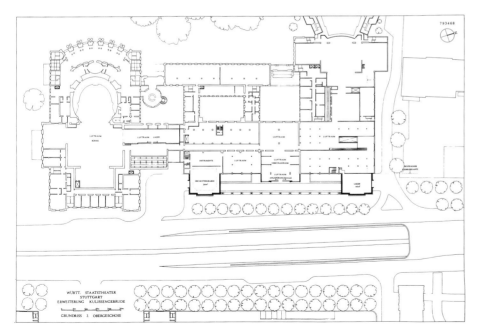

Plan at upper level of the colonnade

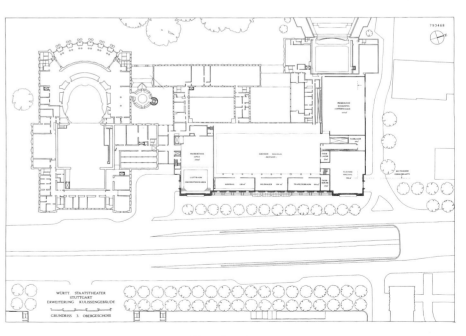

Upper floor plan

The loggia seen from the east end of St. Paul's

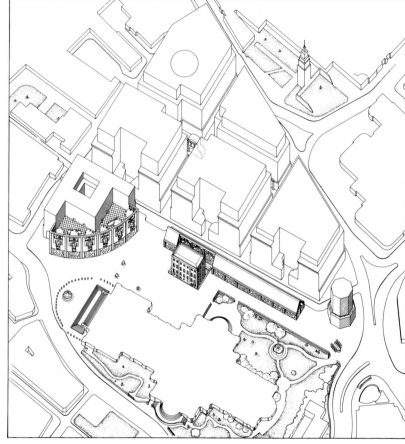

Down view (cathedral removed)

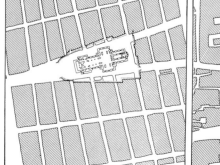

Wren's plan of 1666

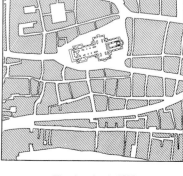

The situation in 1916

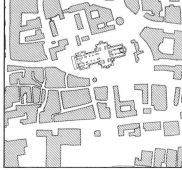

The situation in 1986

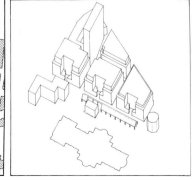

Phase 1

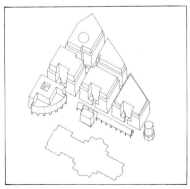

Phase 2

Six office buildings are arranged in an urban pattern, with tree-lined pedestrian streets linking St. Paul's Cathedral to Newgate Street behind, giving a humane working environment and interesting walks through colonnaded shopping areas. The new frontages to the cathedral are set back to create the maximum public space for the large numbers of tourists who visit this national monument. A curved building with an arcaded front and upper-level restaurants offers views of the main west front for people to watch dignitaries arriving for important occasions of state. A long "market" arcade in stone and timber accommodates flower sellers and newspaper vendors and gives a covered route to the underground station and a good vantage point for viewing the cathedral's northern side. The stone pillars of the arcade, seen obliquely, create a visual screen between the office buildings and the church. The basement connection to the underground station is extended to give a direct access into the cathedral crypt, with an information shop for visitors.

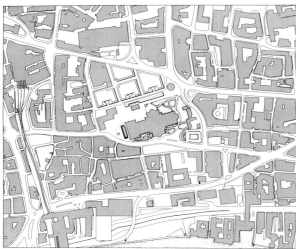

Location plan

Site plan

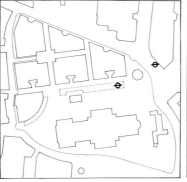

Public areas

St. Paul's garden extended

Exits from the Underground

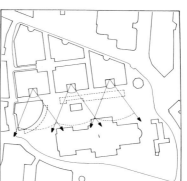

Views from the offices

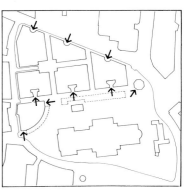

Office entrances

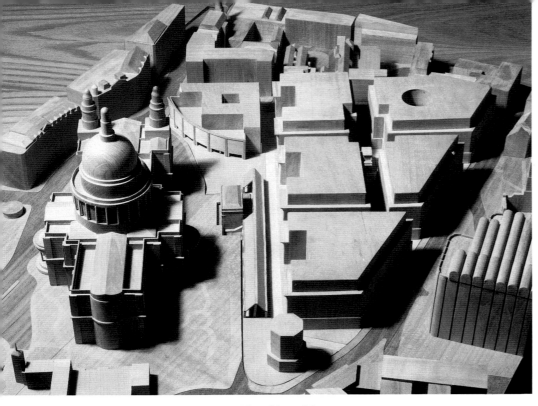

View of the model

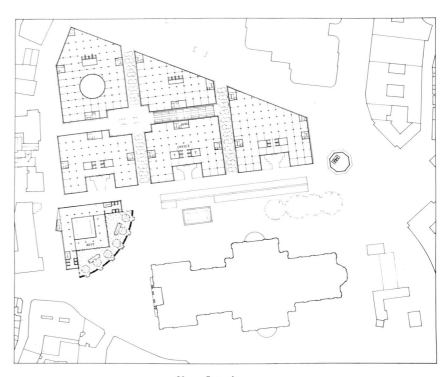

Upper floor plan

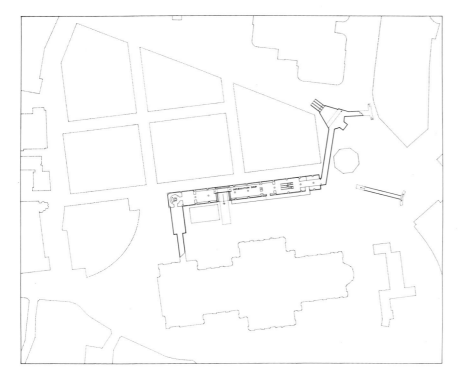

Basement of the loggia with links to the Underground and St. Paul's Cathedral

Basement plan at service level

1986 London: redevelopment of Paternoster Square

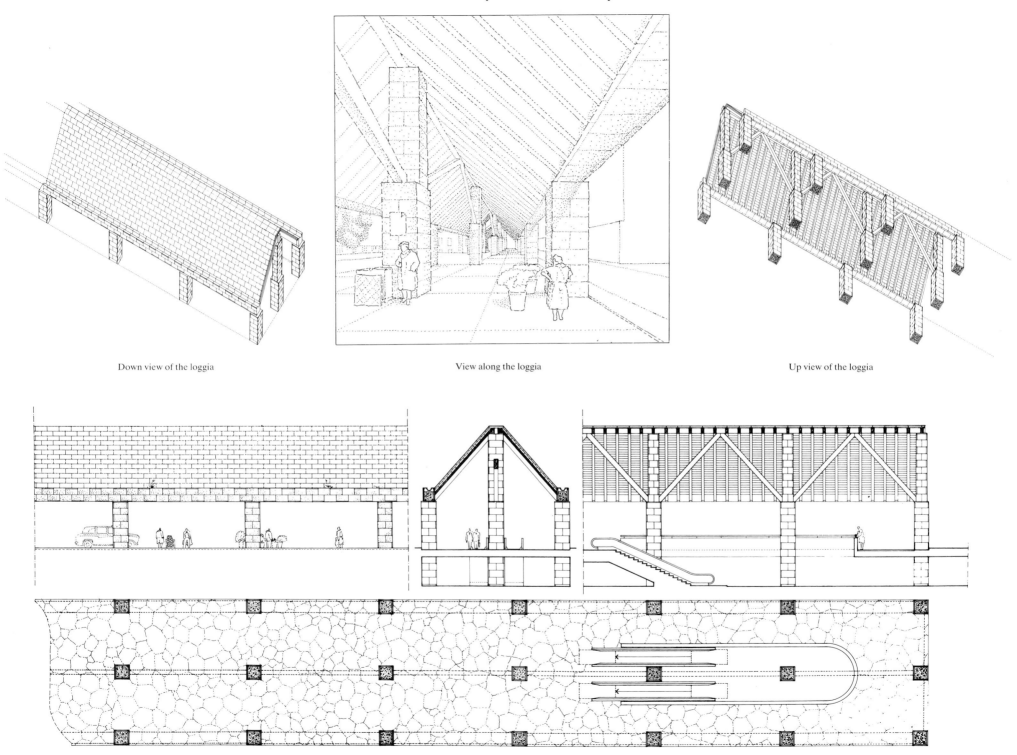

Down view of the loggia

View along the loggia

Up view of the loggia

Plan of the loggia with longitudinal and cross sections

Bracken House was a project for an office building near St. Paul's Cathedral, and was subject to height restrictions protecting the view of the dome. Some decorative elements from the previous 1950s building are conserved and re-used in the new design. The irregularly-shaped site is stabilised by four corner pillars which contain all stairways, services and toilets. The principal entrance allows cars to drop passengers off without impeding traffic, and a secondary entrance has easy vehicle access, with a refuse collection point. A central lightwell gives good daylighting to all floors and allows the interior layout of the offices to be either cellular or open. The building is planned for subdivision into half-floors with stock-market dealing floors at the lower levels. The top floor has a semi-circular wall enclosing a roof garden and adjoining the staff restaurants, which have views over the garden.

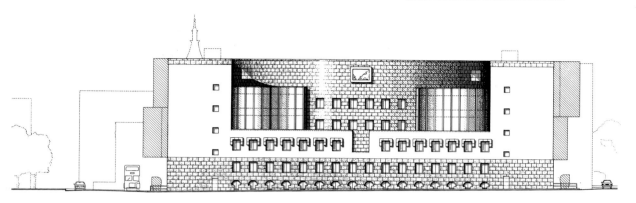

Front elevation

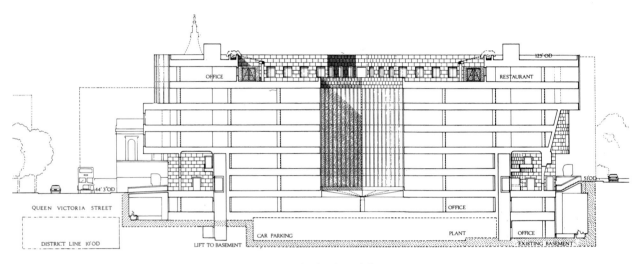

Section through the entrances

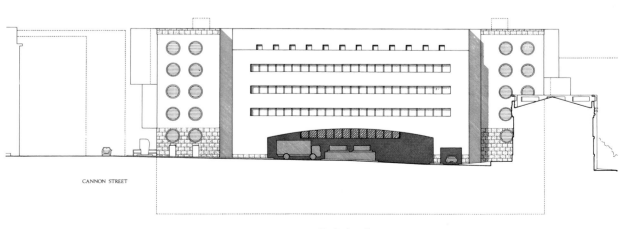

Back elevation

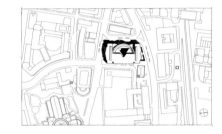

Location plan

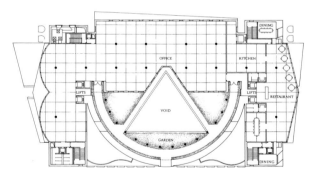

Upper level office plan

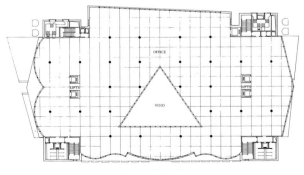

Typical office plan

1986 London: Bracken House

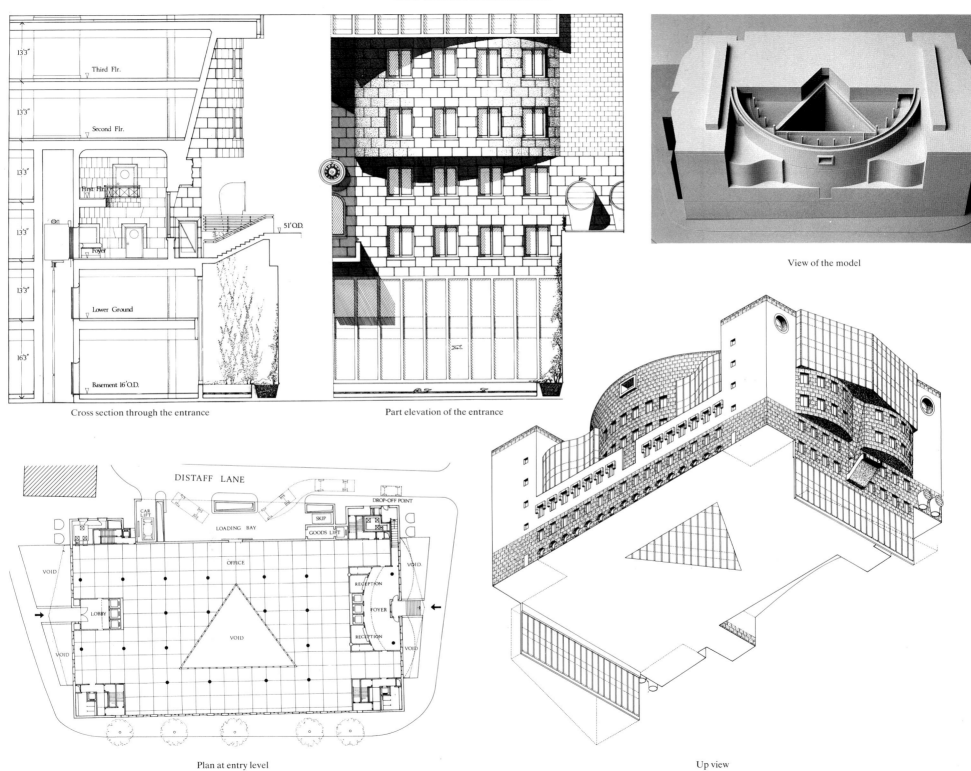

Cross section through the entrance

Part elevation of the entrance

View of the model

Plan at entry level

Up view

The Kaiserquelle imperial baths once stood on this site, where excavated remains of Roman baths mark the original settlement of Aachen. The project incorporates three elements: a square spa house, a semicircular restaurant/café, and an arcaded exhibition building with a ramp leading to the Roman and mediaeval remains below. The paving of the plaza is based on the Roman grid, and the public space enclosed by the new buildings is crossed by pedestrian routes connecting the two parts of the old town. A ramp along the arcaded building descends to the Roman cellar where artefacts can be viewed. The use of arched niches and masonry columns recalls Roman construction; changes in the paving denote different uses and circulation routes. A wedge-shaped media room provides seating for 64 people. Adjacent to a fragment of mediaeval wall, a semicircular space identifies the Roman apse, where the fountainhead can be seen through an opening. The spa house sits above. It is partially surrounded by water and enclosed by "walls" made of beech hedges. The hot water gushes up in a funnel, filling the air with its humid, sulphurous smell.

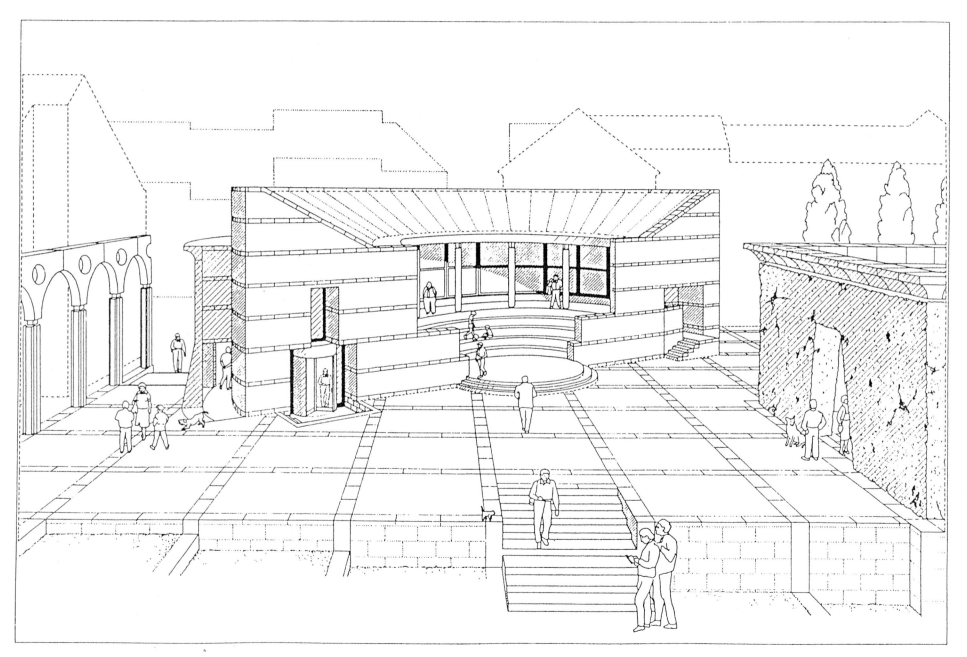

Perspective of the restaurant building

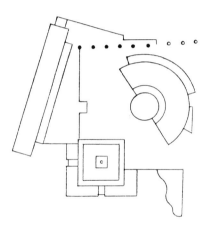

Schematic plan

Shadow plan

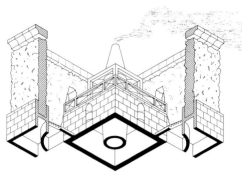

Up view of the fountainhead building

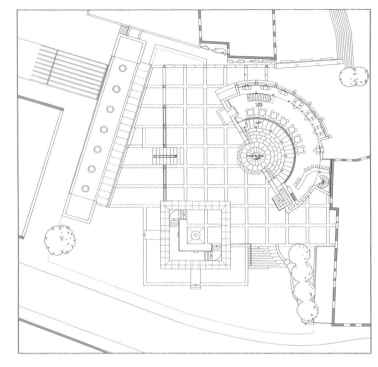

First floor plan

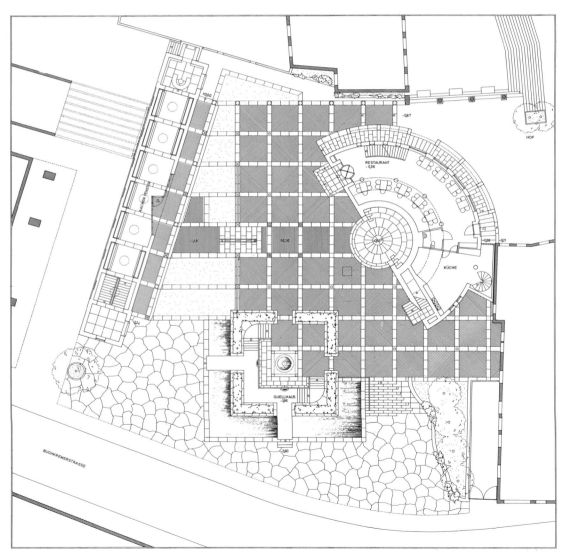

Plan at plaza level

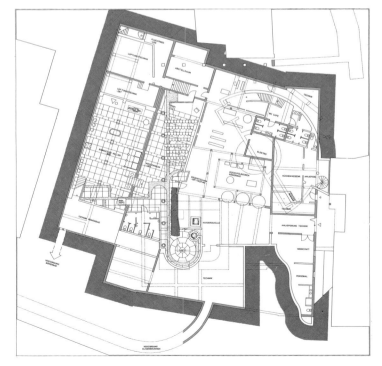

Basement plan

188

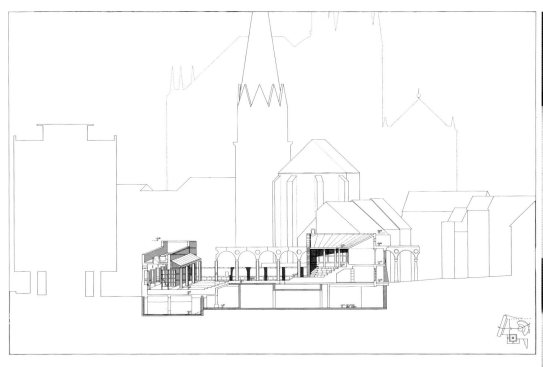

Cross section of the plaza

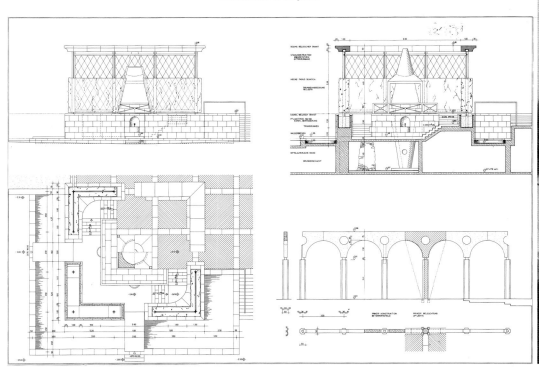

Details of the fountainhead building

View of the model and the context

The new buildings and gardens are added to the Neue Staatsgalerie and incorporating the existing *Landtag* building as one edge of a plaza, framed by the Theatre Academy with the Music School as its backdrop. The plaza has ramped entrances from the front and from Urbanstrasse, and a passageway following the curve of the Theatre Academy which leads to Eugenstrasse and the Staatsgalerie. Where the Staatsgalerie was all about blank walls, the Music School and Theatre Academy are all about windows, randomly positioned according to room sizes inside, with a stone grid superimposed to establish order. The tower contains a theatre for lectures and chamber music, a concert hall, a library, departments of Musical Theory, Composition, and Pitch, and a Senate Room with its own rooftop terrace for receptions or small concerts. Like a cork out of a bottle, the tower relates to the voided courtyard of the Neue Staatsgalerie and is a landmark building adding another to Stuttgart's collection of stumpy towers. It is entered from the main foyer via stairs and lifts which descend to the concert hall and theatre, or rise to the library. The foyer provides multiple connections, acting as main public vestibule, box-office, and cloakroom for the theatre, and providing a walk-through from the plaza to the street, as well as the reception rooms and student refectory at ground level of the Music School. The rest of the nine floors contain teaching and practice rooms with soundproof "room in a room" construction and splayed walls or angled corners.

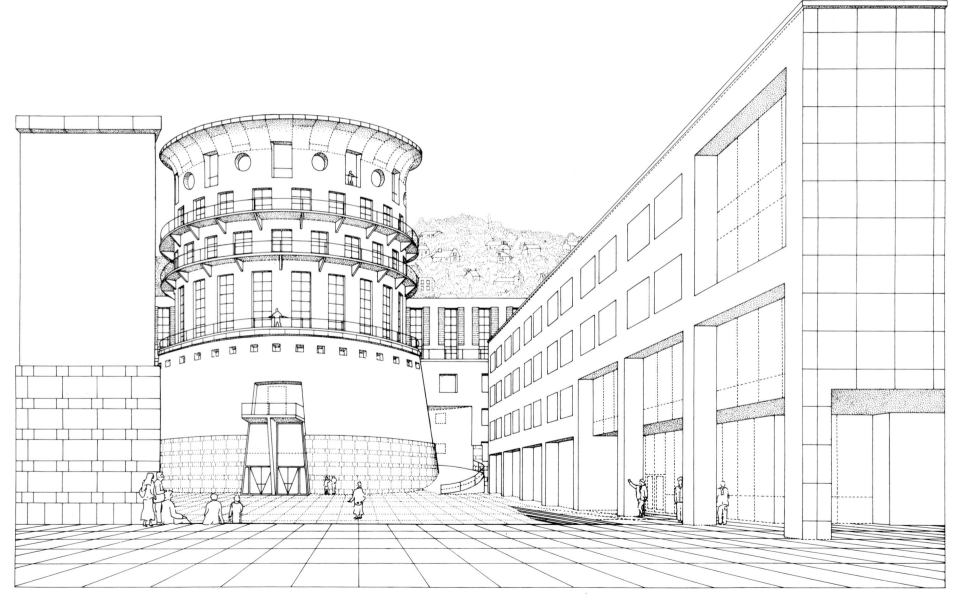

Perspective of the plaza (existing *Landtag* building on the right)

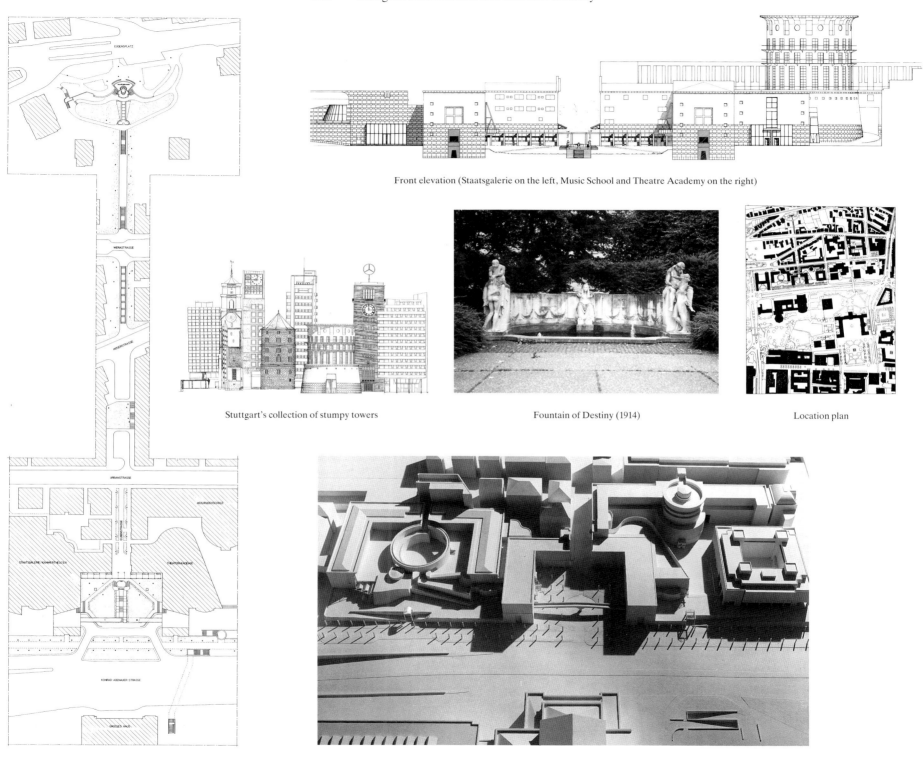

Front elevation (Staatsgalerie on the left, Music School and Theatre Academy on the right)

Stuttgart's collection of stumpy towers

Fountain of Destiny (1914)

Location plan

Galatea Fountain (top of hill)
Fountain of Destiny (bottom of hill)

Left ro right: Staatsgalerie, new garden, Music School and Theatre Academy, *Landtag*

191

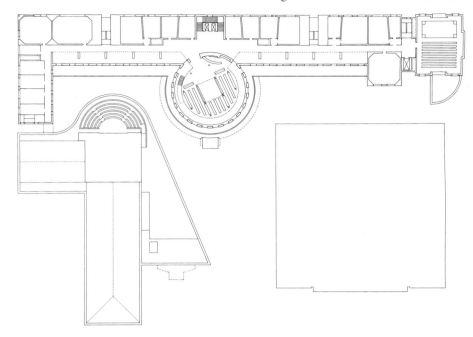

Plan at library mezzanine

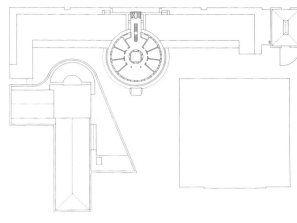

Plan at upper offices in the tower

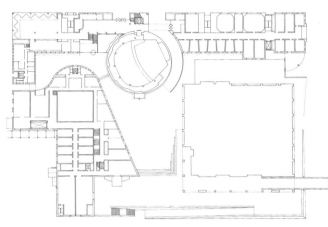

Plan at upper level of the auditorium

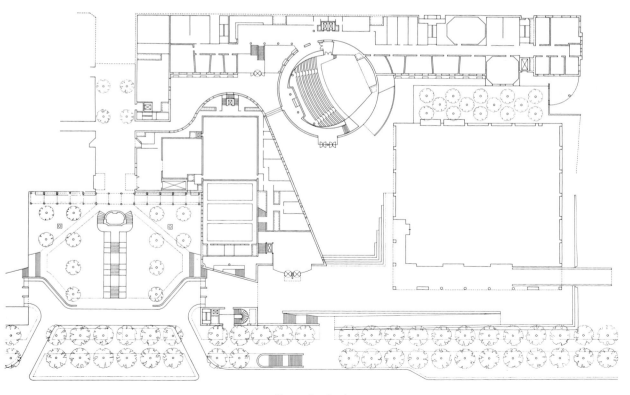

Plan at plaza level

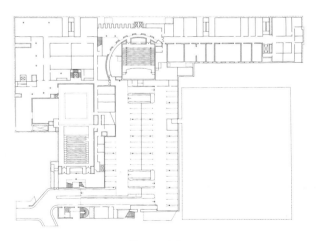

Basement plan

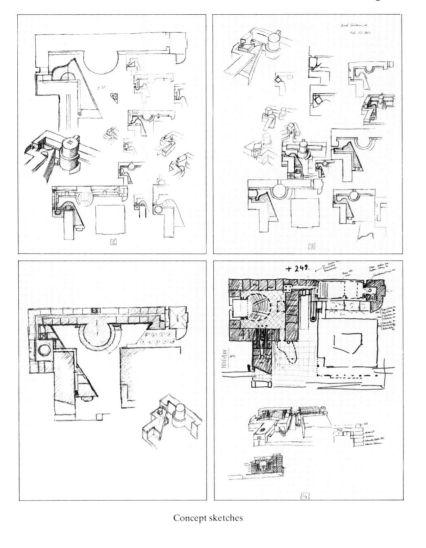

Concept sketches

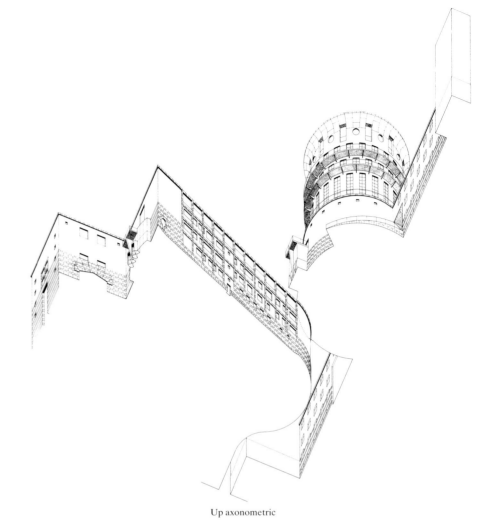

Up axonometric

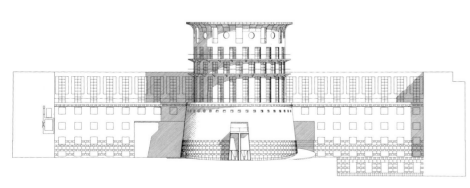

Front elevation

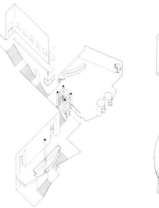

Down axonometric:
Theatre Academy entrance

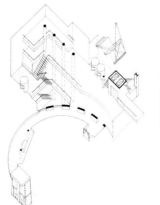

Down axonometric:
Music School entrances

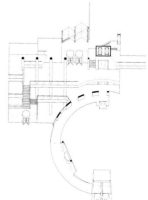

Down axonometric:
Music School entrances

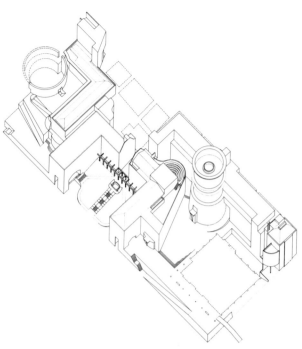

Down view

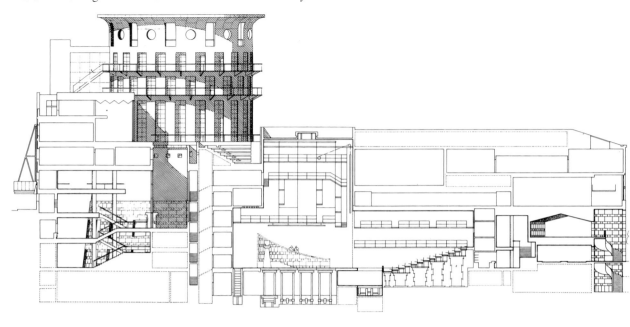

Longitudinal section through the Music School (left) and Theatre Academy

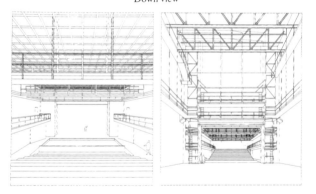

Interior perspective views of the
teaching theatre in the Theatre Academy

Rear view of the model

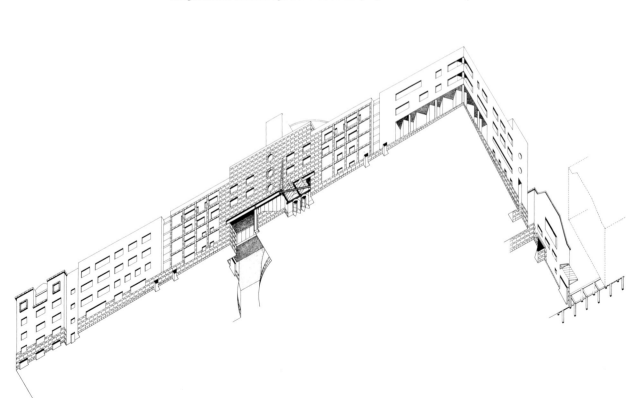

Up axonometric showing the entrance and side elevation of the Music School

1987 – Stuttgart: Music School and Theatre Academy

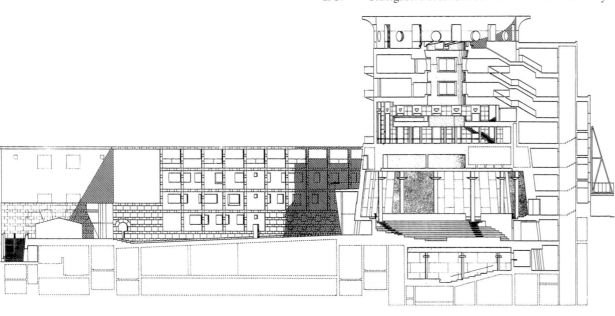

Longitudinal section through the plaza and the Music School (right)

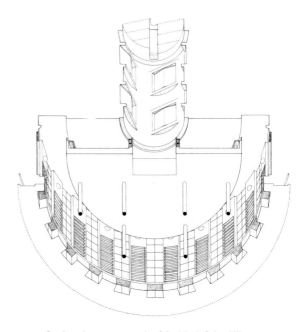

Sectioned up-axonometric of the Music School library

The auditorium

Down view of the model

Study model of the auditorium in the Music School

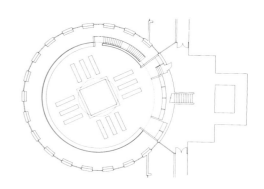

Mezzanine level of the library

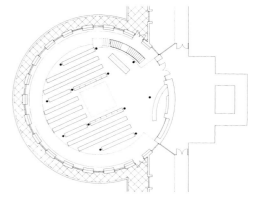

The main floor of the library

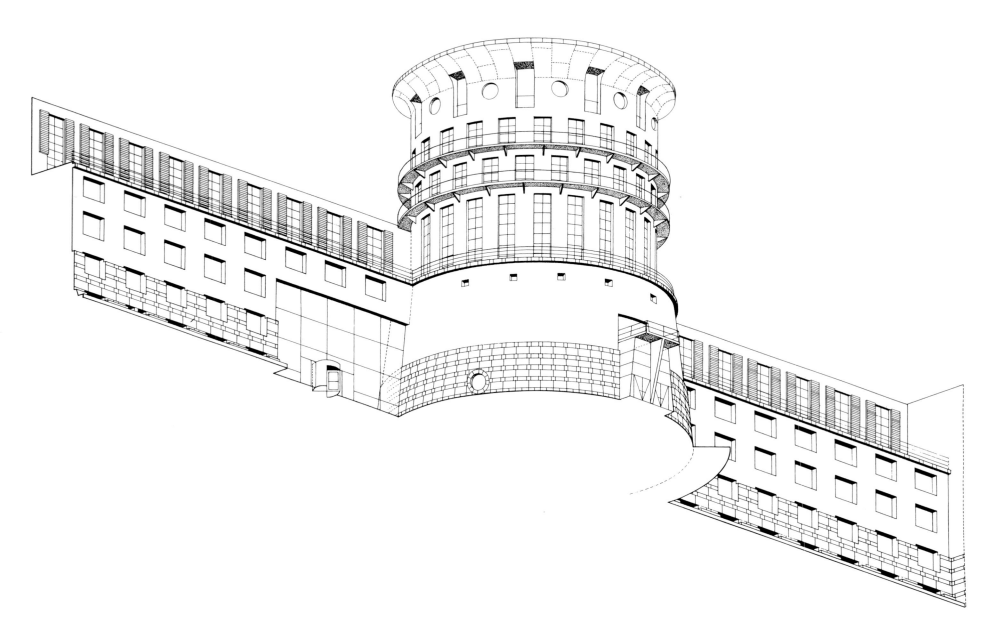

Up axonometric of the Music School

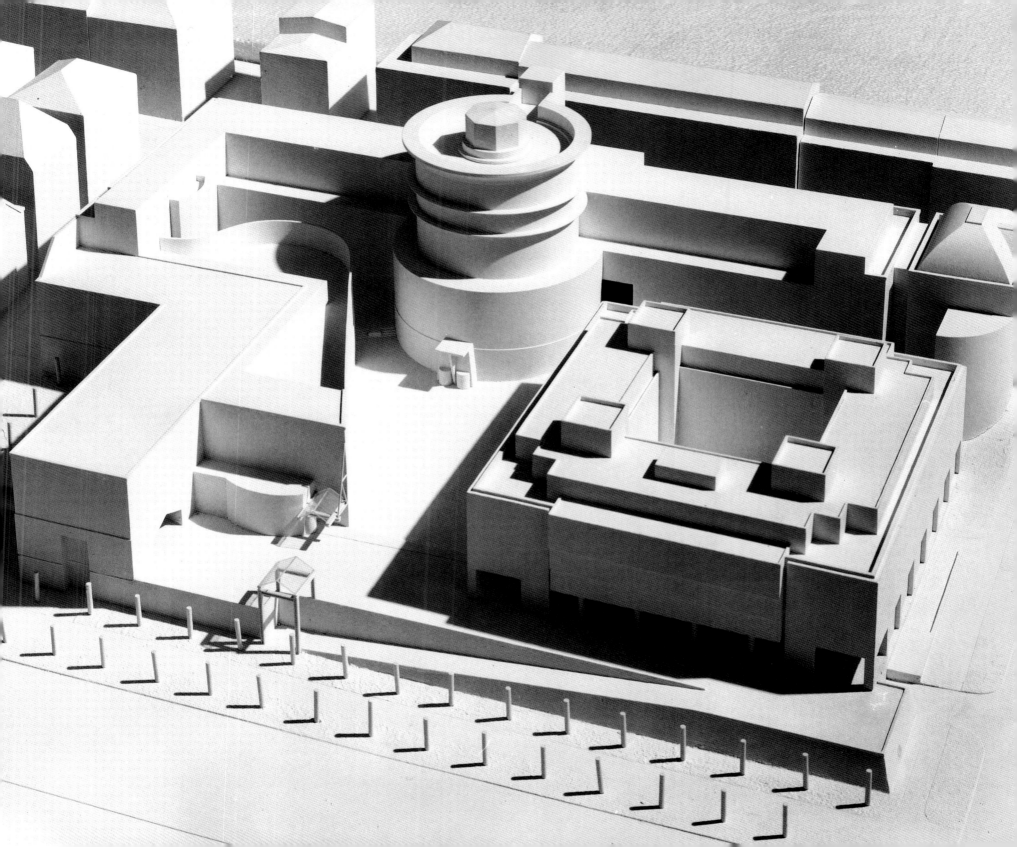

This outline scheme belongs to our series of projects for enlarging the Tate, including the Clore Gallery (designed and built 1980–1986) and the Museums of New Art (1985). The new library will cover British art from the XVI century onwards and foreign modern art from c. 1870, and will also house an archive of XX century British Art. The building completes the enclosure of the sculpture courtyard and will incorporate an Edwardian pavilion refurbished to make a new entrance hall, with lobbies at each level which give access to the study rooms, offices, and the stacks for the library and archive.

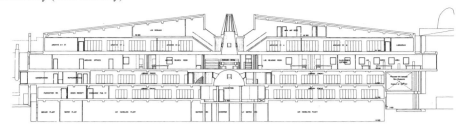

Longitudinal section

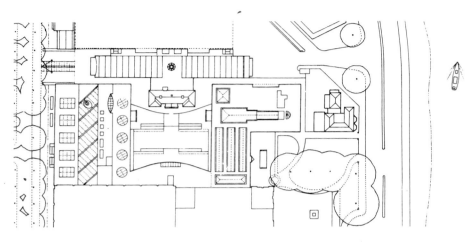

Site plan (existing Tate Gallery bottom, Clore Gallery on the right)

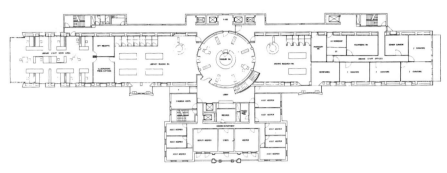

Plan at upper floor

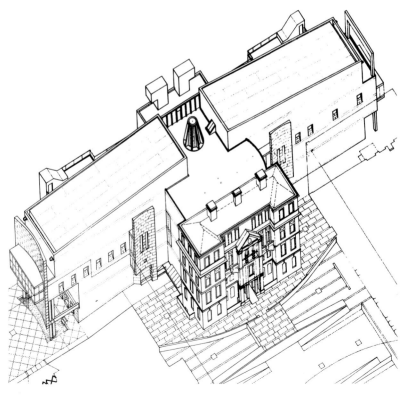

Down view

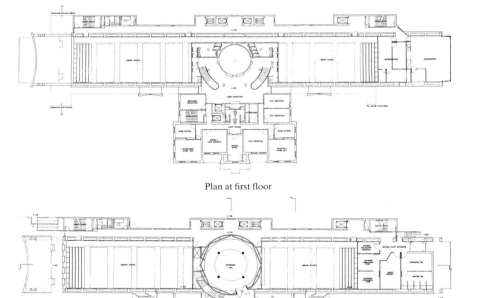

Plan at first floor

Plan at entrance level

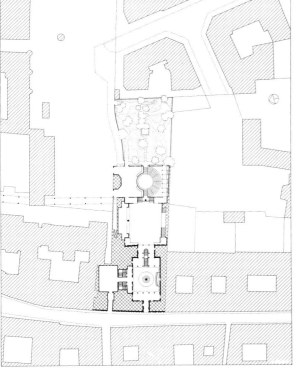

Location plan showing the palazzo and garden

Perspective of the new roof over the courtyard

Views of Via Brera and Palazzo Citterio in 1987

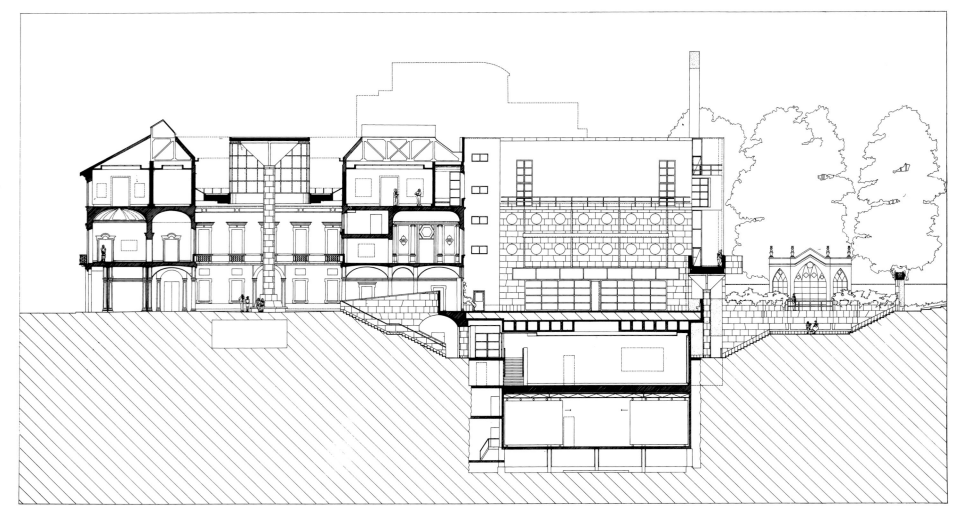

Longitudinal section through courtyard, central staircase,
Changing Exhibition gallery, and steps up through amphitheatre to garden

The new garden courtyard in summer

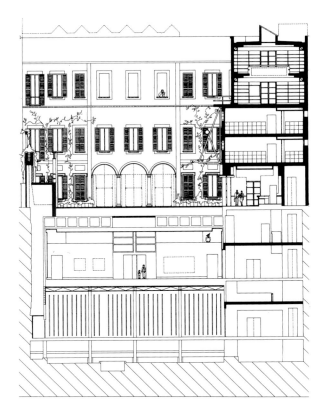

Cross section through garden courtyard

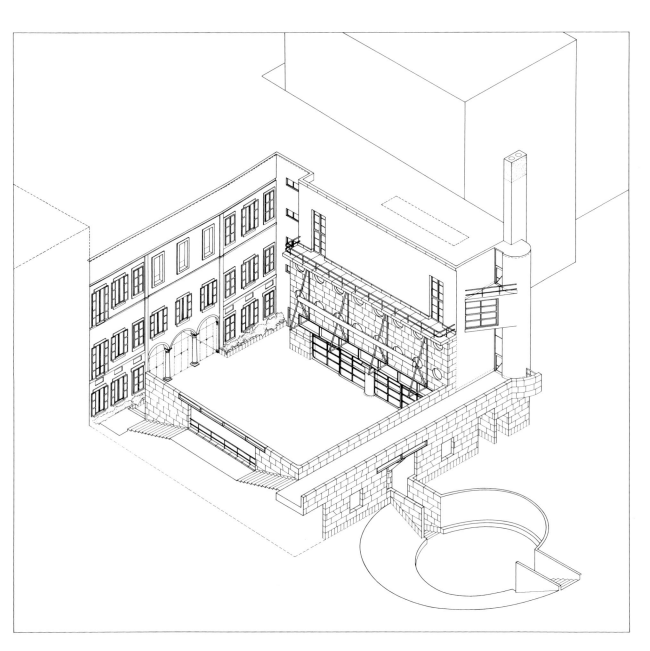

Axonometric view of the garden courtyard, new archive building, and amphitheatre. The staircase and raised bridge form the beginning of a walkway which will be extended to link with the nearby Brera Museum

1987– Milan: Palazzo Citterio (Pinacoteca di Brera)

Palazzo Citterio is in Via Brera, near La Scala and the *Galleria*. Originally an eighteenth century patrician residence with a formal garden, it was frequently transformed, rebuilt, and redecorated to reflect changes in taste and use, right up to recent times. This has left only fragments of the original building as parts of a *collage* of internal and external reconstruction, some of it very radical. Our project reorganises it as a museum with new spaces for temporary exhibitions and donated collections, and lecture rooms, a bookshop, and cafeteria. Specialised functions include a restoration workshop, picture store, administrative offices, a photographic archive, catalogue department, and reading room. The state of the existing building and the need to incorporate the new requirements led to the insertion of a number of new architectural "pieces" grafted in where previous transformation works had already radically changed the building and conservation was not at issue. In particular, an unattractive extra upper storey had been added to the central courtyard in the 1970s and could not be removed. To conceal this and restore correct proportions to the space, a new roof was added, with a glazed lantern supported by a central column, making a covered hall entered via an existing neoclassical vestibule. This hall contains all ticket, information, bookshop, and cloakroom facilities, and acts as an extension of the street outside: a focus for public arrival and informal socialising prior to visiting exhibitions, or during intervals in lec-

View out from the cafeteria into the garden courtyard

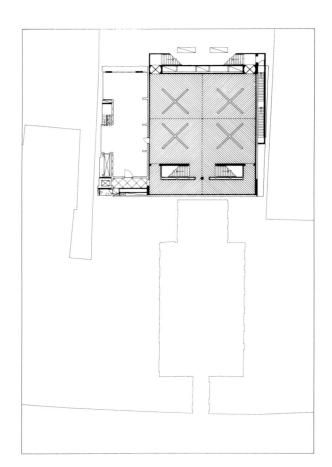

Basement changing exhibition room

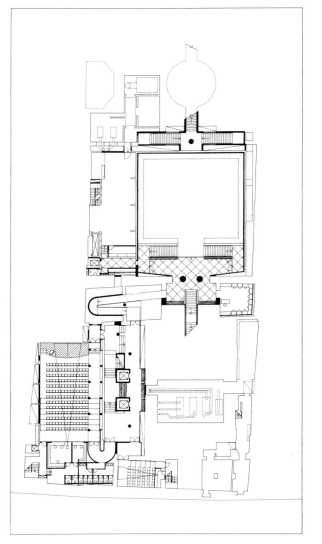

Basement lecture theatres, foyer, and ramp

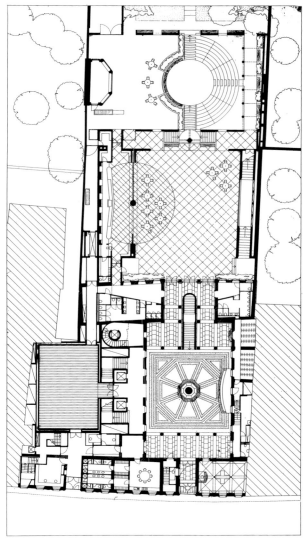

Entrance, gallery, and cafeteria at ground floor

tures, etc. The existing monumental doors opening off the courtyard have been re-utilised, and circulation throughout has been improved and simplified. Access to an existing basement is facilitated by adding a new axial stair leading to one of three large temporary exhibition galleries. A new core of public stairs and lifts, on the cross-axis of the courtyard, ensures clear and easy vertical circulation between the entrance hall, the exhibition galleries at the upper floors and two lecture/seminar rooms in the basement. An informal public promenade leads from Via Brera, through the covered courtyard, into a new outdoor court, and then the gardens. A new wing overlooking the outdoor court contains a cafeteria, typically Milanese in style, with a long bar at which

aperitifs, snacks, and coffee are served, and some small tables for conversation; by walking in from the street through the entrance hall, the general public can use this cafeteria without visiting the museum. In good weather, the front of the cafeteria can be left open with the sunblind wound down, and the tables spread to occupy the courtyard. The upper floors of the new wing are reached from a reserved entrance off the interior courtyard, and leading to specialised, facilities for museum staff, researchers, and art historians. At the top is a double-height art-history reading room, daylit from above and surrounded by a balcony, with an outdoor terrace to the courtyard. Consulting tables are arranged in a bay window overlooking the gardens.

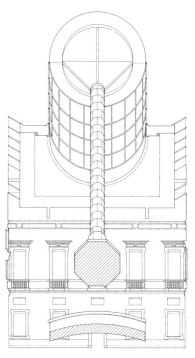

Up view of new courtyard roof

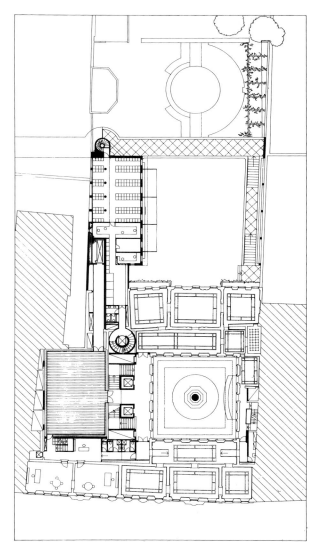

Exhibition rooms and offices at first floor

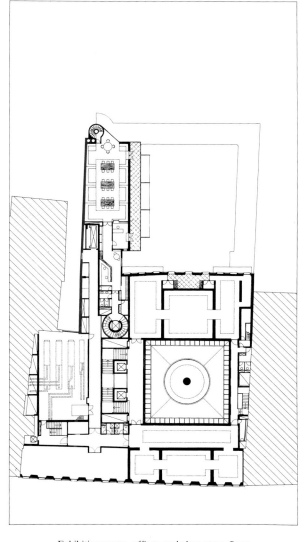

Exhibition rooms, offices, and plant at top floor

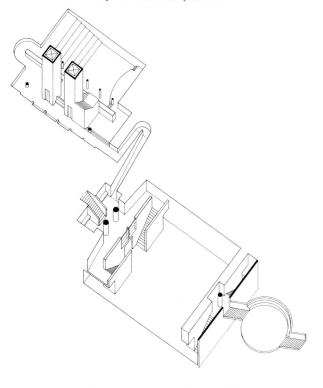

Lecture theatre, foyer, ramp, gallery, amphitheatre

Perspective view showing new glazed link and existing buildings beyond

"Glyndebourne" is a respected institution in the English musical world: an opera house in the grounds of a country house in Sussex, two hours' drive south from London. An increase in the audience for opera has made the existing auditorium too small, necessitating construction of a larger hall and the reorganistions of access and restaurant facilities. In the new project, visitors leave their cars in a parking area and approach by way of an entrance pavilion, standing as a marker at one end of a new glazed corridor which overlooks lawns and gardens, and connects the old and new buildings together in a unified functional *ensemble*. Built in timber and stone, and having glazed sides which can be opened in good weather, it becomes a long *loggia* or open promenade in summertime, and acts as the foyer of the auditorium. It leads on towards the older opera house building, reconverted for use as restaurants and bars, with views of the main house and gardens. The new auditorium provides 1150 seats on three levels of a "courtroom" format around a proscenium arch stage, which provides intimacy and good cross-views for the audience. The rectangular plan, sloped ceiling, and timber panelling give the best acoustics for this type of music and maintain something of the previous character and "out-of-town" ambience of this country auditorium.

Front elevation (existing buildings at centre left)

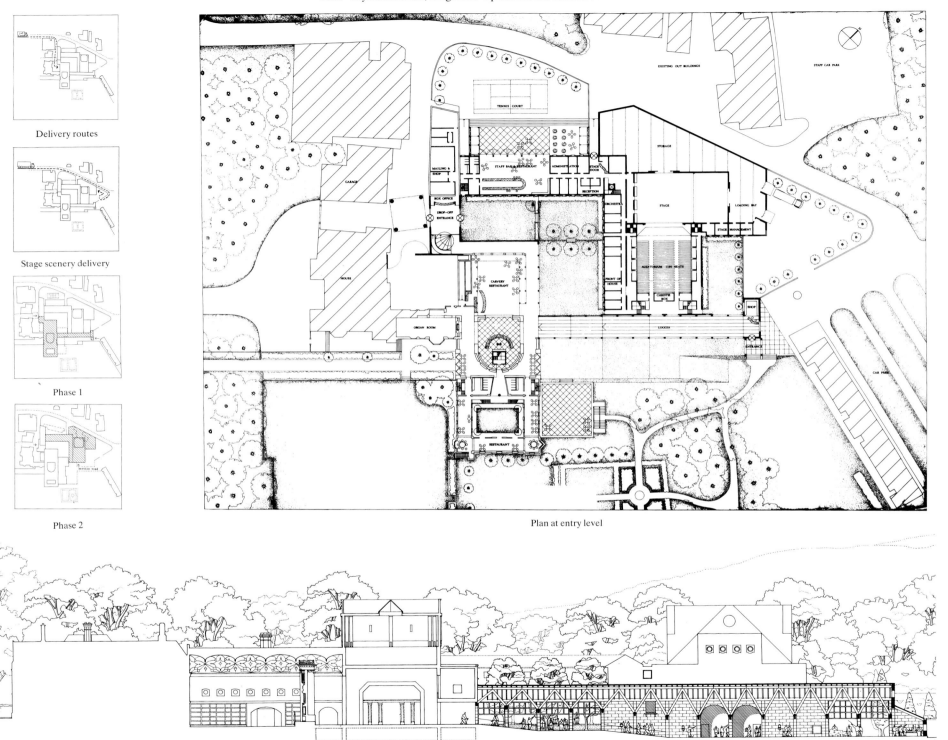

Delivery routes

Stage scenery delivery

Phase 1

Phase 2

Plan at entry level

Longitudinal section along the new glazed link

New restaurant in the existing building

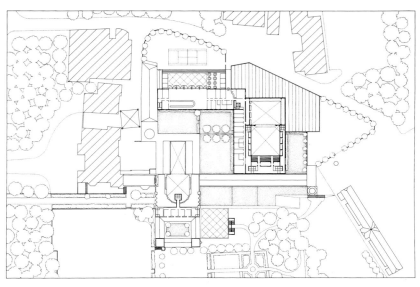

Roof plan

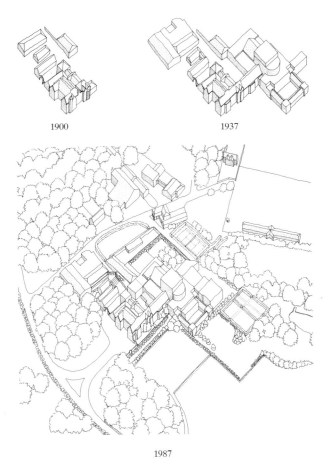

1900   1937

1987

Cutaway axonometric

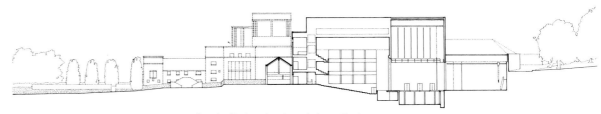

Cross section through the auditorium

Longitudinal section through the auditorium

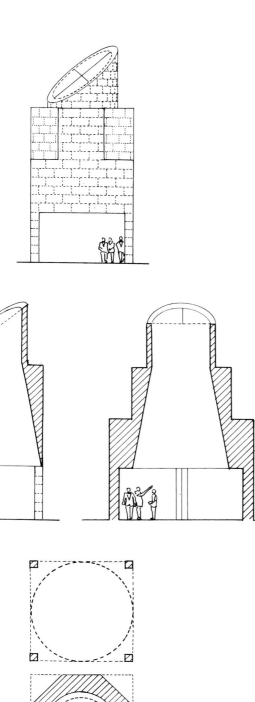

Elevation, sections, and plans of the "lipstick" tower

Cutaway perspective view of the new glazed link

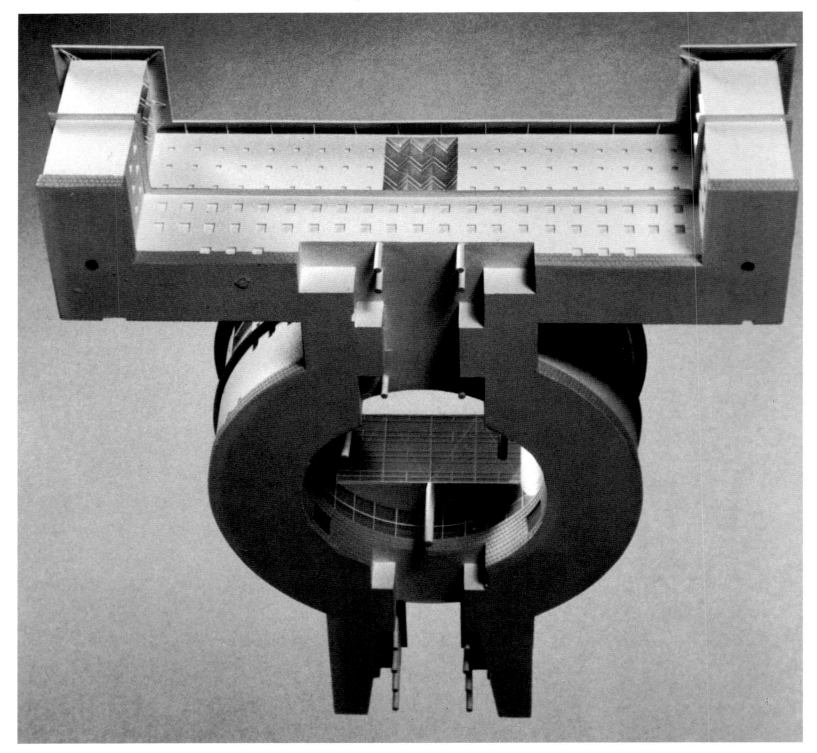

Worm's-eye view of the model

Our new Science Library is specific to the tradition of the master plan of radial Malls emanating from the hub of the campus. At our suggestion, it was moved from the site proposed, to this position astride the axis of the Bio-Science Mall. It responds to the design objectives of developing better urban quality, a sense of place, and increased variety of pedestrian experience. It is highly visible from all directions and creates a portal to the future Bio-Sciences Quadrangle; its extended passage-ways and courtyard create a spatial sequence for visitors entering or leaving the Library and for those passing along the Bio-Science Mall through the building: a place for all. 24-hour activity in the Library enlivens the Mall, making this a safe route across campus. The circular form centres the composition, allowing the building to face in two directions, its narrow end looking towards the Ring

Mall and a wide façade opening the opposite way. The entrance colonnade is one of a sequence of expanding and contracting spaces which encourage entry and passage through the building. Its splayed walls focus towards the central courtyard which brings daylight into the heart of the building and enables the entrance to be located in the middle, equidistant from all departments. Accommodation is on six floors, with exhibition space in the entrance hall, reader and stack areas, catalogue, loan and reserve counters, a reference library, and administrative offices. The internal organisation is unlike that of a city-centre library, where there is often a single grand reading room; instead, various types of study spaces and stacks are distributed throughout. Readers usually find themselves close to windows, seated within a small group of colleagues, rather than in a vast array of tables.

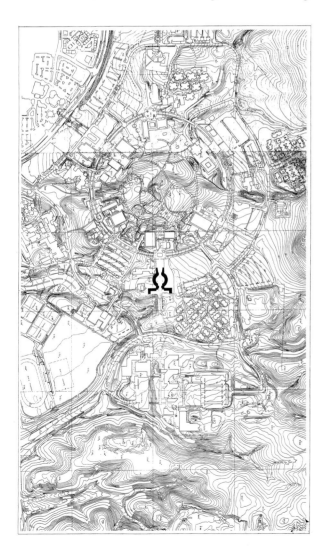

Campus location plan

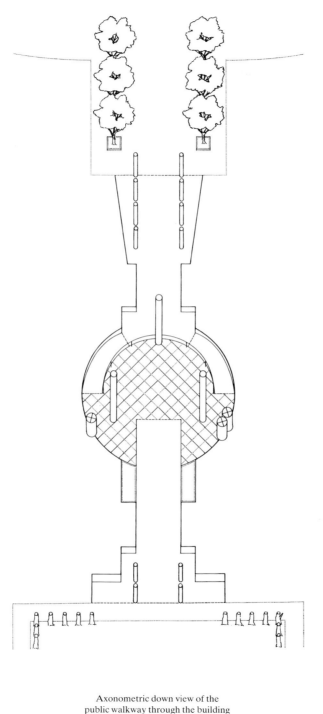

Axonometric down view of the
public walkway through the building

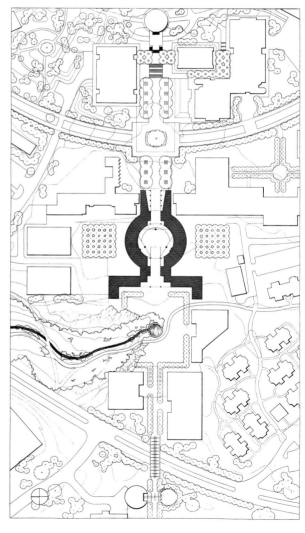

Site plan

209

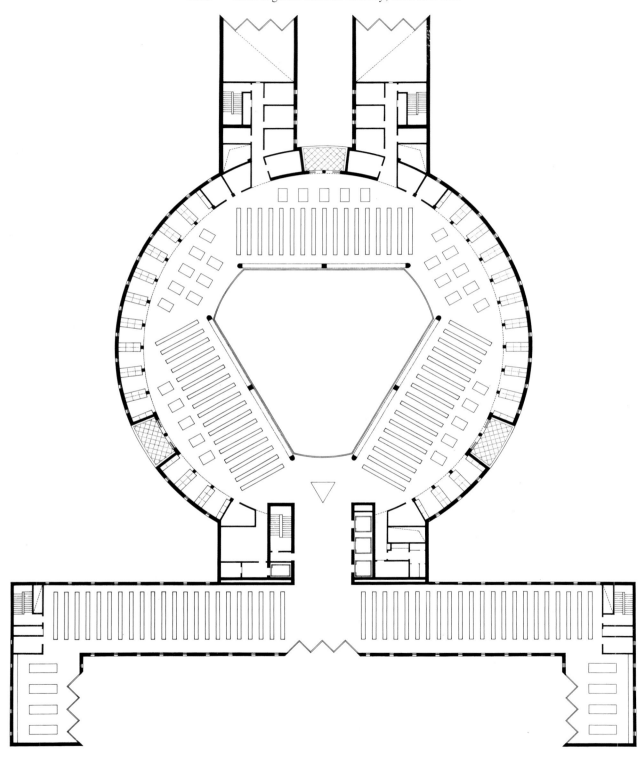

Typical upper floor plan

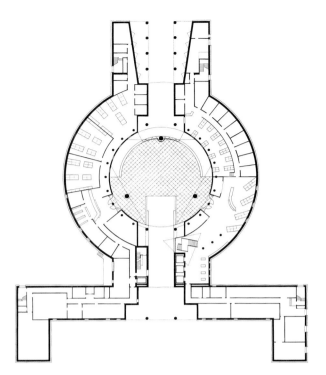

Plan at entrance level

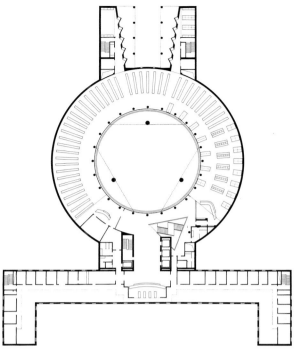

Reference/periodicals libraries and main lending desk

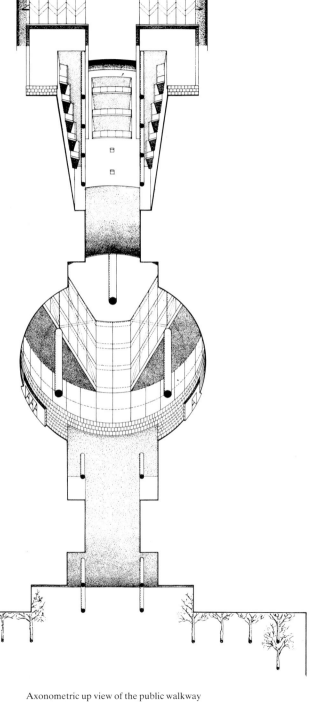

Perspective view

Axonometric up view of the public walkway

211

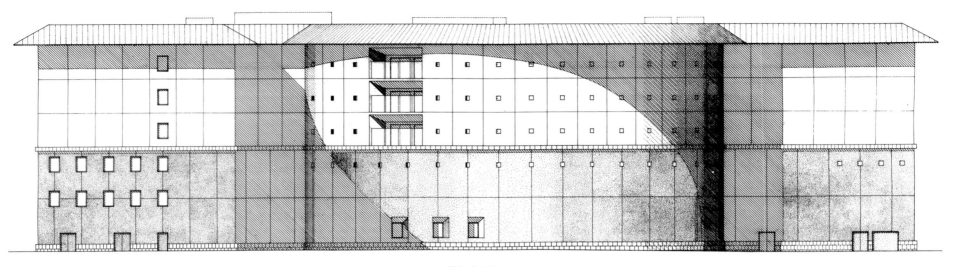

Side elevation

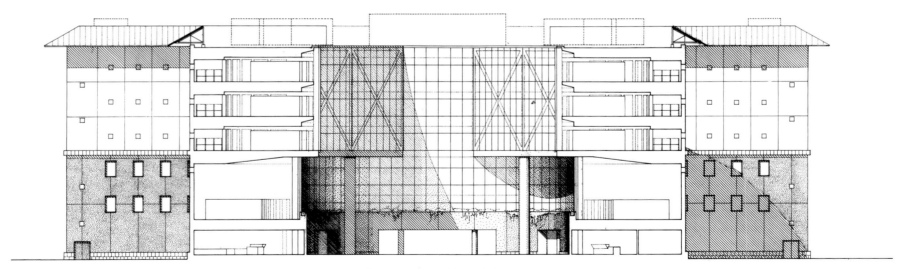

Cross section through the central courtyard

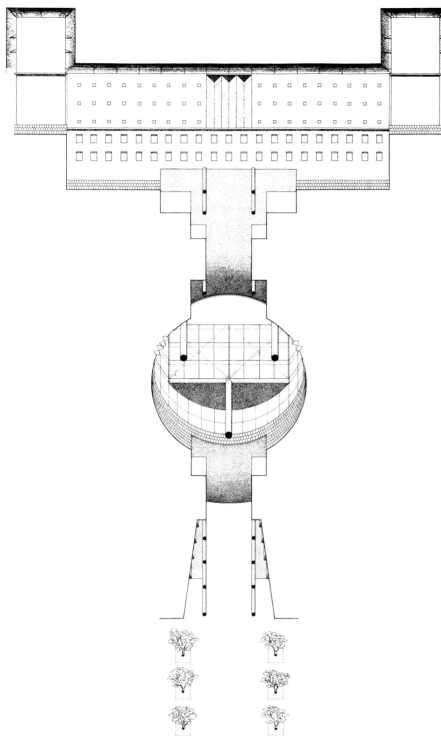

Axonometric up view of the public walkway

Worm's-eye view of the model

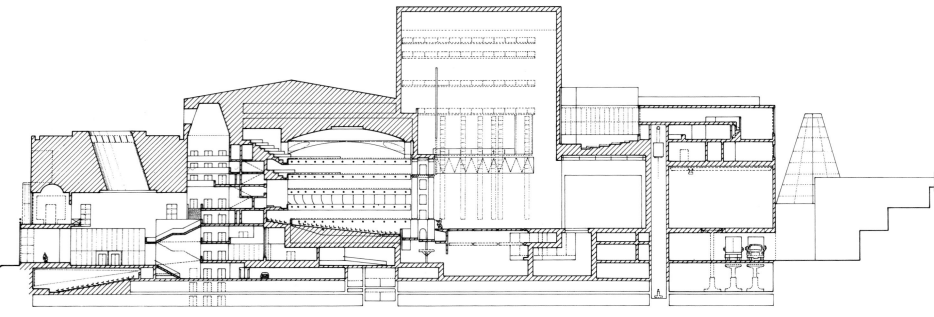

Longitudinal section through the auditorium

This building in downtown To-ronto combines the monumental with the informal. Opera-goers or casual visitors arrive from the street or from underground parking, into a spacious rooflit concourse, con-ceived as an extension of the sidewalk; a bustling centre of activi-ty throughout the day, lined with box offices, shops, a café, a restau-rant, and a museum, and a large window which provides an informal stage for lunchtime recitals. From the concourse, a grand staircase leads to the various levels of the auditorium. A suite of clubrooms, suitable for first-night receptions, surrounds the concourse and con-nects to the auditorium by an inner gallery. Private members' lounges also connect directly to the au-ditorium. Clubrooms around the edges of the concourse have private stairs to the boxes. The auditorium is of the traditional "shoebox" type with proscenium arch, orchestra pit, and tiered balconies. Backstage areas are served from the rear.

Frontal view of the model

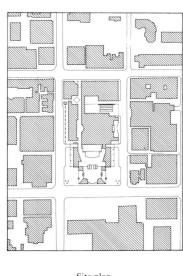

Site plan

1988 Toronto: Ballet and Opera House

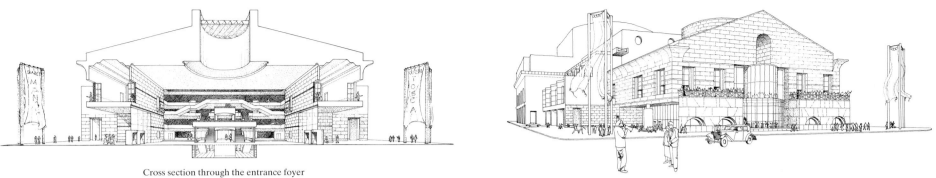

Cross section through the entrance foyer

Perspective view

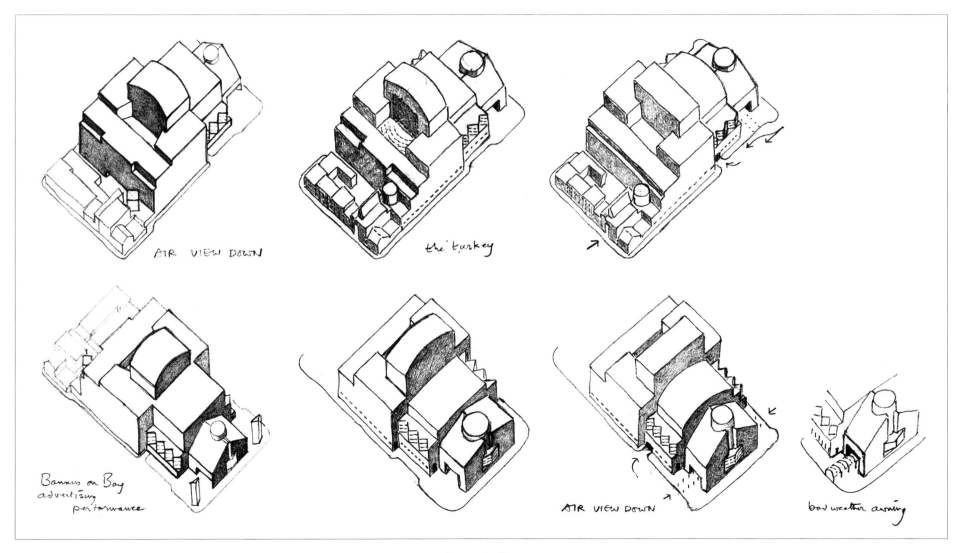

AIR VIEW DOWN

the turkey

Banners on Bay
advertising
performance

AIR VIEW DOWN

bad weather awning

Concept doodles

Perspective view of the developer's previous proposal

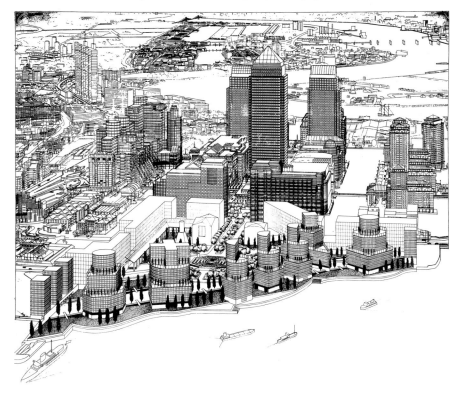

The same view with our alternative proposal

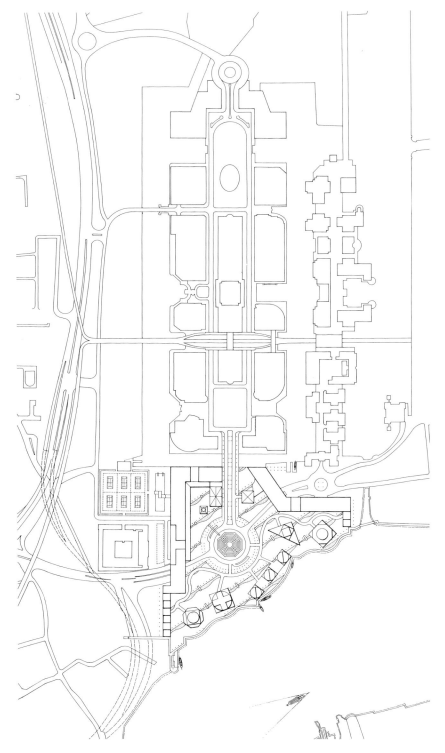

Site plan

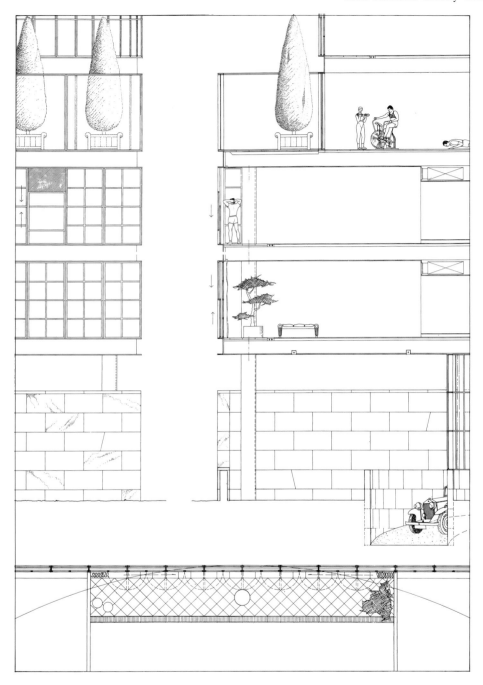

Details of residental buildings

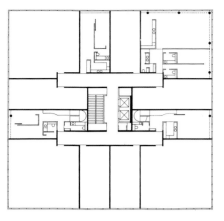

Typical plan of a square block

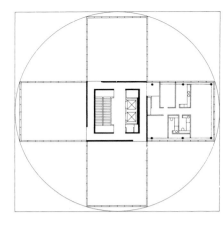

Typical plan of a cruciform block

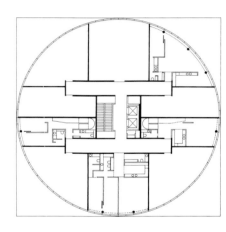

Entry level plan

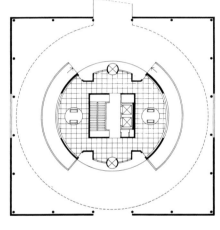

Typical plan of a cylindrical block

Our design proposes a large riverside park with terraces, stepping down to the Thames and enclosed by linear buildings containing offices, shops, and a hotel. The new park contains apartment towers ranged informally along the river and incorporating an existing roundabout, to which we have added a hedgerow maze at the centre, sunk into the stepped terraces. The airy spaciousness of the park creates a gateway to Canary Wharf. Residents, office workers, and visitors could enjoy impromptu events on the terraces, which are alternately surfaced in grass or gravel with stone retaining walls, trees, and shrubs. A covered pedestrian route leads from the nearby offices through the park, to a pier for commuters using the river bus. The residential buildings along the water's edge are designed as a series of "mini towers" of varied form whose reflecting glass surfaces should create a dramatic river-front along the edge of the Thames. These are radically different to the solid massing of the adjoining Canary Wharf office development, but produce the same residential density; their site planning as individual buildings would allow flexibility in investment and implementation and their varied form would give each a distinctive, recognisable appearance. They step vertically to give a variety of apartment types, with roof terraces adjoining club/restaurant facilities. Residents would enjoy views of the Thames, the City of London, the West India Dock, and the commercial centre of Canary Wharf.

Underground parking and service level

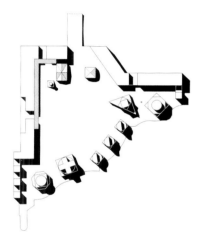

Shadow plan

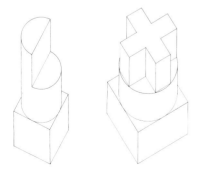

Residential blocks

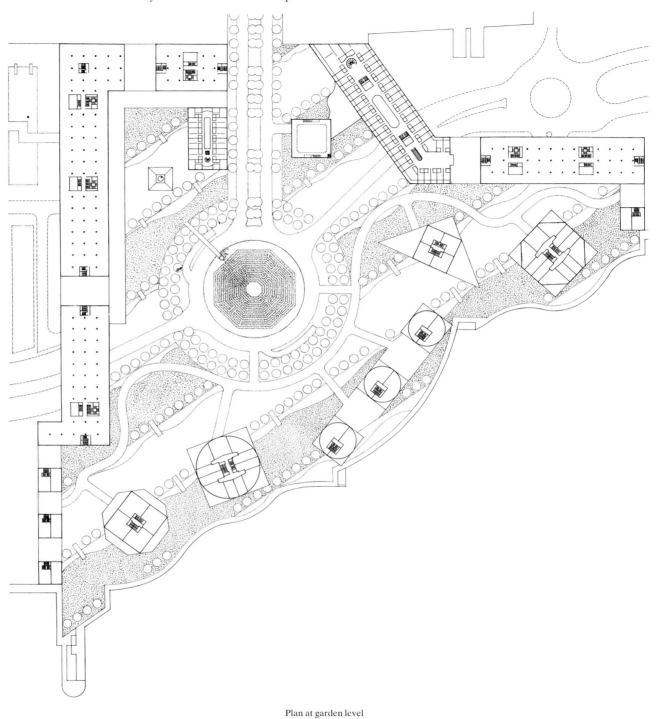

Plan at garden level

1988 London: Canary Wharf residential development

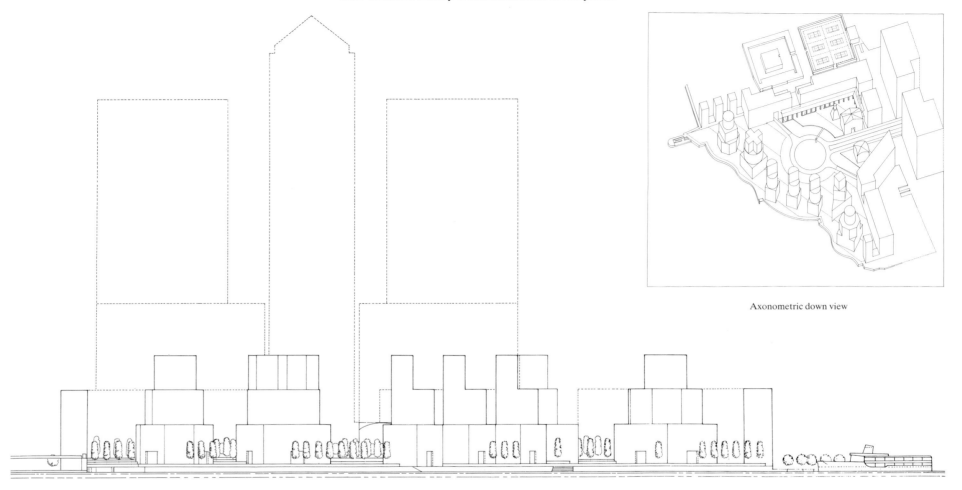

Axonometric down view

Elevation seen from the river Thames

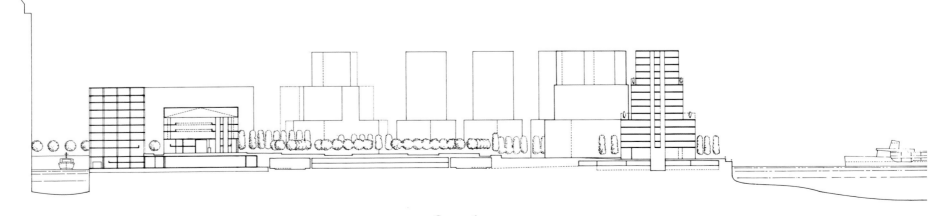

Cross section

The LA Philharmonic Hall is related to the tradition of monumental public buildings and to the populist aspect of today's places of culture and entertainment. It is designed as a focal point, symbolising the importance of music in the cultural life of the city: a highly visible and accessible public place encouraging community involvement in the arts. The design is an *ensemble* of architectural forms related to the functional elements of the programme: a city in microcosm, unified by a concourse at ground level, ablaze with light for evening performances and animated by recitals, lectures, and people moving about at different levels. The circular, stepped concert hall is the centrepiece of the composition, and together with the Chamber Hall and the Support Facilities Building, it forms a trio of primary elements. Three smaller pavilions containing Gift Shop, Box Office/Cinema, and Grand Stair/Club Lounge are arranged along First Street and define the northern entrances to the building. An electronic billboard above the Gift Shop announces current events. Three sides of the Support Facilities Building enclose a garden which looks out towards downtown and makes a new edge to the city block. The top balcony level of the concert hall leads to a roof terrace with adjoining bars and restaurants, with views of Los Angeles and the Hollywood Hills.

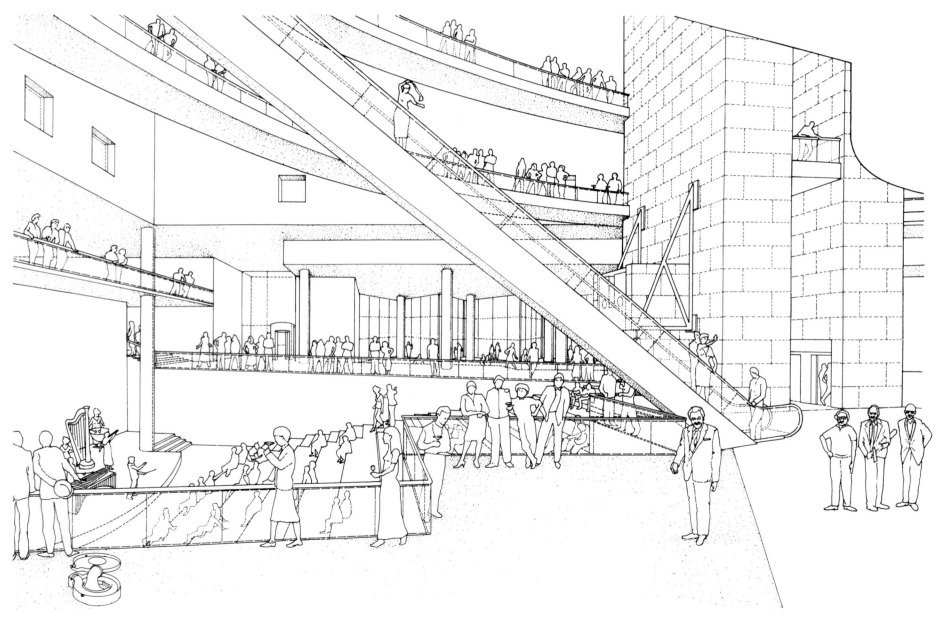

Perspective view of the performance space in the concourse

Perspective view (existing concert hall to the right)

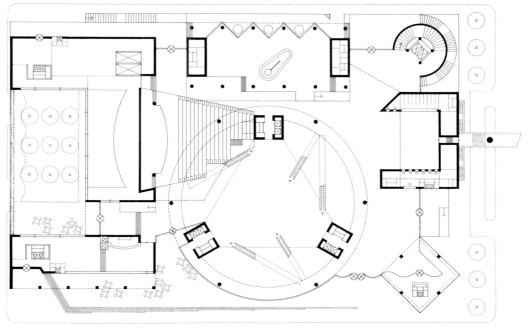

Plan at entrance hall concourse level

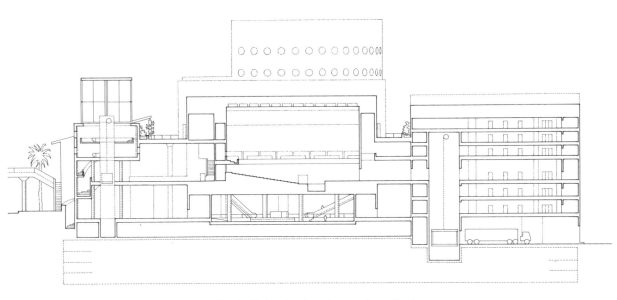

Longitudinal section through the smaller auditorium

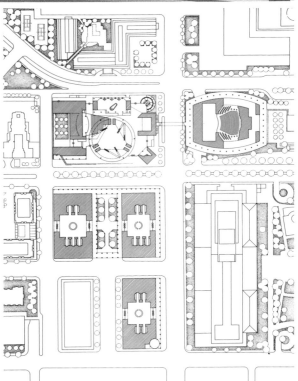

Site plan with new office towers and existing concert hall

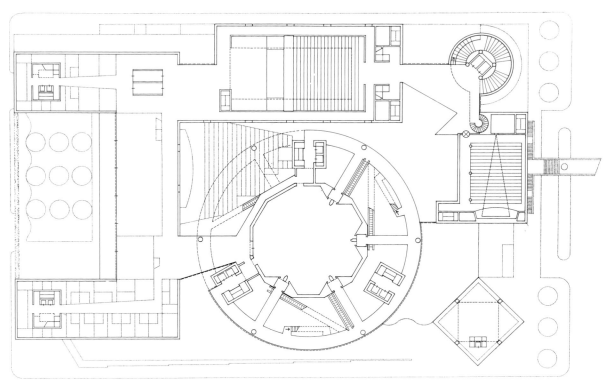

Plan at the main auditorium foyer level

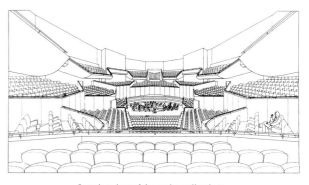

Interior view of the main auditorium

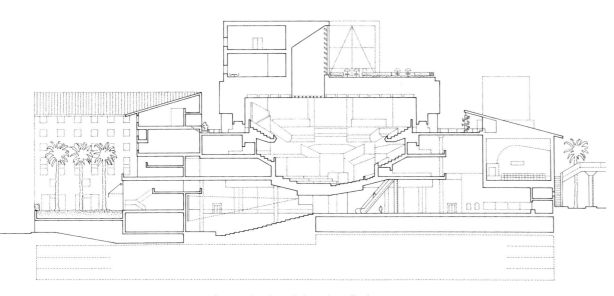

Cross section through the main auditorium

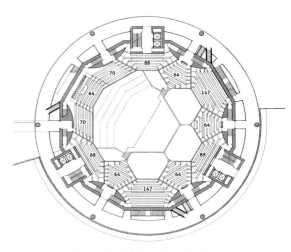

Upper level of the main auditorium

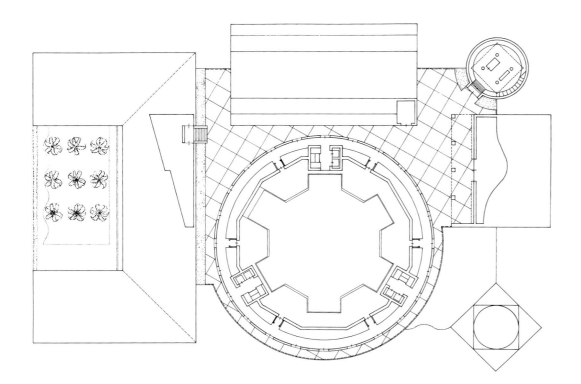

Plan through upper part of main auditorium

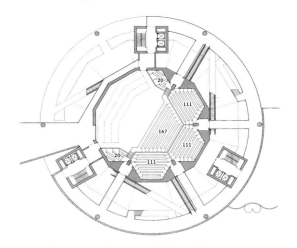

Lower part of the main auditorium at foyer level

225

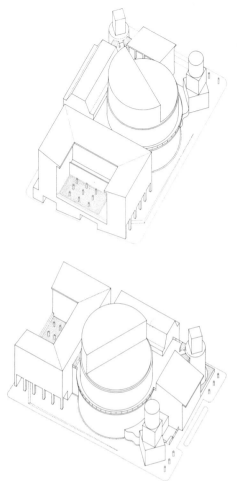

Cutaway view of the model

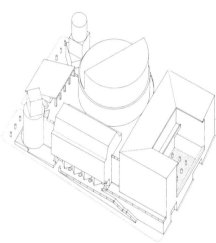

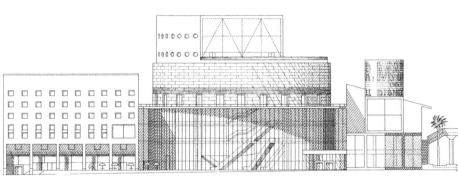

Front elevation

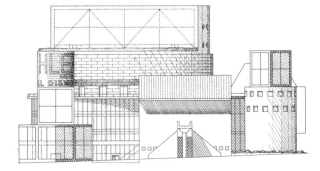

Side elevation

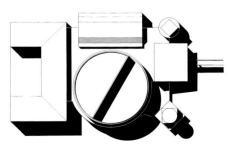

Shadow plan

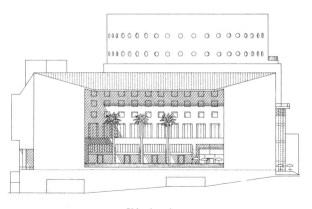

Side elevation

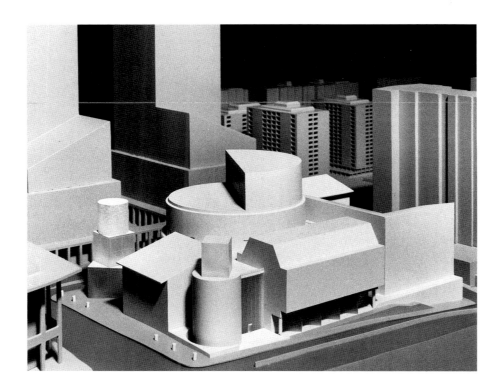

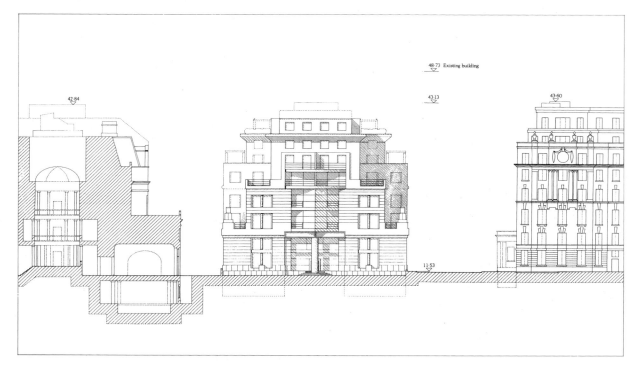

48·73 Existing building

42·84

43·13

43·60

11·53

Elevation to the square

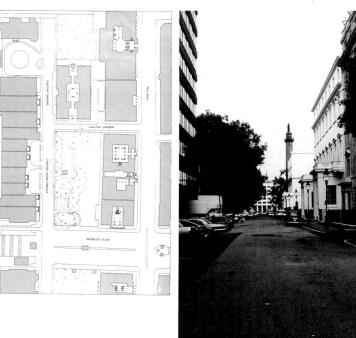

Location plan   (left) Building to be demolished   The model in context

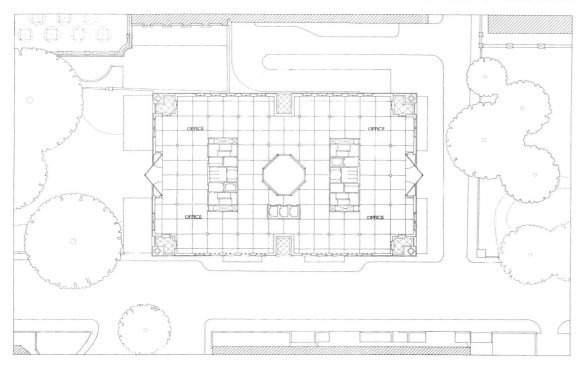

Typical office floor plan

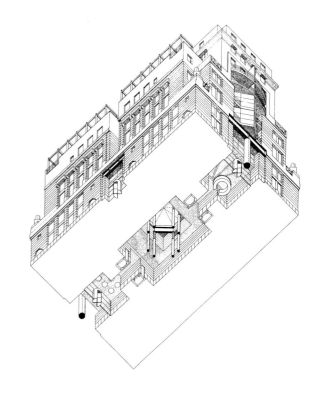

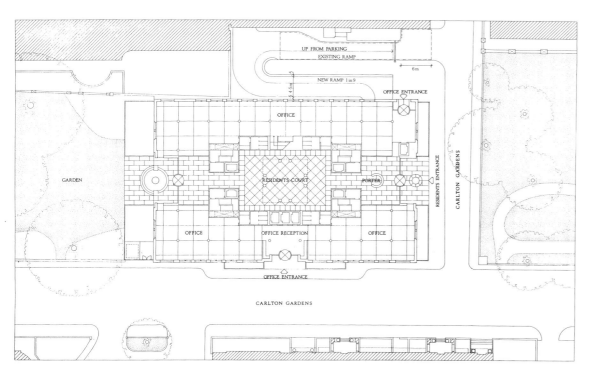

Plan showing residential and office entrances

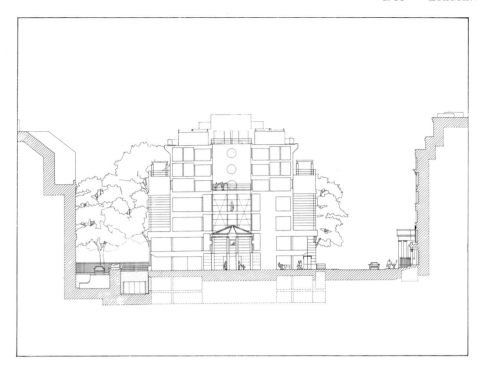

Cross section through the central atrium

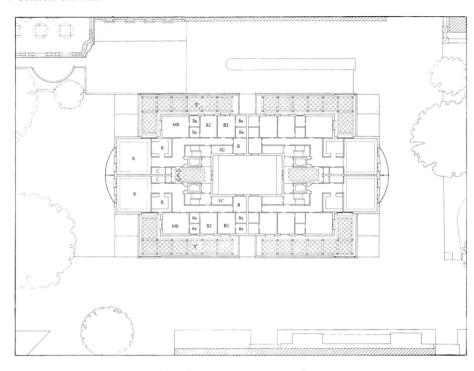

Plan of luxury apartments at upper floor

Plan of luxury apartments at intermediate floor

The site is in St. James's, close to the Athenaeum, Reform, and Royal Automobile Clubs. The planning of these clubs is based on the Italian *palazzo* adapted to the English climate, with the entrance on a central axis leading to a covered inner courtyard. The new building is influenced by these distinguished neighbours and can be understood as a pavilion standing in a park. It is axial and symmetrical in both directions, with two of its façades stepping upwards and backwards off the street, and garden terraces to the luxury apartments which overlook the park. The other façades look towards the street, and the proportions, height, and fenestration of all four reflect those of the adjoining buildings. The offices, which occupy the lower floors of the building, are entered on one of the two axes and are served by lifts connecting to a basement garage. Residents have a completely separate entrance on the other axis, leading by a vestibule into a covered central court from which there are views over the surrounding gardens.

Perspective view

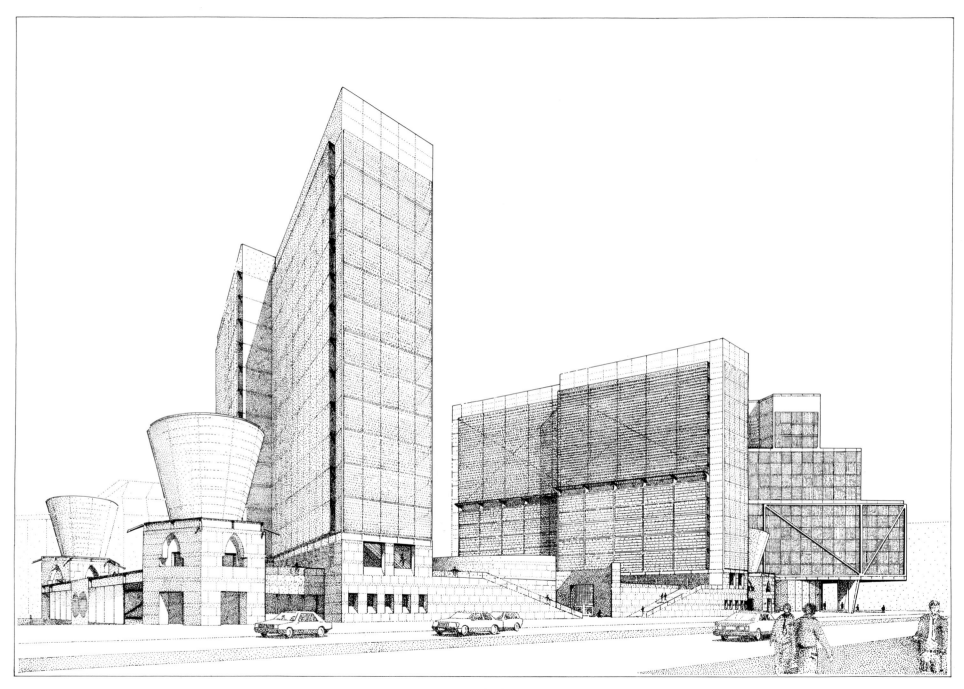

Perspective view

The project is conceived of as a "traditional" podium (clad in local sandstone with strips of terracotta tiles) with a "technological" superstructure and "modern" materials. Crowds going to the stadium pass through a circular plaza from which stairs and ramps lead up to a public terrace on the podium. Under the plaza, a two-storey department store, with two levels of parking, extends across the site. The escalators are sheltered by hexagonal pavilions, decorated inside and out with coloured terracotta tiles, which bring daylight into the entrances of the shopping floors. Two twelve-storey office buildings stand to either side of the plaza. Their curtain walls are shaded by metal sunscreens which occupy a 1,5 m. zone in front of the façades. A structural setback halfway up, clad in terracotta tiles, aligns with the eaves of the stadium and neighbouring apartment buildings. Openings on the façades of these buildings are echoed by vertical structural divisions on the lower part of the office blocks. Above, the louvres reduce their bulk and veil the divisions between floors. On one end of the site, with its entrance on the street corner, sits a 280-room hotel. Each hotel room has a *celosia* (shaded balcony) with sliding metal lattice sunscreens which define the outer face of the building.

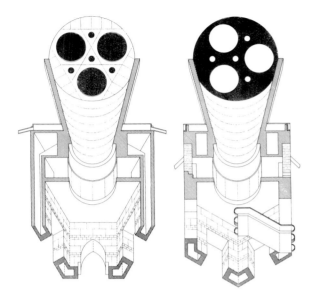

Up views of department store entrances

Location plan (stadium: top centre)

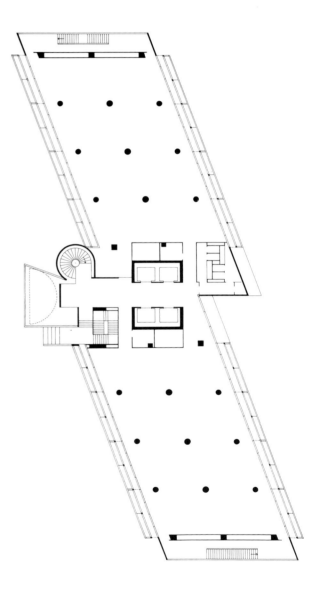

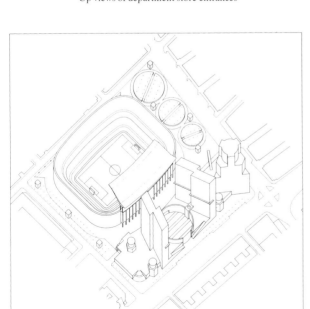

Down view

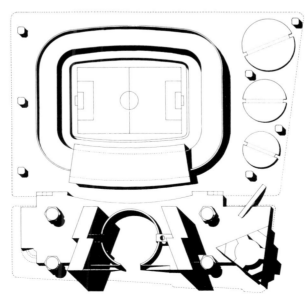

Shadow plan

Plan of the offices at entrance level

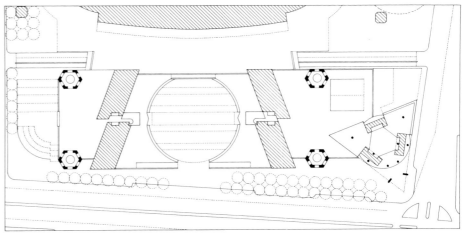

Block plan at podium garden level

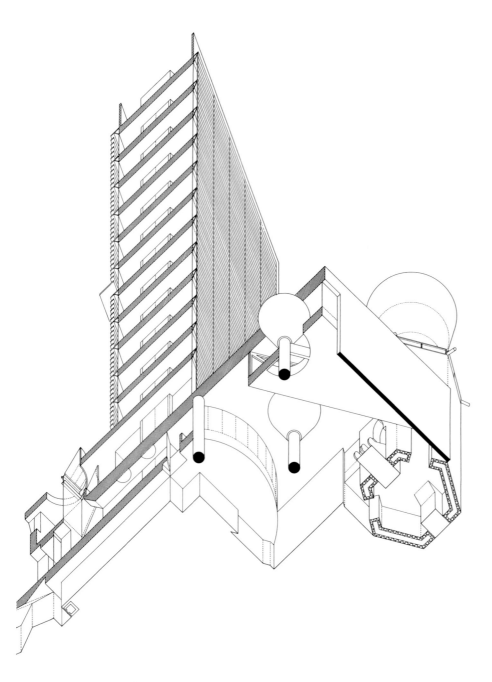

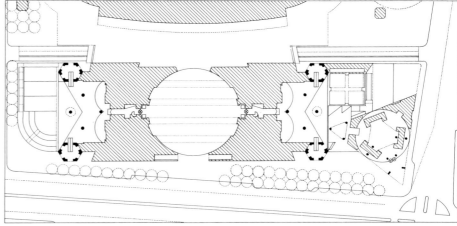

Block plan at entrance level

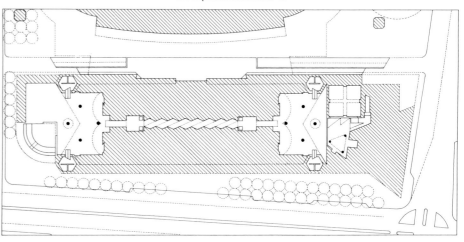

Cutaway up view of office entrance and department store

Block plan at shopping arcade level

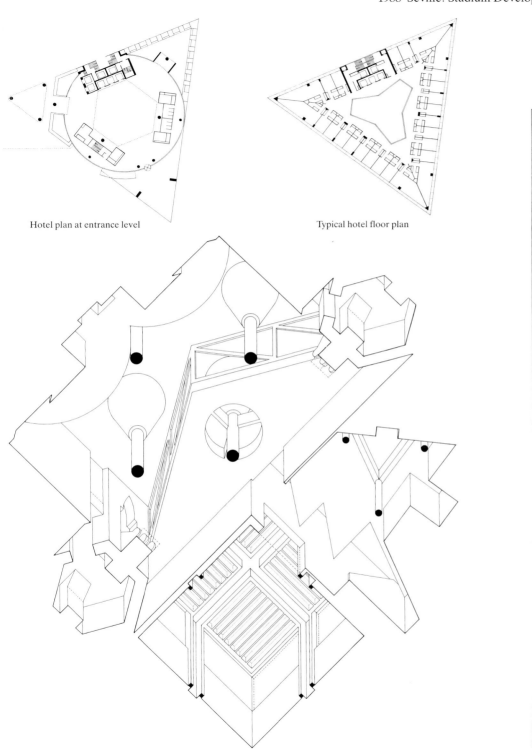

Hotel plan at entrance level

Typical hotel floor plan

Up view of department store, the conference hall, and foyer

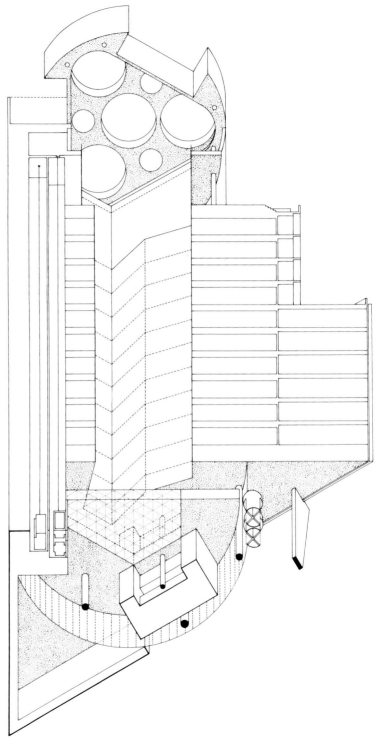

Cutaway up view of the hotel

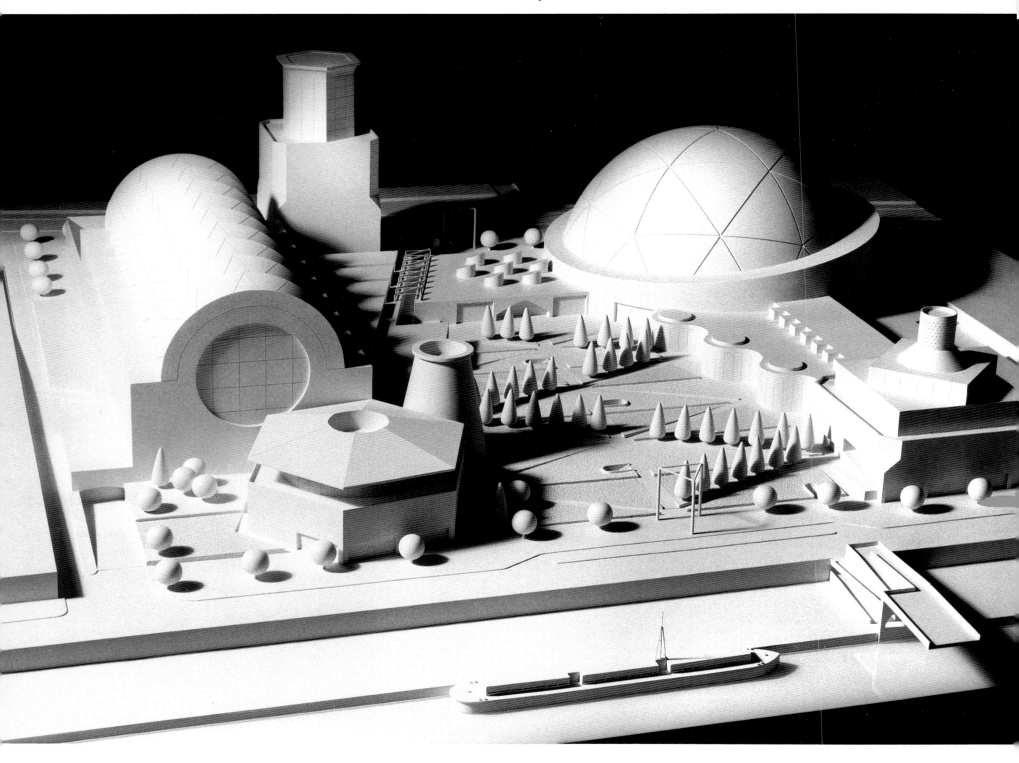

1989 Paris: Bibliothèque de France

The Library is a group of buildings around a park rising in stepped terraces from the river Seine, as a monumental but informal grouping which could become a familiar landmark, reviving this neglected eastern end of Paris; its sculptural forms are intended to establish a "mini-city" and to contribute to the urban skyline. The buildings express a combination of "modern" and "traditional" architecture; at ground level they would be mainly clad in stone, whilst the upper floors would be largely in steel and glass. The dome marks the Recent Acquisitions Library; the vault identifies the Reference Library; a cone-shaped building contains the Catalogue Room; and a hexagonal pavilion houses the Research Library. These principal facilities are backed up by underground book storage, document processing and technical services, and administrative offices with recreation rooms. Access to each department is planned round three sides of a free-form concourse surrounding the central garden. The main entrance, identified by four large cylindrical volumes, is located on the central axis. Two public footpaths enter and cross the Library, passing through the interior without compromising functionality or breaching security. One leads from the rear entrance to the garden terraces in the park, traversing the reception area, where viewing windows allow passers-by to see into the building. The second footpath is designed as a glazed enclosure connecting the river to the Avenue Nouvelle and passing through the Sound and Moving Image Library, the Café, and the Recent Acquisitions Library. This openness and interpenetration between public and private realms is intended to encourage the public and library users to explore and socialise. In addition to the library facilities there are shops, restaurants, bookstores, cafés, exhibition galleries, and a conference centre.

Eastern Paris in 1989. The site is on the right beyond the station

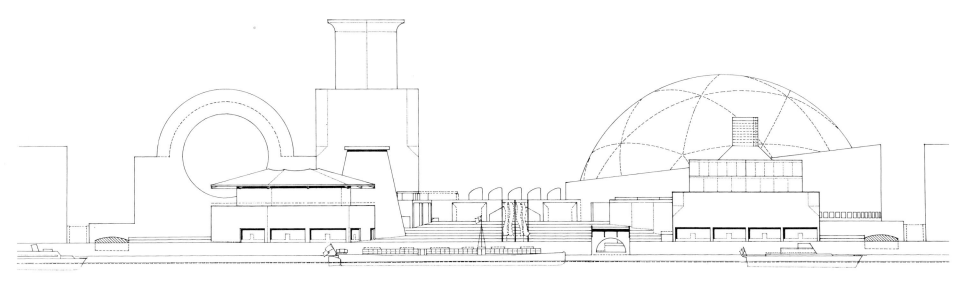

Front elevation seen from the Seine

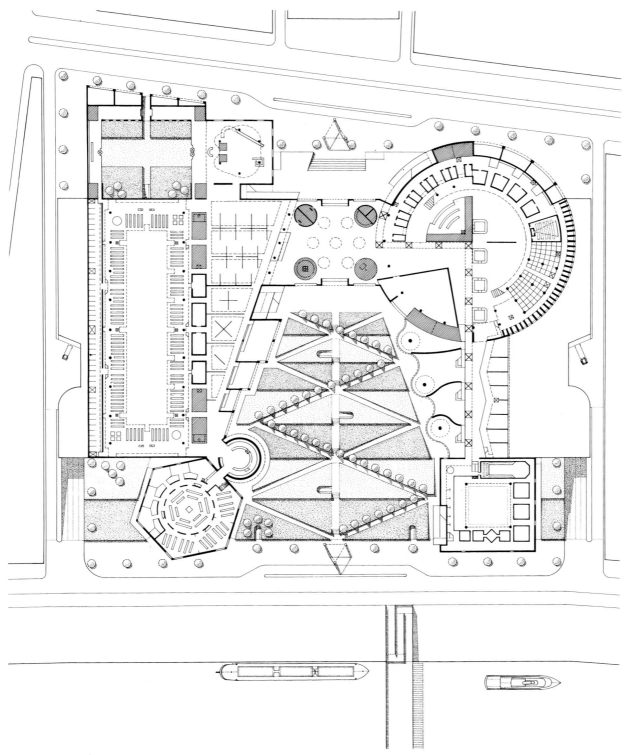

Plan showing the garden and the entrances

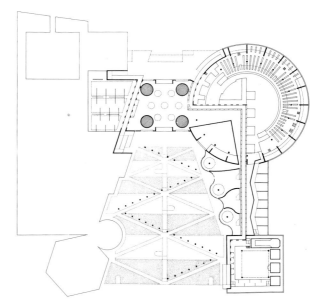

Plan at upper levels

Plan showing public walkway through the building

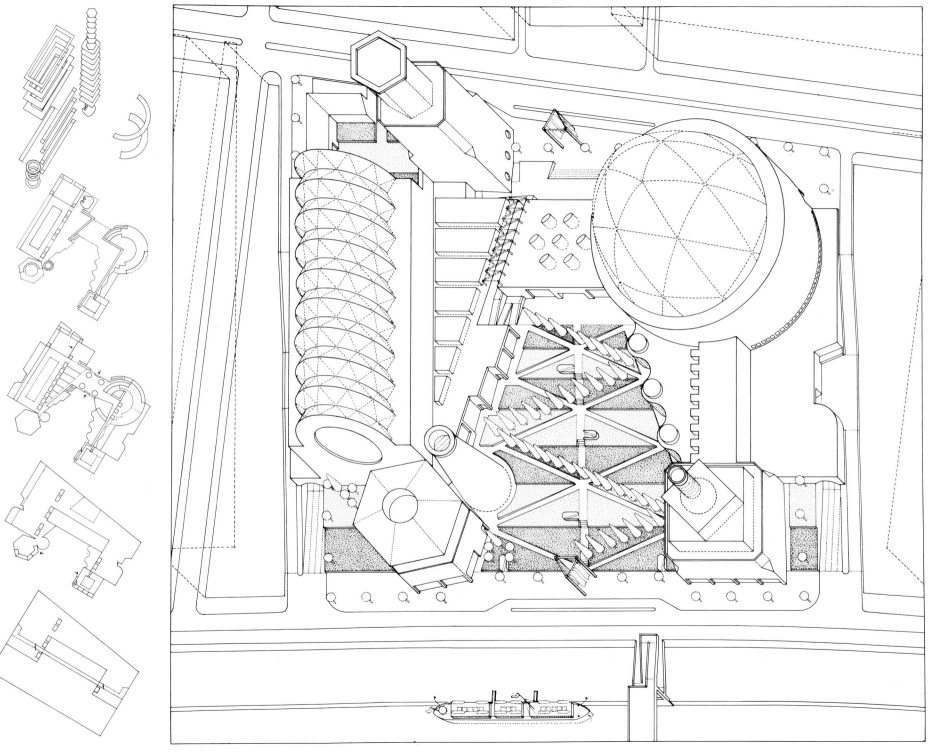

Analytical diagram

Down axonometric

1989 Paris: Bibliothèque de France

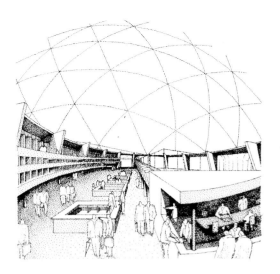

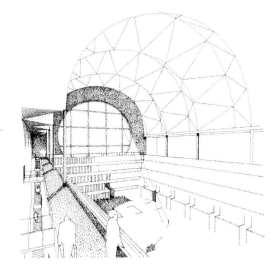

The Recent Acquisitions Library

Interior of the entrance hall

The Reference Library

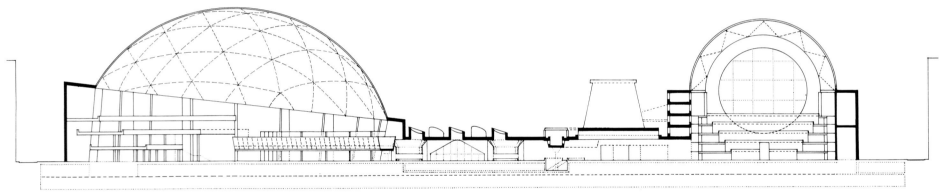

Cross section through the Recent Acquisitions Library, the entrance hall, and the Reference Library

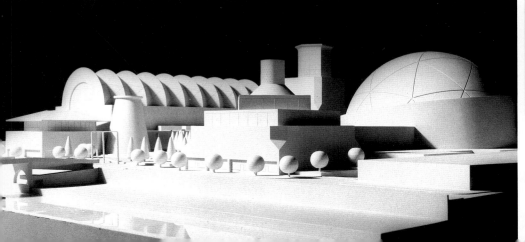

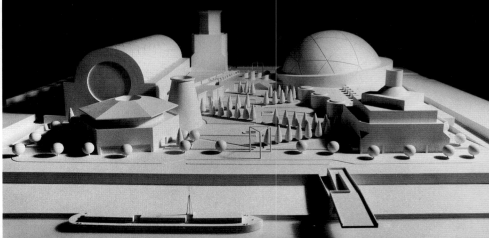

1989 Paris: Bibliothèque de France

The public walkway overlooking the restaurant and cafeteria

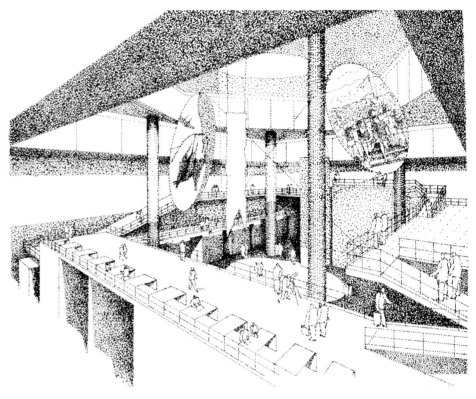

Interior of the Sound and Vision Library

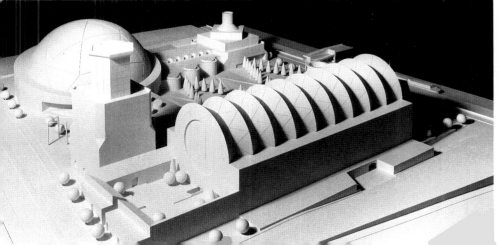

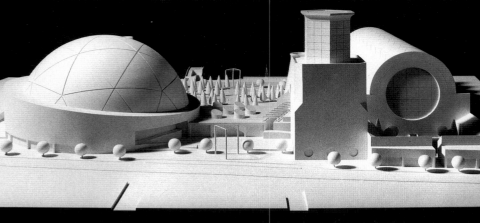

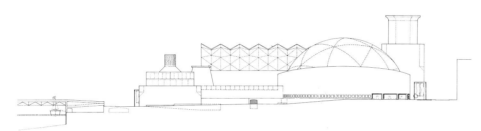

Elevation from the west

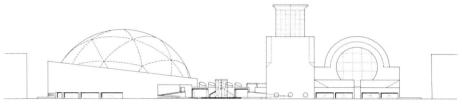

Elevation from the south

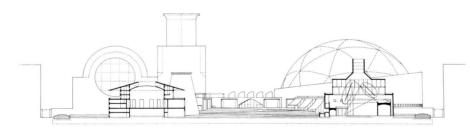

Section through Research Library (left) and Sound and Vision Library (right)

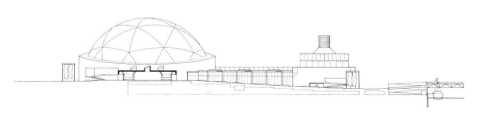

Section through entrance hall (left) and garden

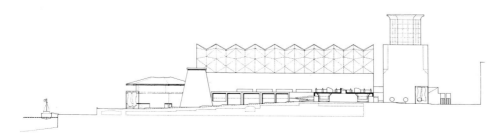

Section through garden and entrance hall

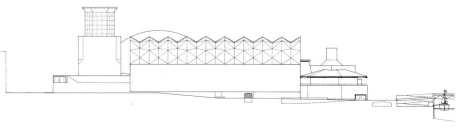

Elevation from the east

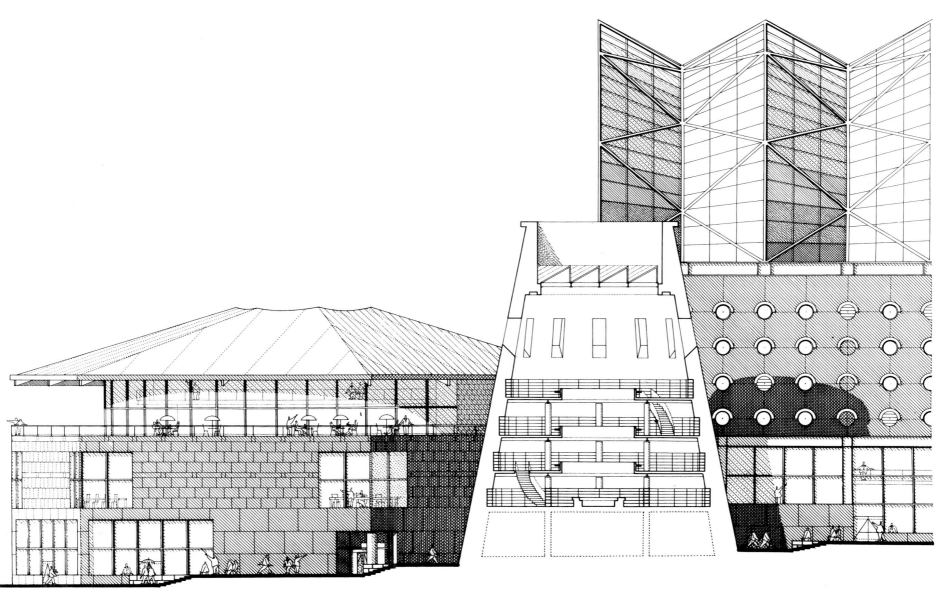

Research Library   Catalogue Building (sectioned)   Reference Library

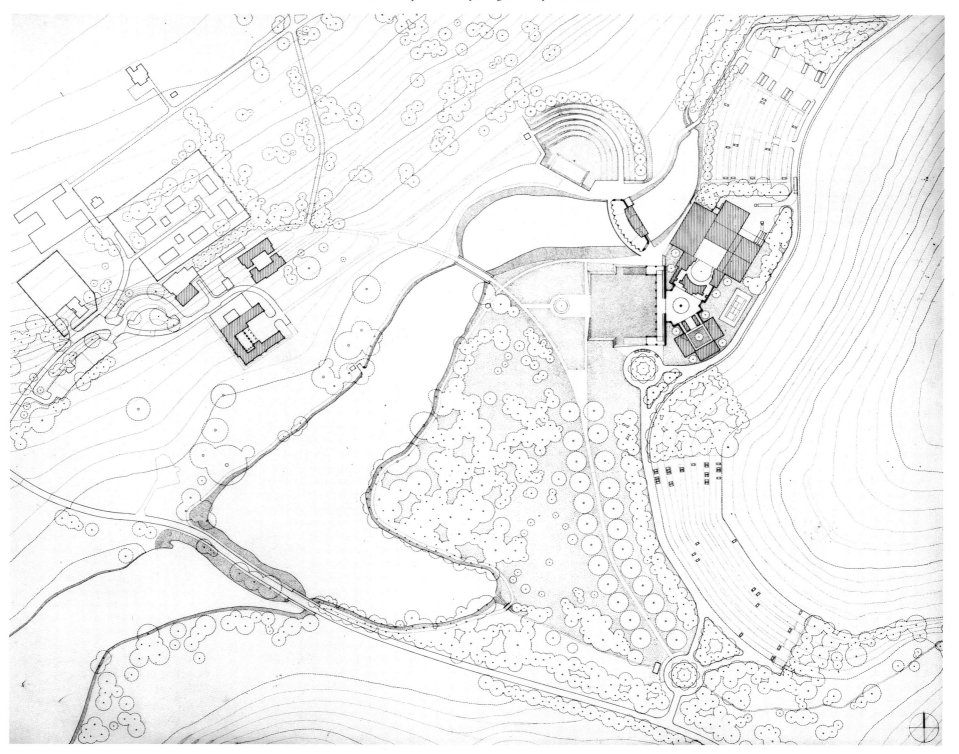

Site plan of the estate. Existing house left, entrance bottom right

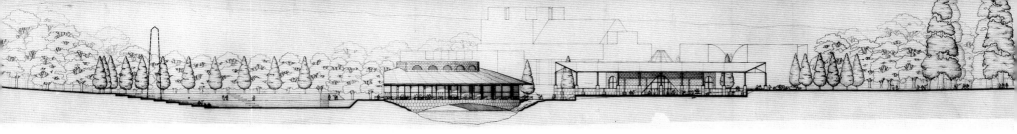

Longitudinal section through amphitheatre showing bridge restaurant and loggia

People disembarking at the gate would walk into the grounds along a curving avenue of sequoias, with dramatic distant views of the house, the lake, and the Adam bridge which crosses it. In inclement weather they could proceed by car or coach as far as a gatehouse drop-off point located close to the Foyer, at the southern end of a Loggia which permits approach to the building from any direction. A footpath connects the Loggia to a new amphitheatre in the garden, thus making possible a variety of walks round the lake. The main Foyer is triangular on plan, with cloakrooms and bookshop to the right and the Box Office and entrance to the main Auditorium to the left. Adjoining it is the administration building, which encloses a garden court. The offices are at first floor, with public facilities at ground level. The fan-shaped restaurant is in the form of a bridge over the lake, with views over the gardens and the water. The intention is to bring the house, the Adam bridge, the lake, and the garden amphitheatre into an harmonious relationship both formal and informal, encouraging dialogue between past and present across the lake. The Loggia, administration building, and the restaurant bridge are placed in front of the auditorium and fly tower to reduce their bulk when seen from the other side of the lake. These new buildings are arranged as pavilions and folies around one end of the lake, and perhaps visitors would enjoy discovering picturesque formal relationships between buildings and landscape.

COMPTON VERNEY,
WARWICKSHIRE.

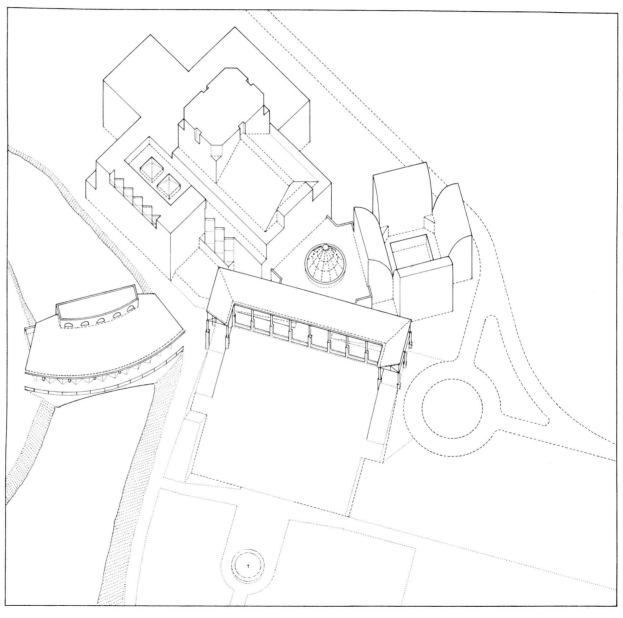

Schematic down view (bridge restaurant on the left)

1989 Compton Verney, England: Opera House

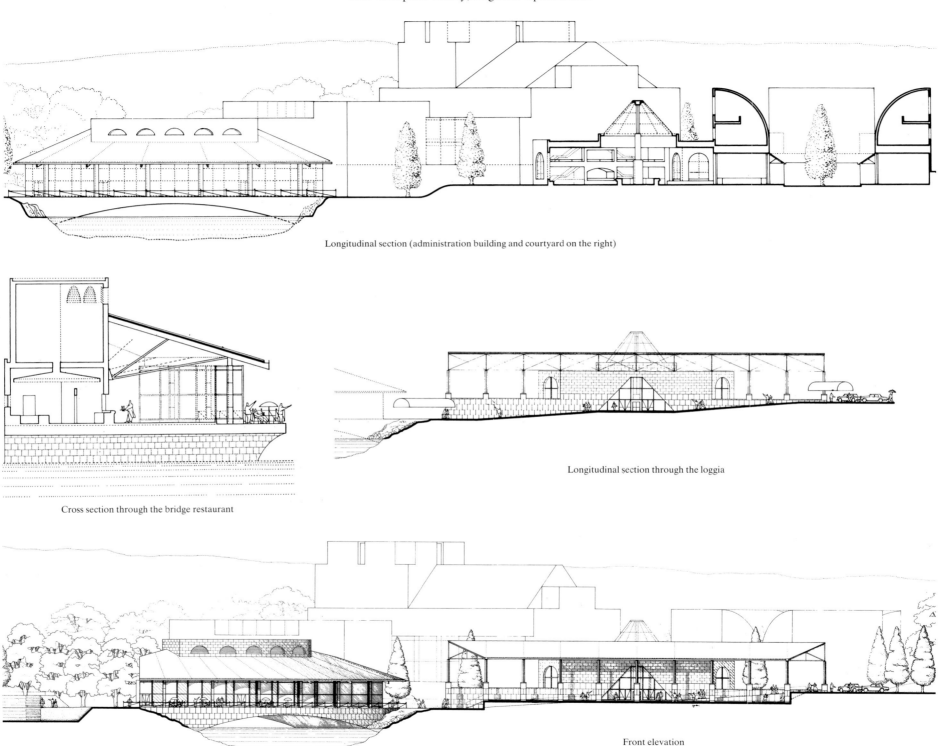

Longitudinal section (administration building and courtyard on the right)

Cross section through the bridge restaurant

Longitudinal section through the loggia

Front elevation

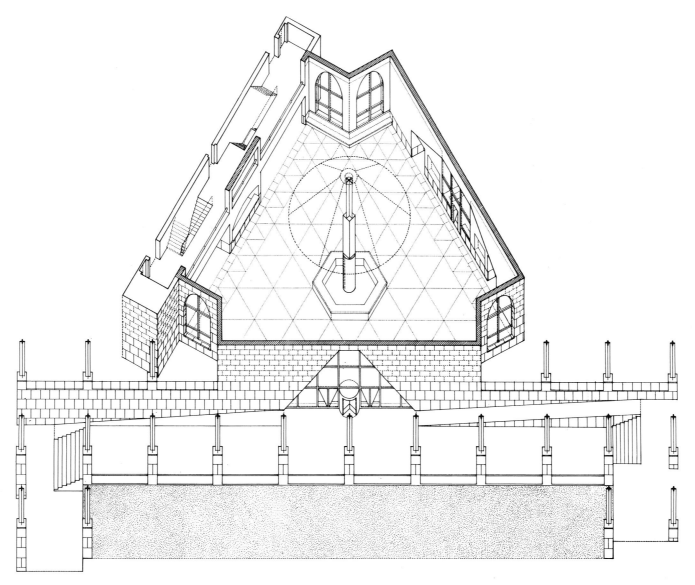

Axonometric down view

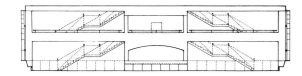

Elevation of auditorium entrance

Elevation of foyer entrance

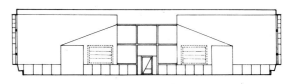

Elevation of entrance to administration offices

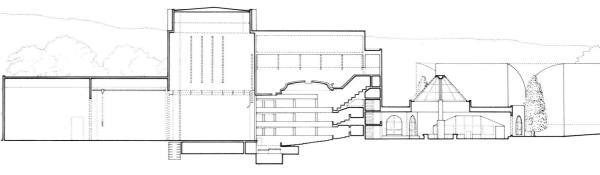

Longitudinal section: backstage areas, auditorium, foyer

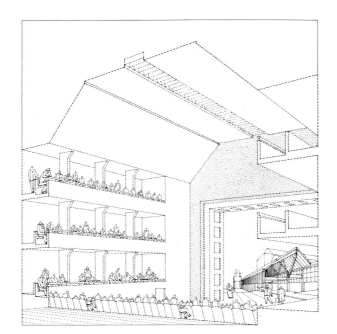

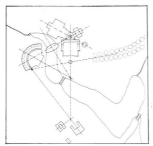

Interior of auditorium

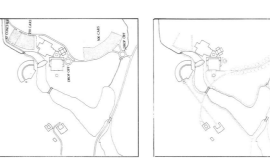

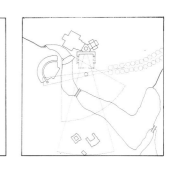

Building axes

Parking areas

Footpaths

Vistas and views

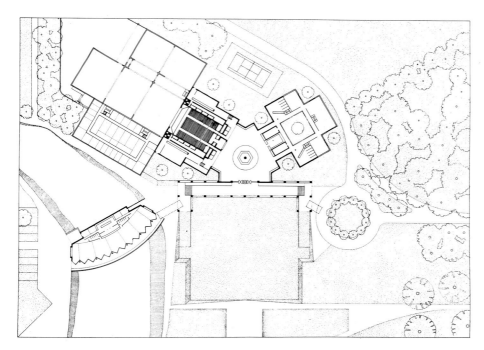

Plan at entrance level

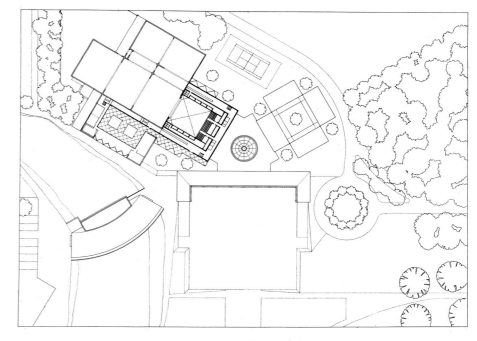

Plan at upper auditorium level

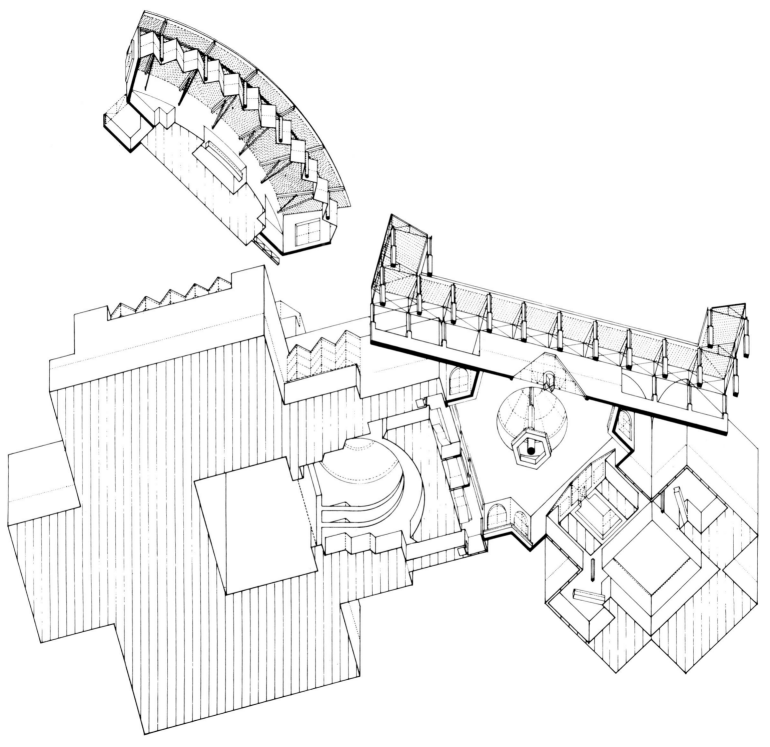

Up axonometric

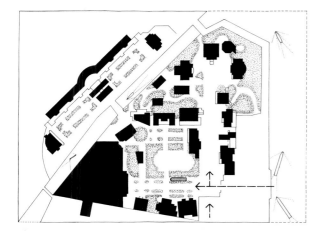

The Biennale Gardens and Bookshop (centre bottom, hatched)

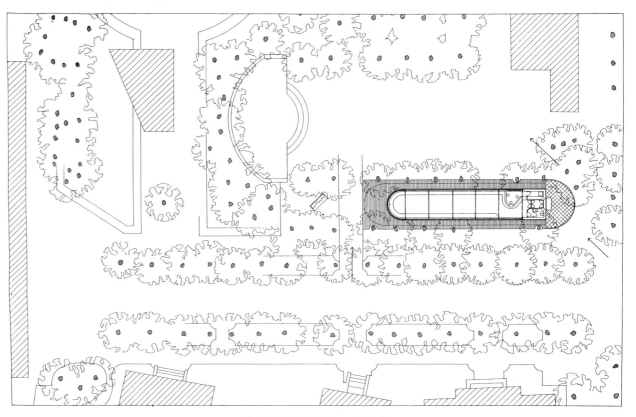

Site plan (Italian Pavilion on the left)

The site is among trees, parallel to the central avenue of the Biennale Gardens, where international exhibitions are held. The 25 pavilions reflect architectural taste over 100 years – from the neoclassical American Pavilion to the brutalist concrete of Sverre Fehns's Scandinavian Pavilion. They remain closed through the winter, coming alive for the busy summer exhibitions, when an international crowd strolls from pavilion to pavilion. This setting of small buildings in a formal garden evoked the idea of the "pavilion in the park" and ideas about nature and artifice, as in the "theoretical" scenes of painters like Claude: landscapes of the intellect where, in artfully-composed "natural" settings, serene beings stand or recline, gratified to contemplate their own appropriateness, combining innocence and sophistication, savagery and nobility. These considerations influence the "modernity" of the Bookshop, but its unmistakably nautical appearance reflects a very different aspect of Venice. The cross-town traffic on the nearby lagoon, heading for the Grand Canal or the Giudecca, is as neurotic as that of any contemporary city; car ferries, supertankers, cruise liners, launches, barges, and tugboats come and go incessantly, and it is an everyday sight to find some gigantic red and blue freighter, empty and sitting high in the water, at anchor right in front of the Doge's Palace, its rusty metal sides contrasting impossibly with that lace handkerchief of a building. Out of these aesthetic conflicts came the Bookshop (or *Boatship*) which happens to be about the same size as a *vaporetto*. Perhaps the fault of modern architecture has been its doctrinaire seriousness, but given a waterside site and a nautical atmosphere, things seem to loosen up; mysteriously, it would seem that the closer modern architecture gets to water and boats, the more amusing it becomes. For it to survive, it will need to reinvigorate itself and become more credible and acceptable. If the Bookshop stimulates the senses and pleases the intelligence, then it may have fulfilled some of that purpose.

251

Entrance elevation

The bull-nosed end

Traditional *cason* in the Venetian marshes

Ceiling duct for air conditioning

Cash desk

Book display

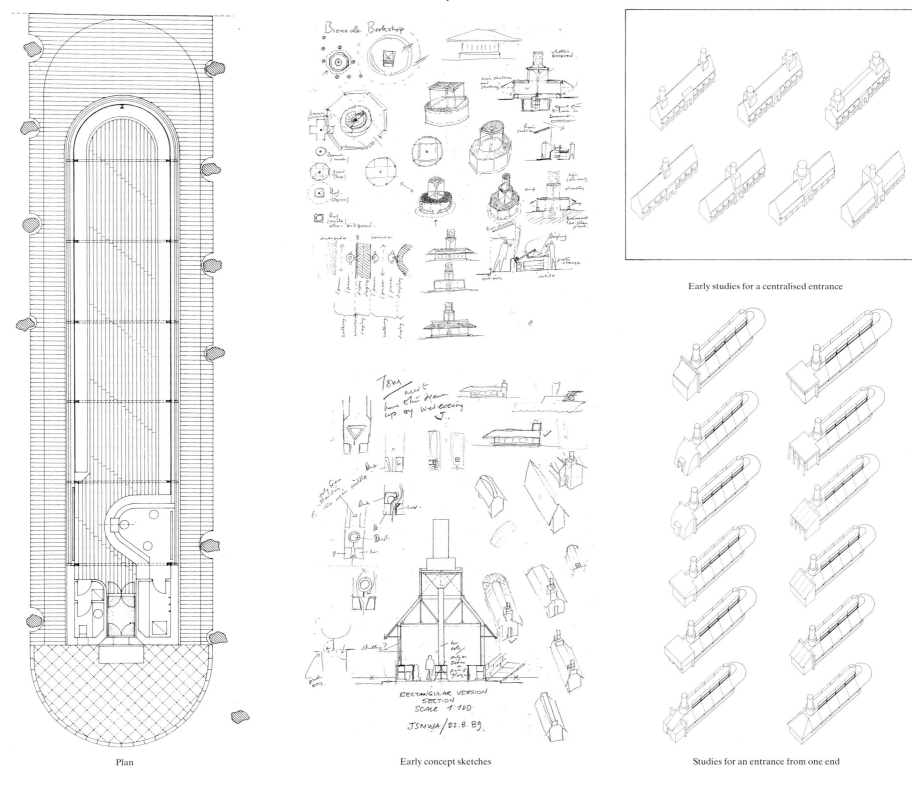

Plan

Early concept sketches

Early studies for a centralised entrance

Studies for an entrance from one end

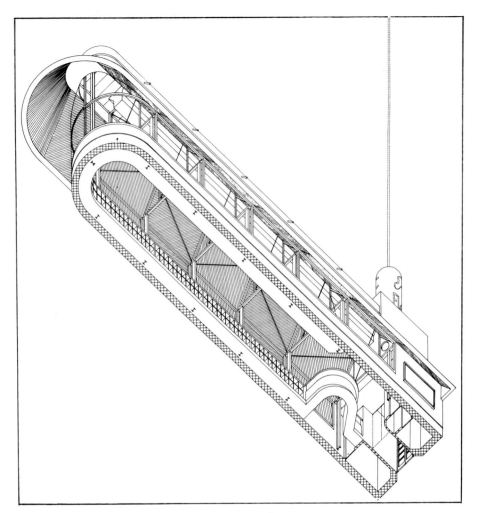

Up axonometric

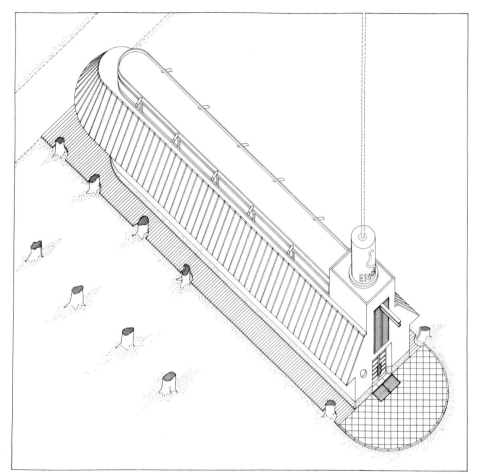

Down axonometric

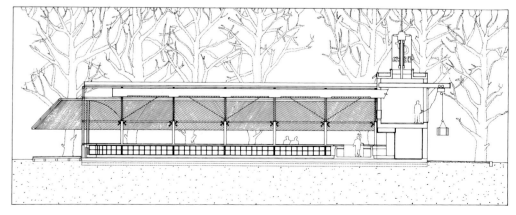

Longitudinal section

The Forum occupies a city block and is arranged symmetrically to face along a street leading to the Emperor's palace. At the rear of the site, shopping passages under the JR railway embankment allow pedestrians to walk through from the busy Ginza district. The complex contains conference centres, concert halls, and associated public facilities. The structure is earthquake-resistant and the entire area is designed for emergency evacuation. Emphasis is therefore given to clarity and simplicity of circulation. The most important functions are accomodated in transparent buildings of "technological" appearance standing on a "traditional" stone-faced plinth. A semicircular glass building overlooking the plaza contains a large hall for 5000 people. In a square building opposite are two more halls seating 1500 and 200 people; both buildings have rooftop restaurants and bars. In the tower at the centre there are additional facilities for smaller conference and meetings. The tower steps upwards in a sequence of hexagonal, circular, and semicircular volumes. The lowest part contains a banqueting hall and a core of double-height conference rooms, surrounded by smaller meeting and tea ceremony rooms with views towards the outside. The semicircular part at the top contains administrative

offices, a VIP suite, and a luxury restaurant with a roof terrace and garden. All conference facilities have separate lobbies and circulation systems which converge in an upper concourse accessible only to those holding tickets. The area for the general public is at street level below, in the main concourse, which is the meeting place for delegates and visitors, with conference ticket desks and information points. From the surrounding streets or the Keiyo and Yurakucho subway stations at either end of the concourse, visitors gather in a central space three floors high, under the tower. Public facilities at this level are planned around a circular courtyard, which can be equipped with temporary seating for open-air concerts and other events. From the concourse, escalators lead down to the large exhibition halls in the multi-level basement. In addition to the exhibition halls with their associated loading and unloading areas, the basement contains car parking, a bus station, delivery areas for the conference facilities, collection points for garbage, etc., all directly accessible from the street by ramps which allow vehicles to drive directly down to the level required. All access and exit points for vehicles are concentrated along the existing street at the rear. This leaves the other three sides free for pedestrians.

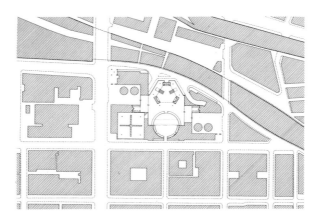

Location plan in central Tokyo

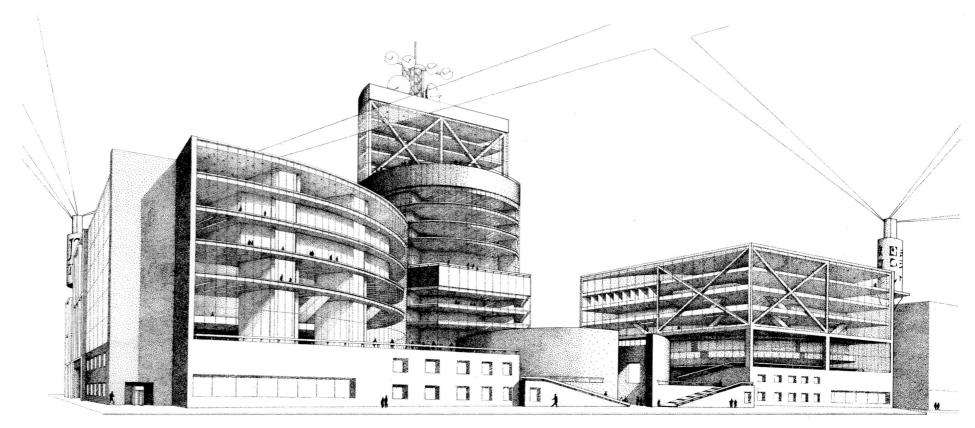

Perspective view

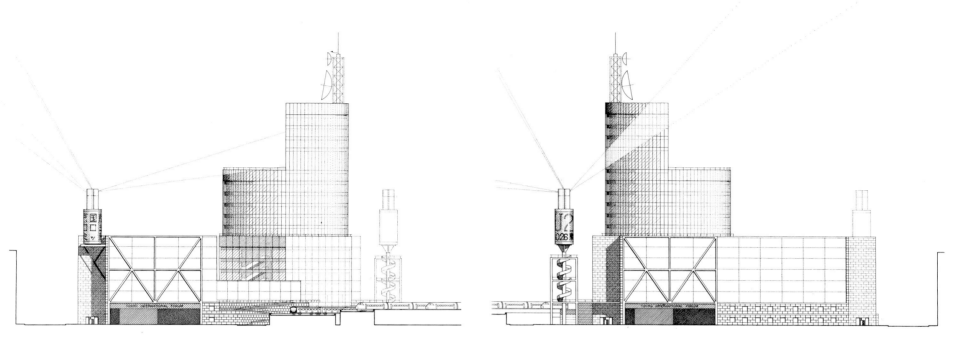

Side elevation

Side elevation

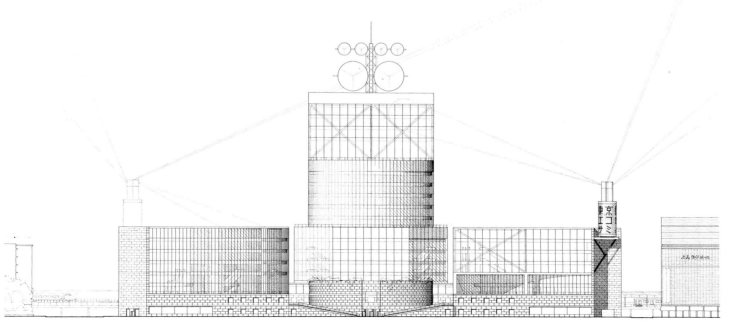

Front elevation

Rear view of the model

Shadow plan

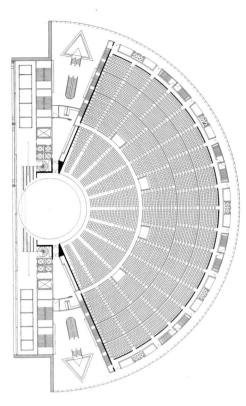

Auditorium seating plan

Auditorium interior

Auditorium cross-section

Interior of the tower entrance hall

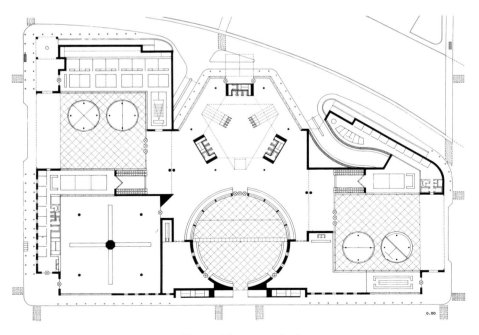

Plan at public concourse level

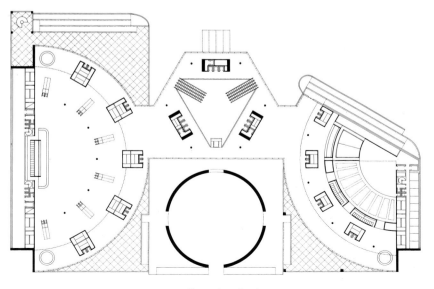

Plan at foyer level

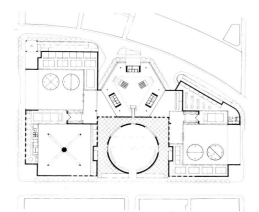

Plan at podium level

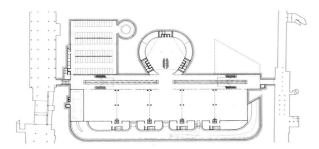

Basement exhibition halls and parking

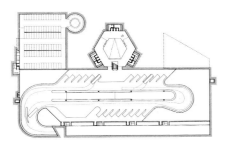

Basement bus station and parking

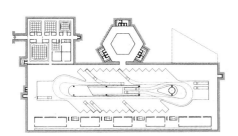

Exhibitions delivery docks and plant

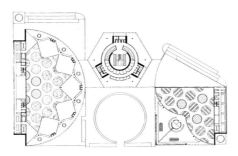

Roof restaurants and gardens

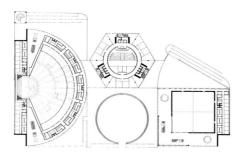

Upper auditorium levels

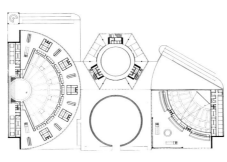

Intermediate auditorium levels

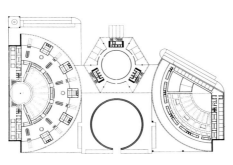

Lower auditorium levels

Rooftop garden

Garden and restaurant

Tower plan

Tower plan

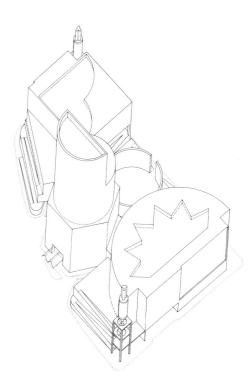

Schematic down view

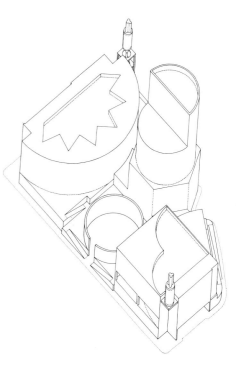

Schematic down view

259

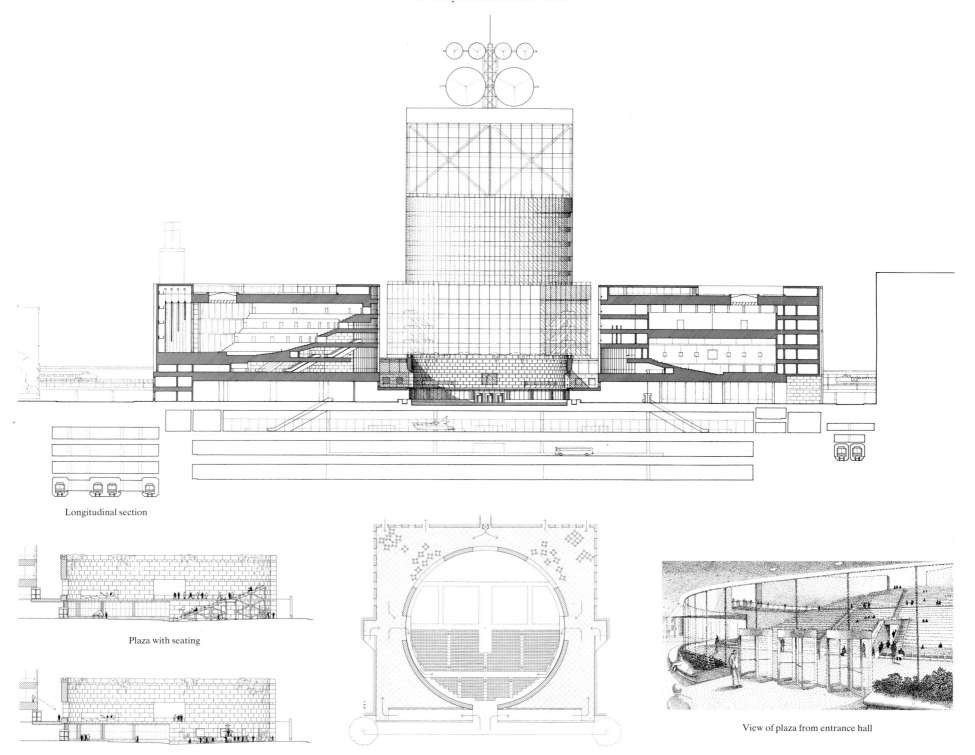

Longitudinal section

Plaza with seating

Plaza without seating

Plan of plaza with seating

View of plaza from entrance hall

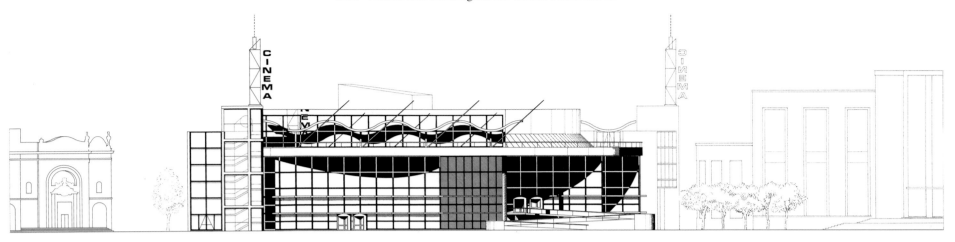

Front elevation

Front view of the model

1990 Venice: new building for the Venice Film Festival

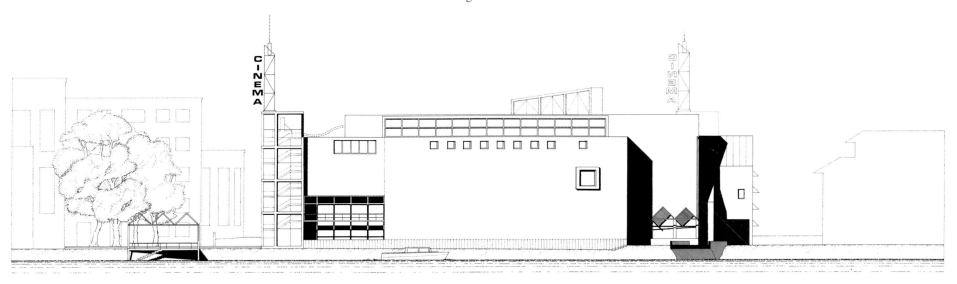

Back elevation

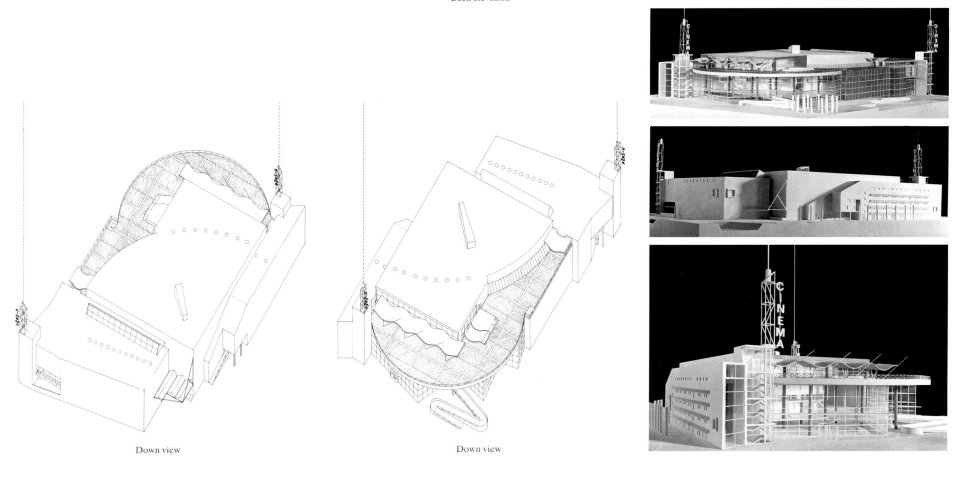

Down view

Down view

The *Mostra del Cinema* in Venice is the most important international venue for the presentation of serious works on film. Producers, directors, technicians and artists gather for discussion and business with journalists and critics. The atmosphere is sociable, elegant, and festive, without the exhibitionism of Cannes. The site is on the Lido between the Excelsior Hotel and the Casino, and enjoys good views of the public space which overlooks the beach. These views determine the asymmetrical layout of the building, which has an open public side facing the lagoon, and a more enclosed side at the back, where administration departments and service delivery points are located adjacent to canals. To make the most of the wide outlooks over the lagoon and the Adriatic, the public side is completely occupied by the foyer, raised above ground level and connected to the piazza by a wide external ramp, winding up in front of the glass wall which zigzags round the whole façade. The building would be used most intensively at night, and the bustle in the brightly-illuminated foyer would be made more dramatic by the arrival or departure of VIPs, actors, and famous personalities promenading up and down the ramp.

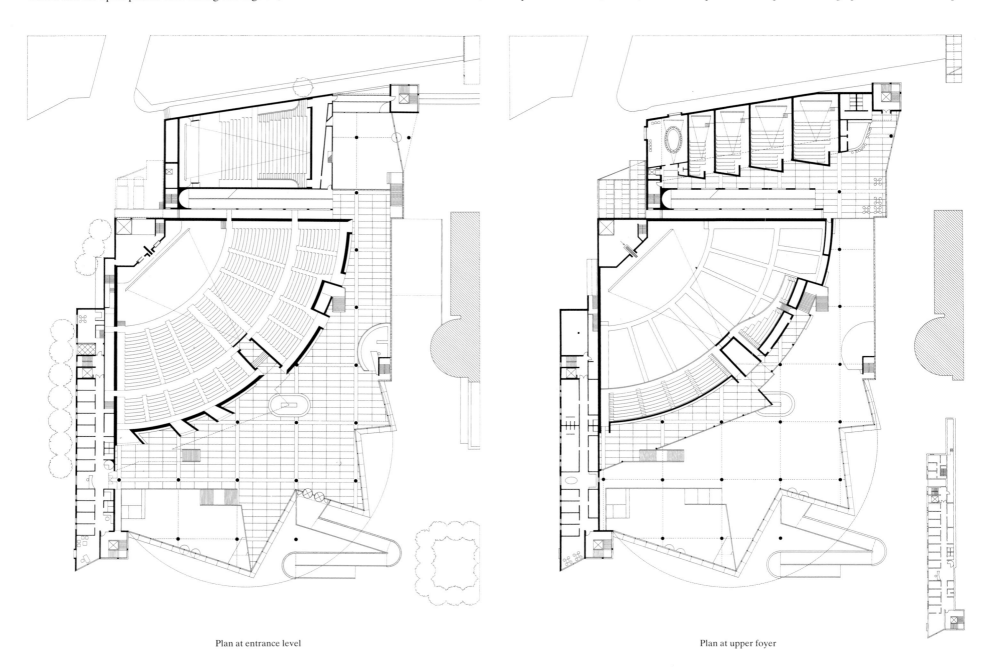

Plan at entrance level

Plan at upper foyer

The foyer wraps round the building, connecting the main arrival points on the seaward side with a secondary entrance and landing stage for those arriving from Venice by canal at the back. The lower part of the foyer can be used for temporary exhibitions, and a wide stair connects it to two large film theatres on the floor above. These can be used separately or combined to make an auditorium for 3000 people, by opening a movable dividing wall and raising it into a glazed enclosure above the roof. Behind the projection booths, a passage leads to a separate wing at the back of the building, which contains a range of smaller cinemas and viewing rooms. These can function independently, and each has a separate foyer connected by a passageway which overlooks a full-height internal hall. A ramp rising through the hall connects all levels and continues up to the press information centre at roof level, where there is a bar overlooking a roof terrace. At the opposite end of the terrace is a rooftop restaurant connected by stairs and lifts to the main foyer. For receptions, parties and special events, up to 3000 people can congregate on the roof terrace and mingle informally, against the spectacular backdrop of the Adriatic.

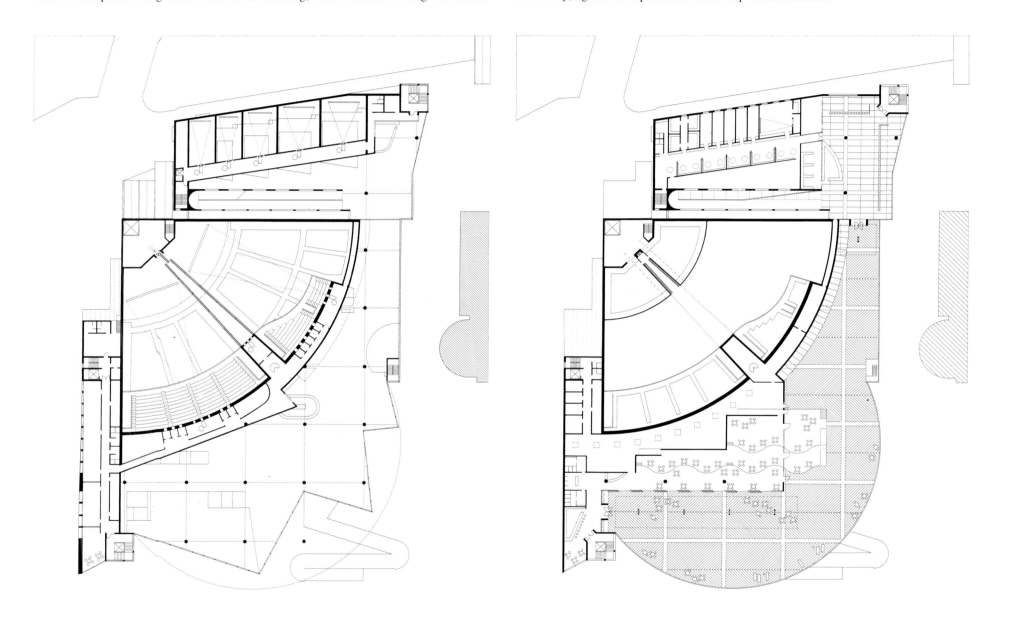

Plan at upper auditorium level

Plan showing roof terrace, restaurant, and bar

1990 Venice: new building for the Venice Film Festival

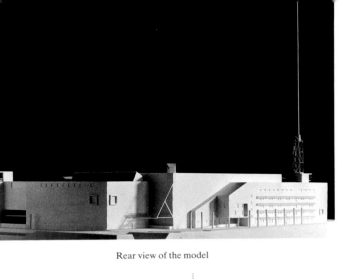

Rear view of the model

Large auditorium (partition lowered)

Large auditorium (partition raised)

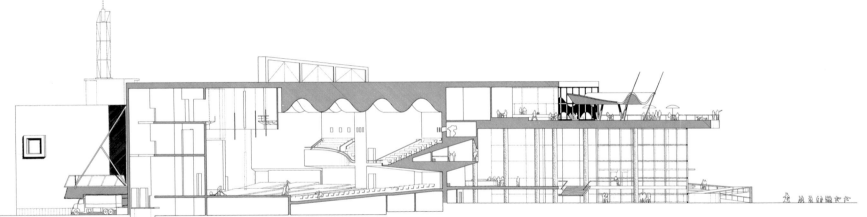

Longitudinal section through auditorium and foyer

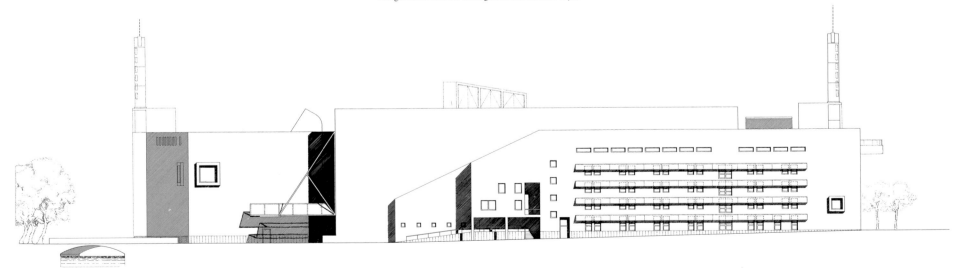

Side elevation

1990 Venice: new building for the Venice Film Festival

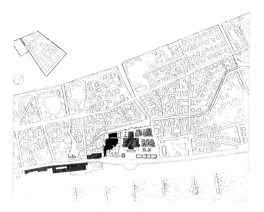

Location plan

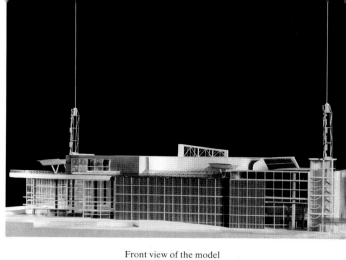

Aerial view with Venice in the distance

Front view of the model

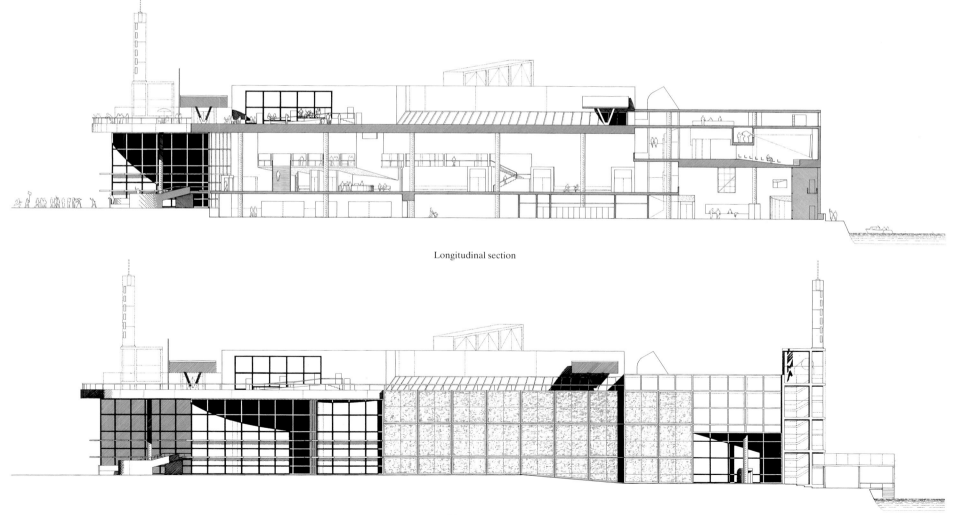

Longitudinal section

Side elevation

A shortcut across the site passes through a plaza overlooked by residential buildings with gardens and playgrounds, and by Channel Four's office and production facilities. The entrance to the programme preview theatre is located under a covered walk-through, flooded by daylight from a light cone above. A curving colonnade leads studio audiences from here to a television studio at the rear, in a pavilion with an octagonal rooftop drum (for air conditioning machinery) and adjacent reception facilities; vehicles can load or unload scenery and equipment at the back. The office entrance for television staff is angled to look out along the main street and leads into a double-height foyer, spacious enough to accommodate the continuous coming and going of visitors and deliveries to this busy television company. Informal meetings can take place in a restaurant and bar on the mezzanine overlooking the foyer and lift lobby. The lifts rise through a light cone, with balconies at each level giving access to three floors of administration facilities. The two light cones ensure good daylighting throughout and the open plan, column-free layout allows flexibility in the use of the space. The stairs and lifts at the corners enable Channel Four staff to reach all production and technical facilities, and permit direct access to the parking under the plaza in the basement.

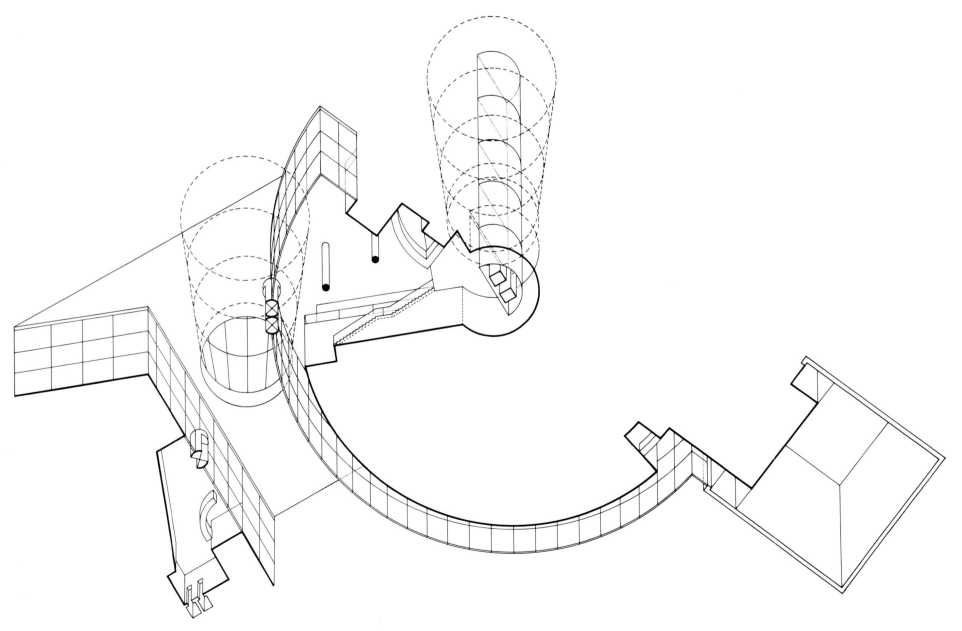

Up view of the foyers and daylighting cones

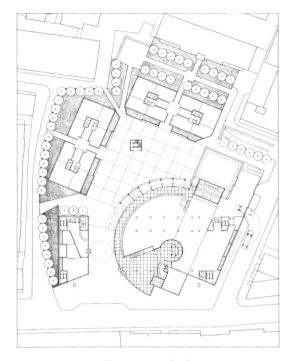

Plan at entrance level

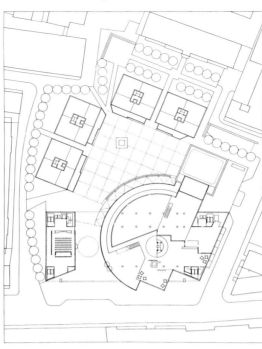

Preview theatre (left) main foyer (right)

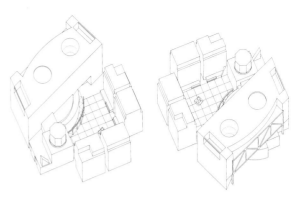

Down view   Down view

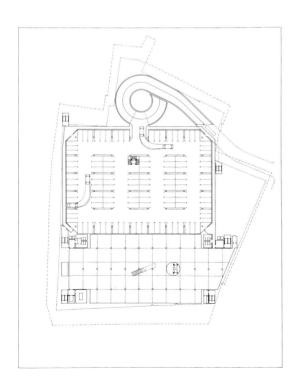

Basement plan with parking

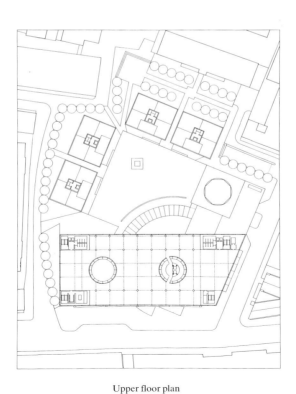

Upper floor plan

Up view

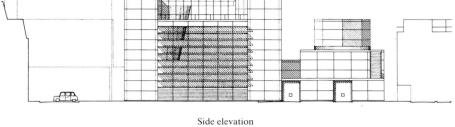

Side elevation

Interior of the foyer

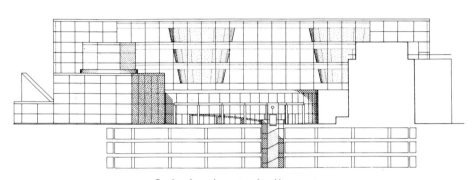

Section through courtyard and basements

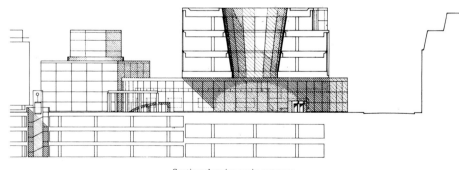

Section showing main entrance

Perspective view

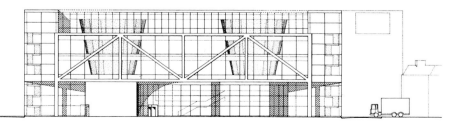

Front elevation

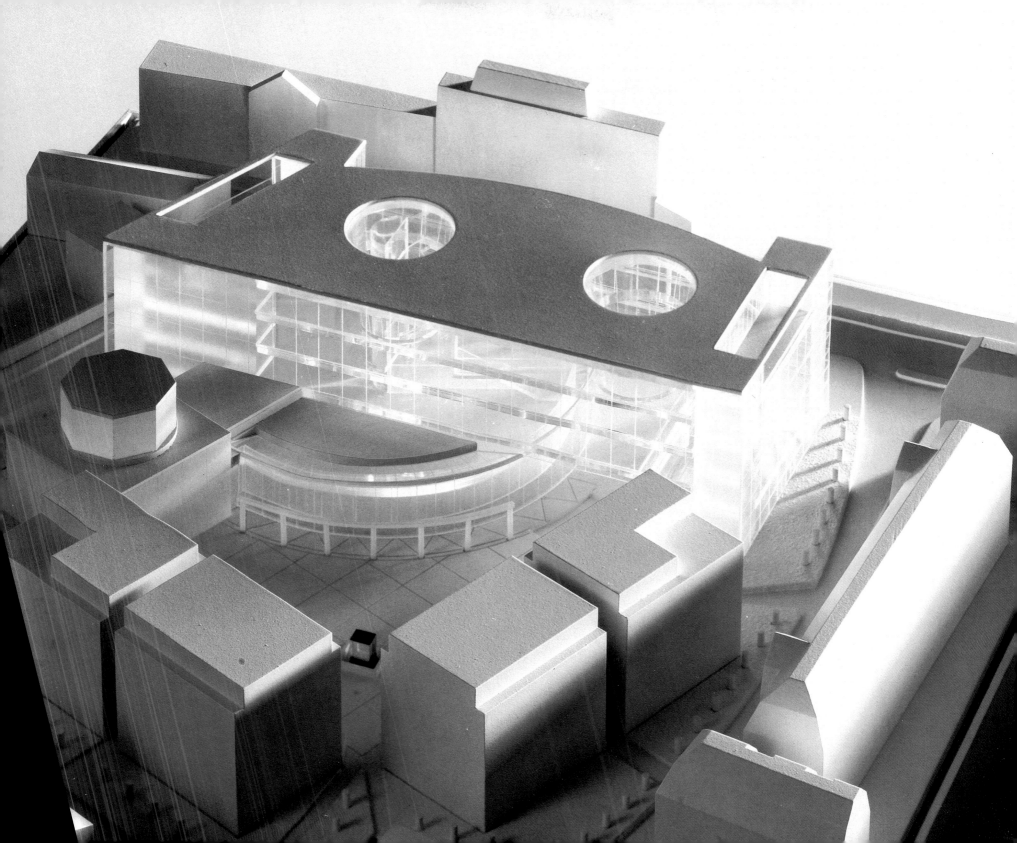

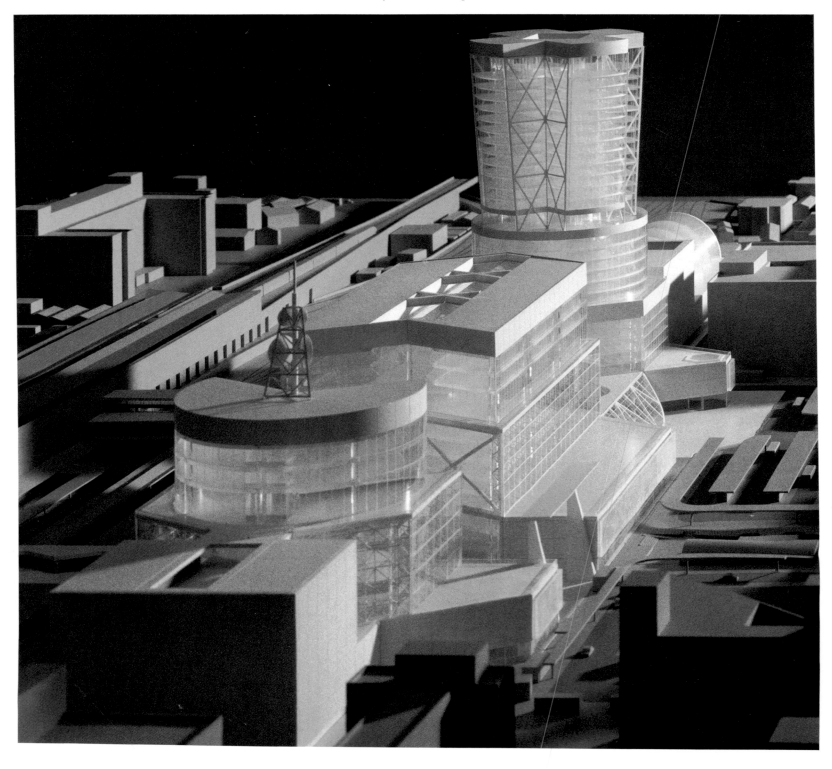

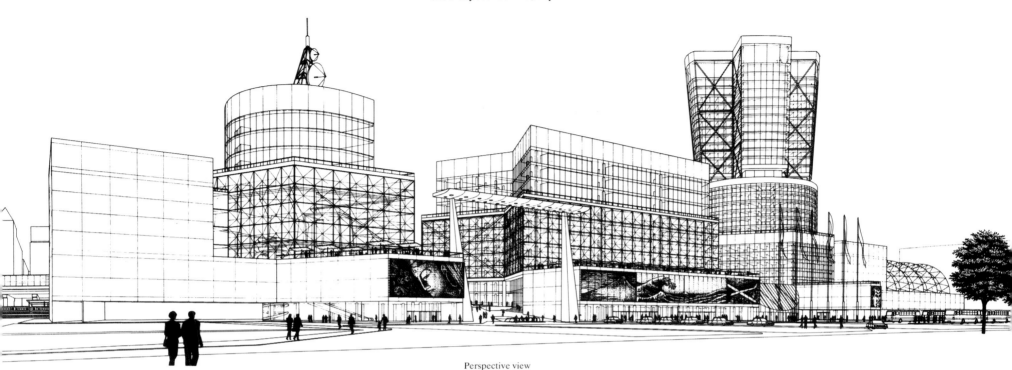

Perspective view

Our design for redeveloping Kyoto station and its flanking sites relates to the symbolic and urbanistic implications of placing a large complex along one side of a city square in the commercial downtown. We see the site as a threshold between the traditional city to the north, enclosed by hills to the east and west, and the future technological city to be built in the south. We propose the creation of symbolic and functional gateways leading to public crossings over the barrier of the railway tracks, which divide the city centre in two. The project includes a new plaza on the north-south axis, designed as a semi-enclosed space connecting with a new public bridge, lined with shops and spanning the tracks between the northern and southern parts of Kyoto. Parallel to the public bridge is a second enclosed bridge connecting the station concourse across the tracks and reserved for passengers only. The tower at one end of the scheme contains a new hotel which, along with the TV tower and the oval plaza, forms a new triangle of city landmarks around the public square. The geometric silhouette of the hotel tower gives the city centre an identifying sign when seen from the temples and gardens in the surrounding hills. The two buildings facing over the oval plaza are the chevron-shaped department store, on ten floors, and a cultural centre containing image facilities, a winter garden, and a large open area for exhibitions and public events. The basement levels contain car parking, service areas, and a shopping spine which connects the two bridges.

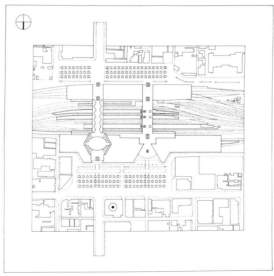

Site plan

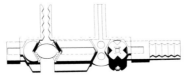

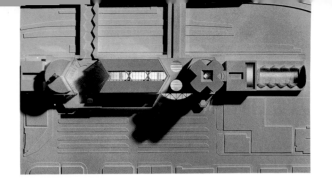
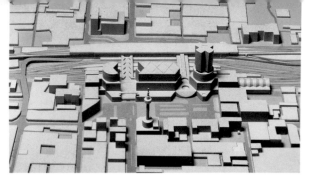

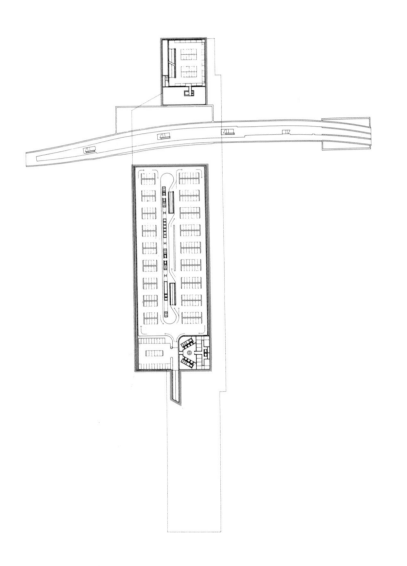

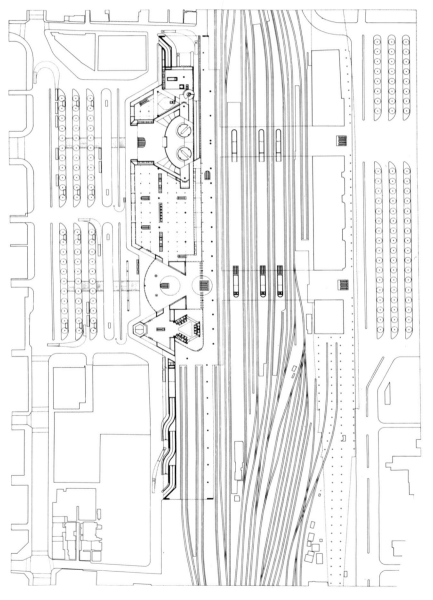

Metro station
Basement car parking

Storage
Metro
Shopping arcade

Plan at entrance level

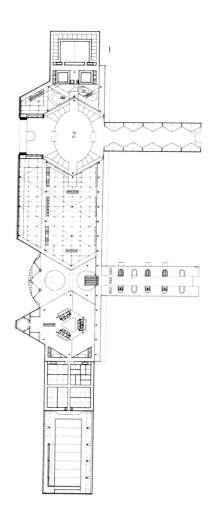
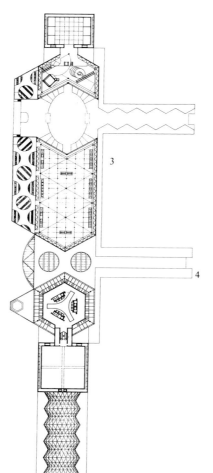
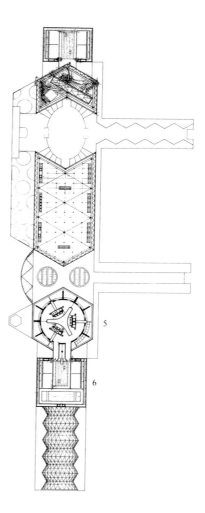
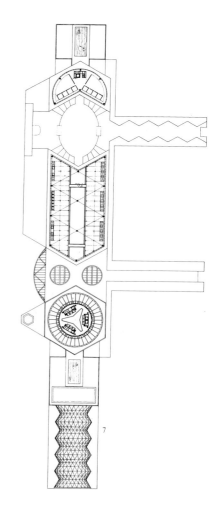

1. Cultural building
2. Plaza

3. Department store
4. JR railway station

5. Hotel
6. Conference/banqueting hall

7. Kansai Airport rail link

1991 Kyoto Centre, Japan

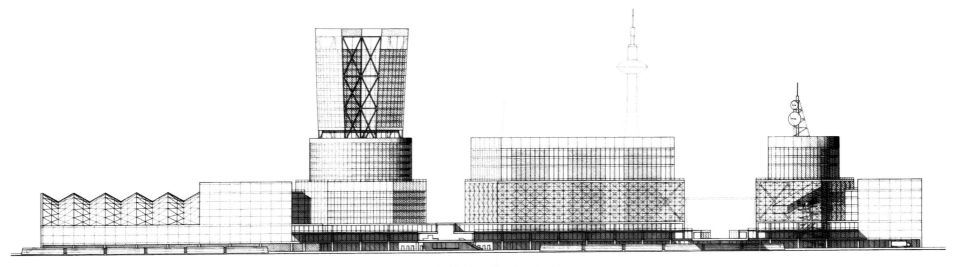

Elevation looking from the railway tracks

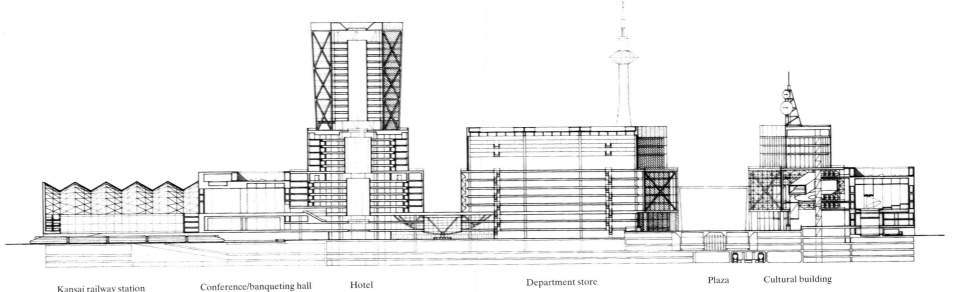

Kansai railway station   Conference/banqueting hall   Hotel   Department store   Plaza   Cultural building

Perspective of the railway station ticket hall

Perspective of the department store restaurant

1991 Kyoto Centre, Japan

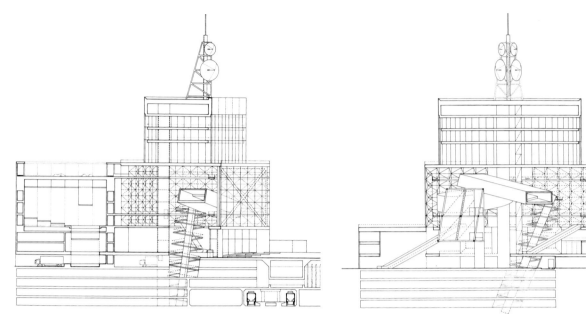

Section through theatre, tourist facilities, metro

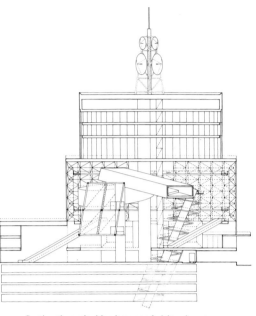

Section through video beam and visitors' centre

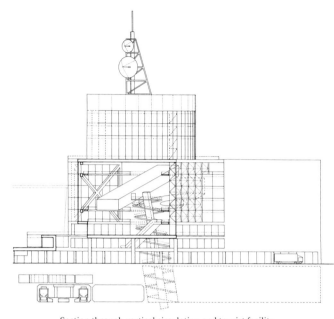

Section through vertical circulation and tourist facility

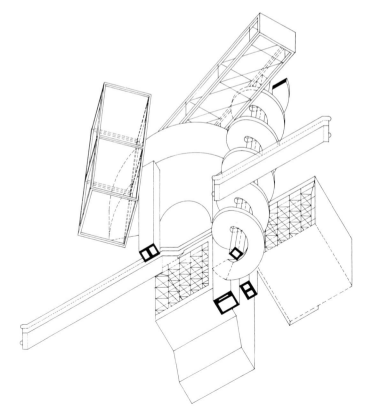

Up view of the Cyclorama, video beam, and tourist facilities

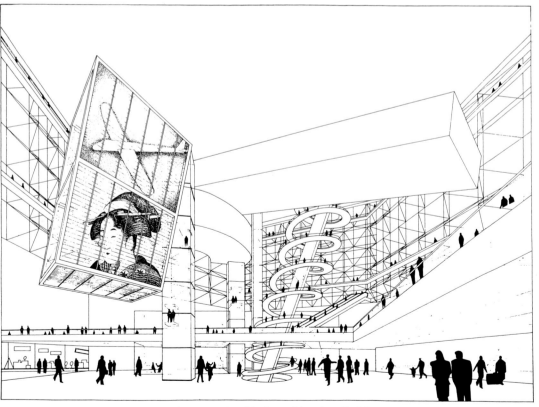

Interior perspective of the foyer of the cultural building

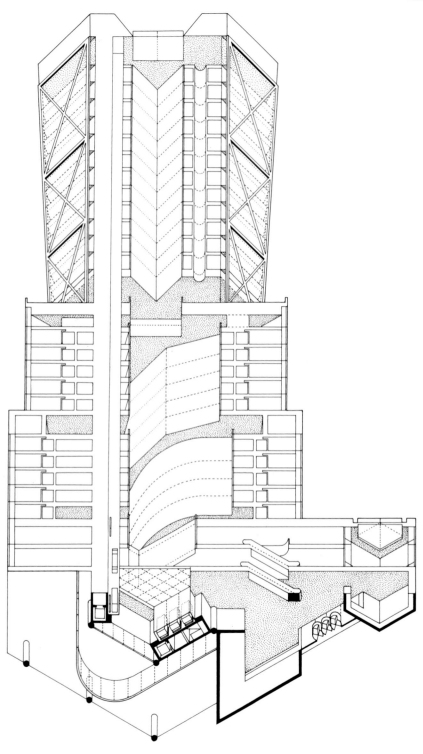

Sectioned up view of the hotel

Plan of hotel rooms

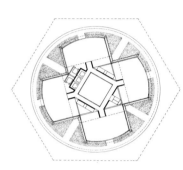

Plan of tea ceremony rooms

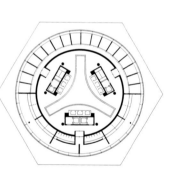

Plan of hotel rooms and bars

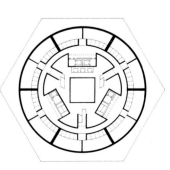

Plan of wedding suites

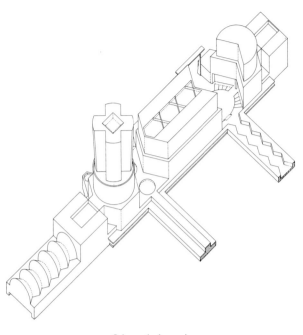

Schematic down view

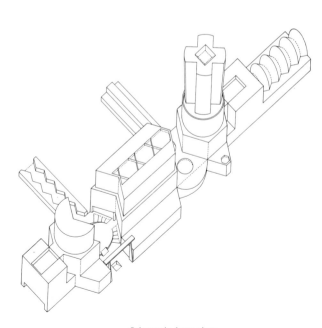

Schematic down view

Perspective looking through the plaza

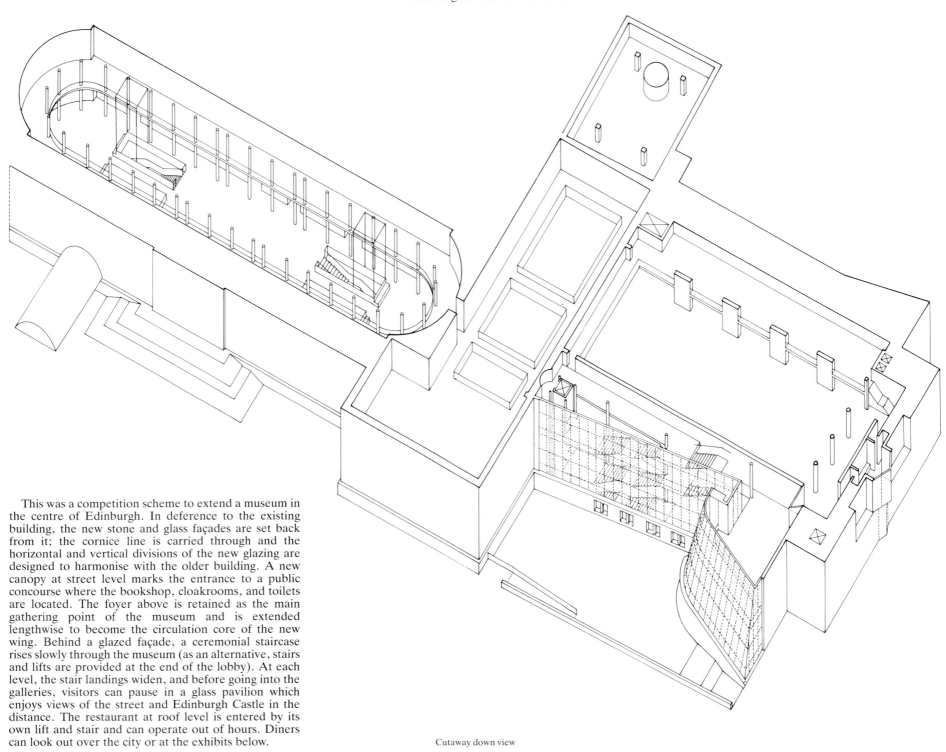

This was a competition scheme to extend a museum in the centre of Edinburgh. In deference to the existing building, the new stone and glass façades are set back from it; the cornice line is carried through and the horizontal and vertical divisions of the new glazing are designed to harmonise with the older building. A new canopy at street level marks the entrance to a public concourse where the bookshop, cloakrooms, and toilets are located. The foyer above is retained as the main gathering point of the museum and is extended lengthwise to become the circulation core of the new wing. Behind a glazed façade, a ceremonial staircase rises slowly through the museum (as an alternative, stairs and lifts are provided at the end of the lobby). At each level, the stair landings widen, and before going into the galleries, visitors can pause in a glass pavilion which enjoys views of the street and Edinburgh Castle in the distance. The restaurant at roof level is entered by its own lift and stair and can operate out of hours. Diners can look out over the city or at the exhibits below.

Cutaway down view

1991 Edinburgh: Museum of Scotland

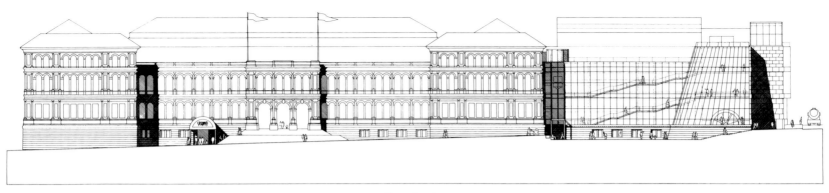

Front elevation

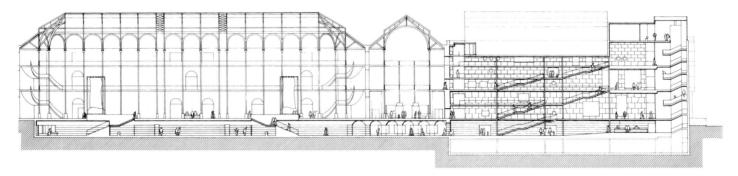

Longitudinal section

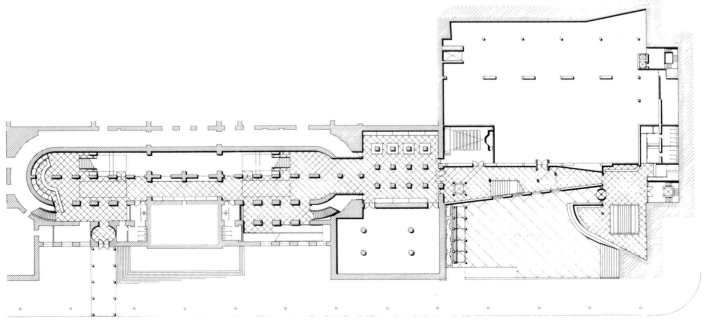

Plan at foyer level

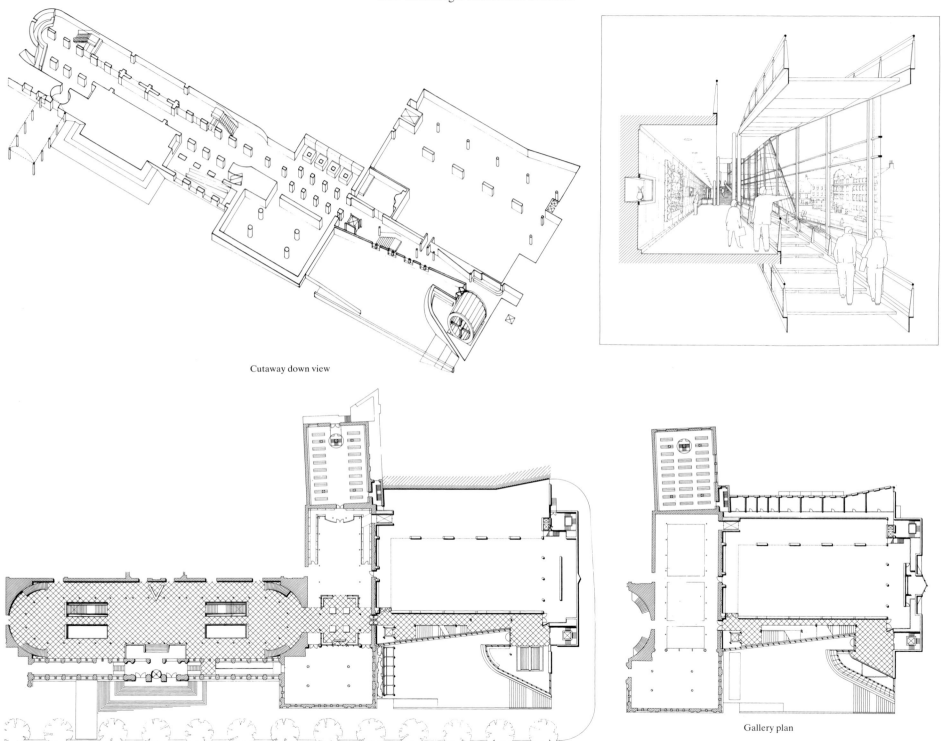

Cutaway down view

Plan at upper foyer and galleries

Gallery plan

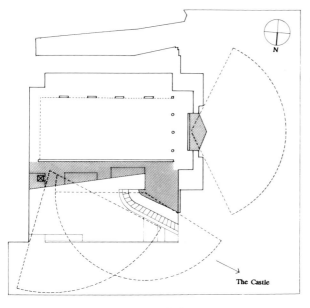

Views out from the foyer

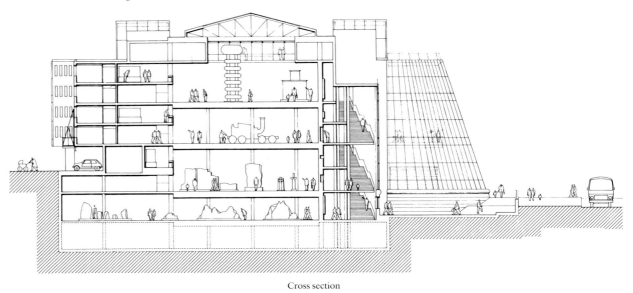

Cross section

Plan of restaurant and balcony

Perspective

With its four schools (Applied Science, Business, Design, and Technology) and its population of 13,000 people, the polytechnic stands in landscaped gardens with other buildings for residential, sporting, and leisure purposes. This "city of learning" is connected to the public domain by a horseshoe-shaped public plaza. Underneath are two public auditoria: a hall for 600 people and a multi-purpose theatre for 250 with a common foyer to the street. The open space of the plaza is overlooked by the administration building, which stands on *pilotis*, giving shade to the four school entrances. Shopping, banking, and public exhibition facilities are located near these entrances. Through an opening are views over a triangular garden, where the Refectory and Student Centre stand in arcadian surroundings, with the library tower rising above. The most intensive activities in each school are planned along concourses. Staff and students intermingle here, sheltered from the tropical monsoon climate.

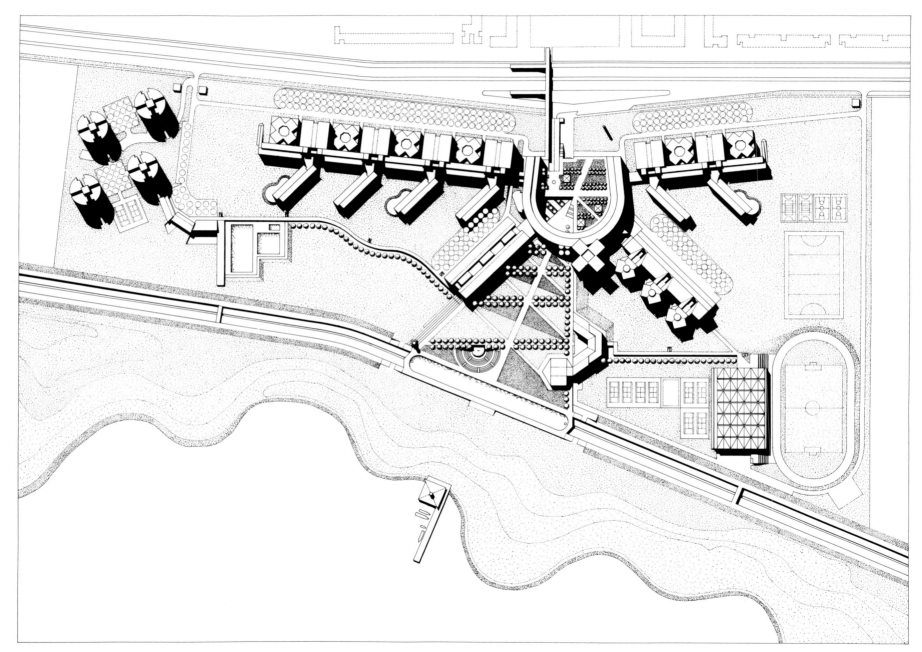

Site plan with shadows

1991–   Singapore: Temasek Polytechnic

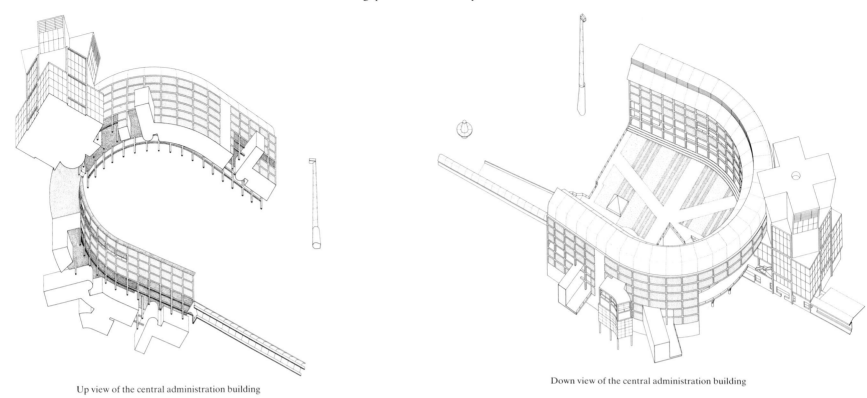

Up view of the central administration building

Down view of the central administration building

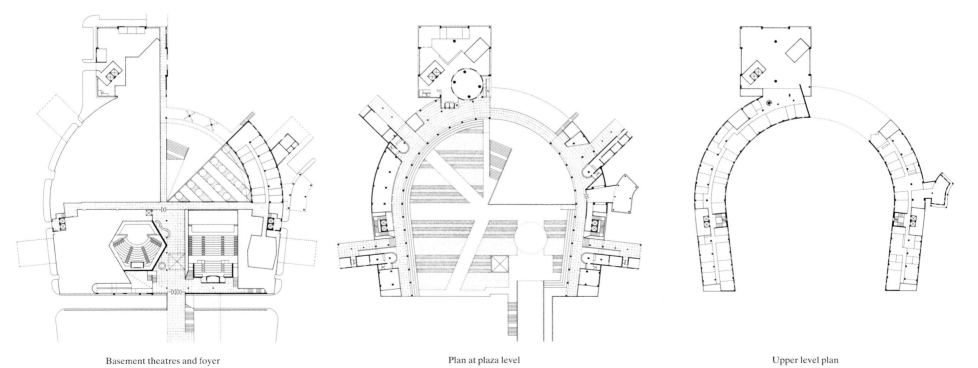

Basement theatres and foyer

Plan at plaza level

Upper level plan

285

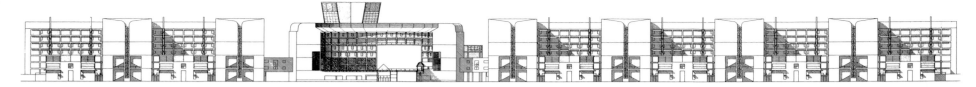

Street elevation

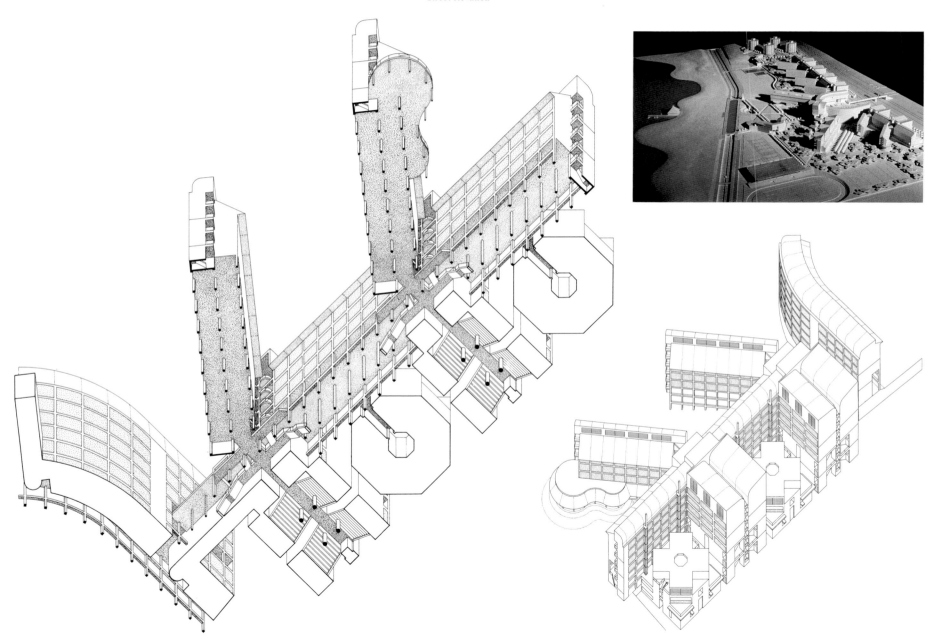

School of Applied Science: up axonometric

School of Applied Science: down axonometric

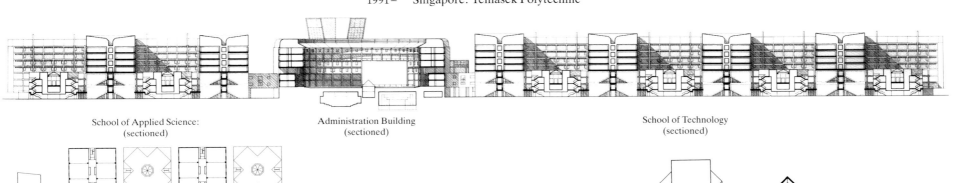

School of Applied Science:
(sectioned)

Administration Building
(sectioned)

School of Technology
(sectioned)

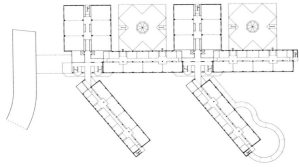

School of Applied Science: upper level plan

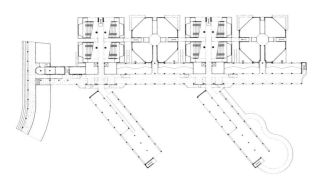

School of Applied Science: concourse level

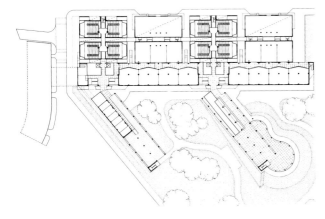

School of Applied Science: lecture theatres

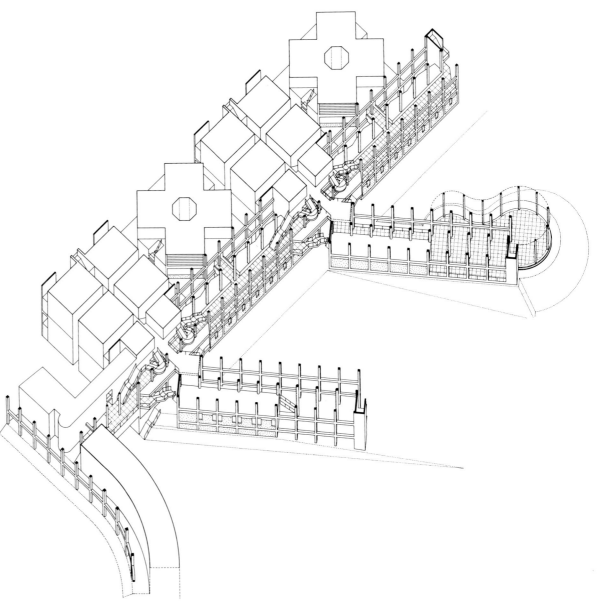

School of Applied Science: cutaway down axonometric

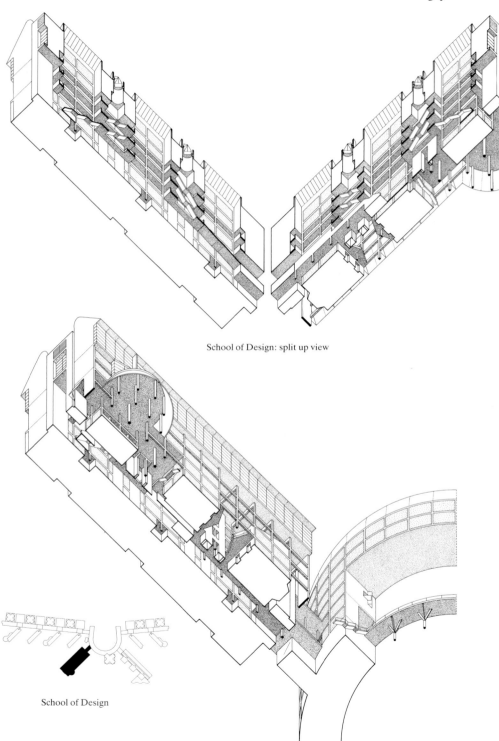

School of Design: split up view

School of Design

School of Design: upview showing the garden elevation

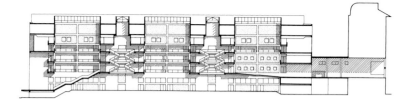

School of Design: longitudinal section

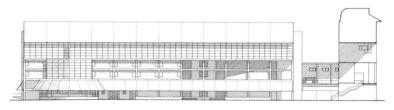

School of Design: garden elevation

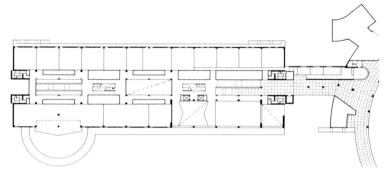

School of Design: plan at concourse level

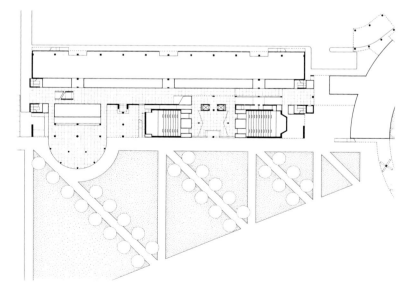

School of Design: plan showing workshops, refectory, lecture theatres

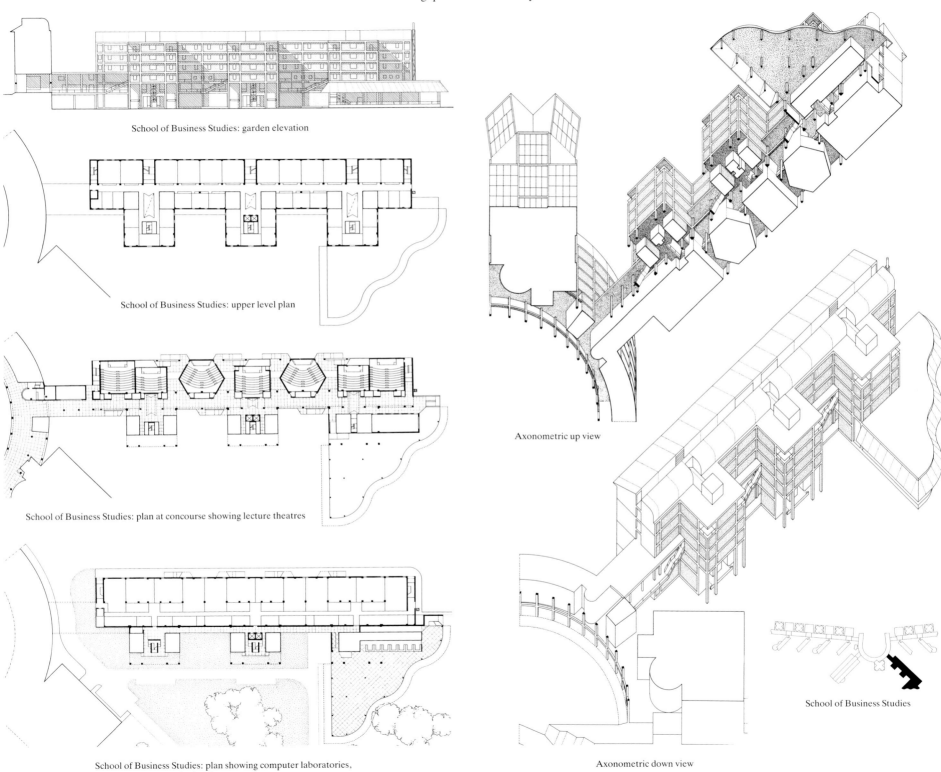

School of Business Studies: garden elevation

School of Business Studies: upper level plan

School of Business Studies: plan at concourse showing lecture theatres

School of Business Studies: plan showing computer laboratories,
audiovisual rooms, refectory

Axonometric up view

Axonometric down view

School of Business Studies

Administration Building   Library tower   Student Centre

Up axonometric view of the Student Centre

Up view: Design School (left) Student Centre (right) Administration and Library (centre)

Plan of Student Centre and Refectory

Model showing Faculty Club at far left

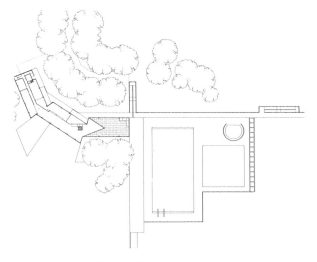

Faculty club: upper level plan

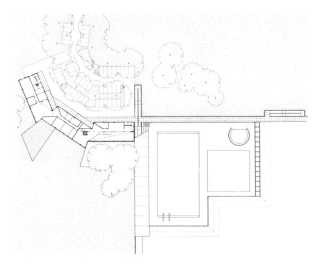

Faculty club: lower level plan

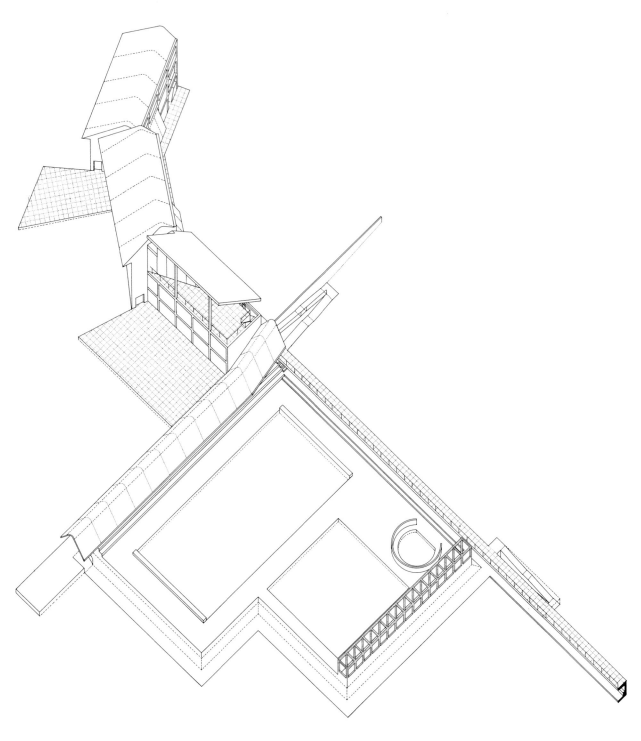

Faculty club: down axonometric

291

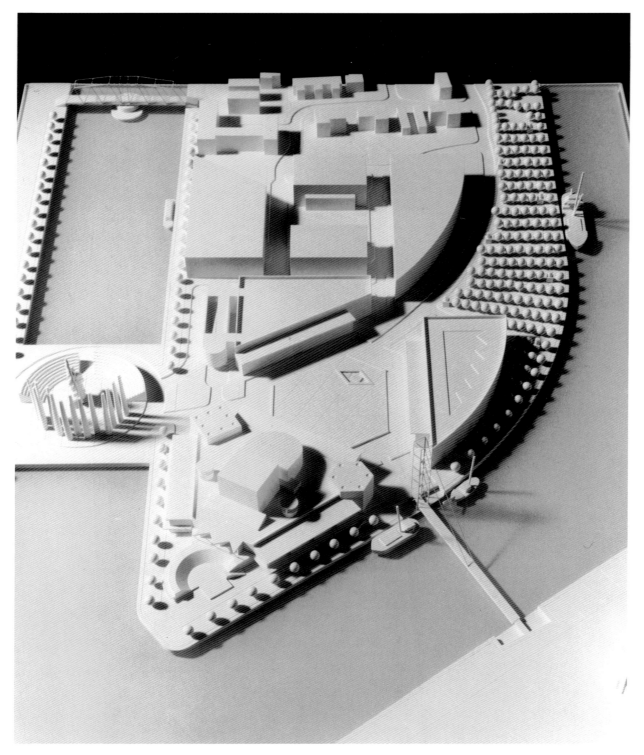

The site in 1992

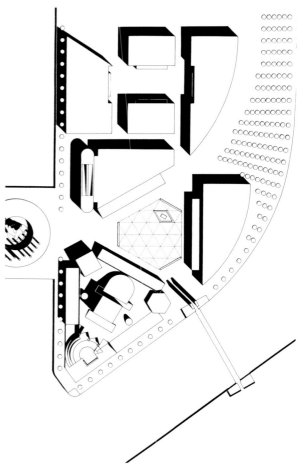

View of the model

Shadow plan

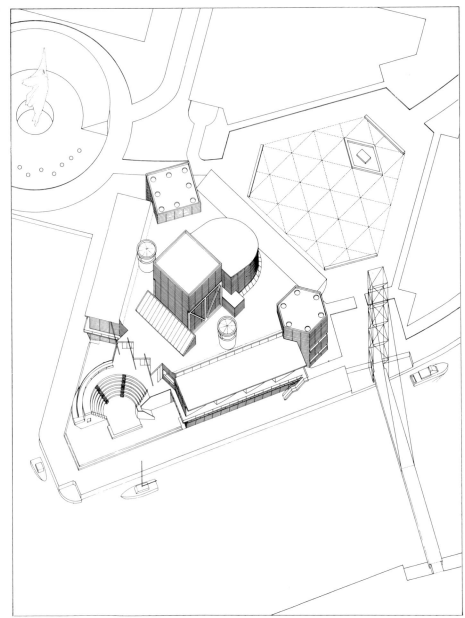

Down view

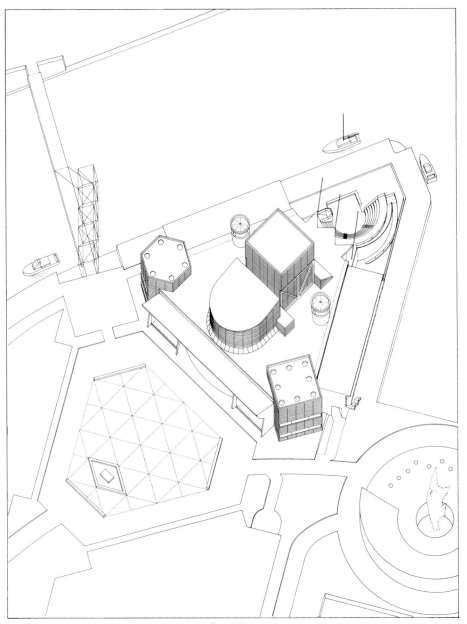

Down view

The disused canal port of Salford, near Manchester, has been redeveloped for housing, and our new master plan integrates this by adding a Performing Arts Centre and Museum, parking, a hotel, offices, and a public garden. The arts centre sits on a point with good views over the canals, and will enhance opportunities for social interaction within the community. From parking and drop-off points in the triangular plaza, visitors walk into a spacious double-height public foyer which extends across the whole site, and is surrounded by the entrances to the various facilities: a 1200-seat opera house; a 400-seat flexible theatre in the square building; cloakrooms and bars in the hexagonal pavilion. Lifts or stepped ramps lead to an upper-level balcony overlooking the foyer, and giving access to a gallery for changing exhibitions, a restaurant (with an external terrace which overlooks the waterfront) and a museum for the city's collection of paintings by L. S. Lowry. An amphitheatre on the point is separately accessed, with its own bar and café facilities. Technical and backstage areas at the lower level are accessed from a perimeter road.

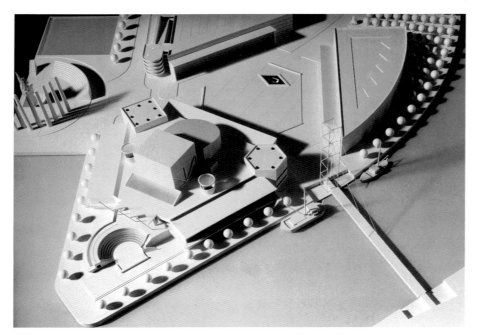
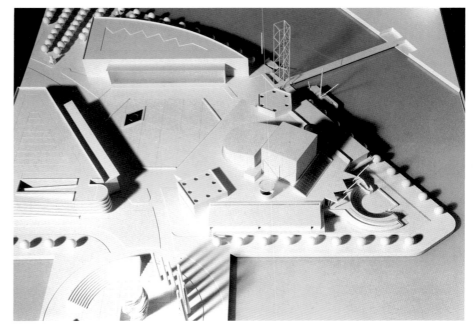

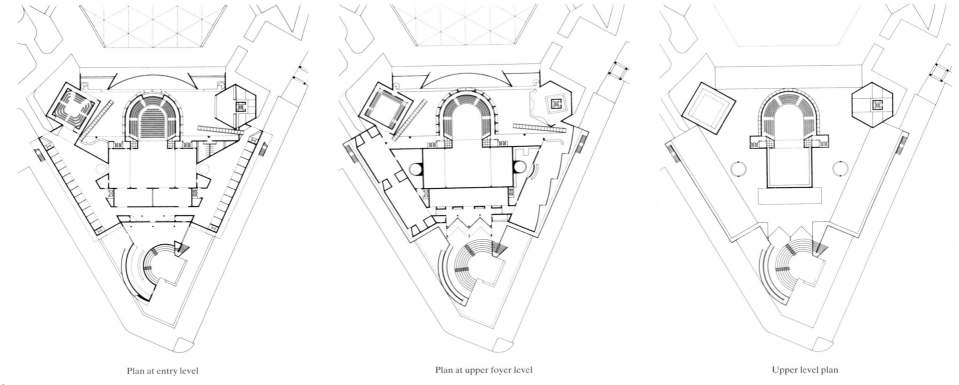

Plan at entry level

Plan at upper foyer level

Upper level plan

1992–   Salford, England: Arts Centre

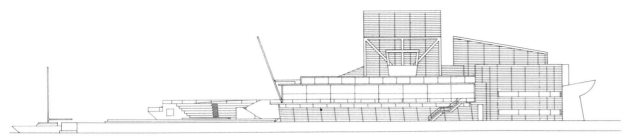
Elevation to the canal

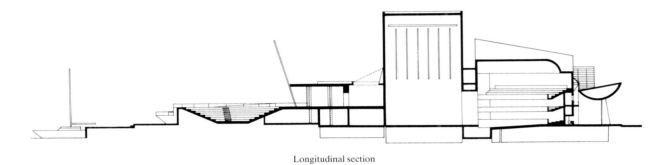
Longitudinal section

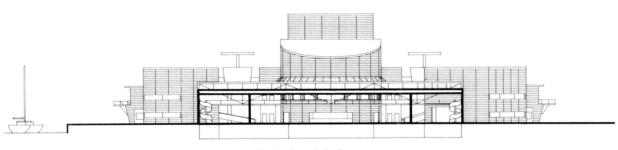
Section through the foyer

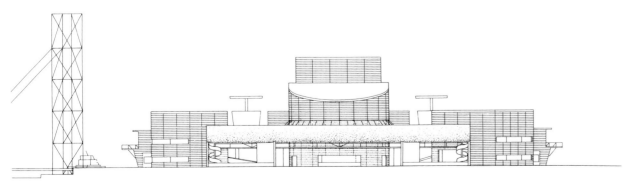
Elevation of the entrance

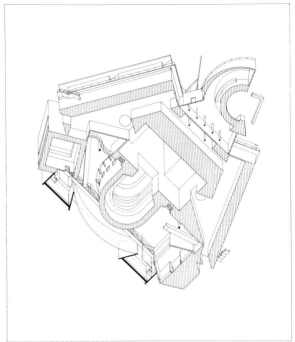
Up view

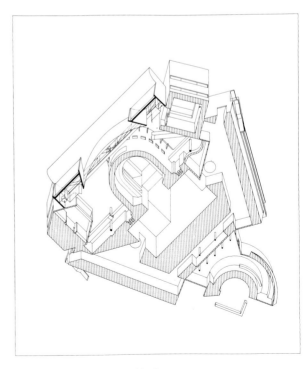
Up view

Projects

First date: initial design
Second date: completion

1972

Runcorn New Town: Southgate Housing (Phase 2)

p 18

James Stirling/Michael Wilford

David Falck
Crispin Osborne
Peter Ray
Brian Riches
Ulrich Schaad

Davis Langdon & Everest
F. J. Samuely & Partners
R. Travers Morgan & Partners
Runcorn Development Corporation
(Civil and Services Engineering
Departments)

1975

Düsseldorf: Nordrhein-Westfalen Museum

p 22

James Stirling and Michael Wilford

Russell Bevington
Robert Livesey
Crispin Osborne

1975

Cologne: Wallraf-Richartz Museum

p 30

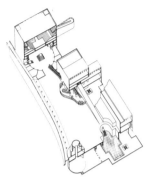

James Stirling/Michael Wilford

Russell Bevington
John Corrigan
Werner Kreis
Robert Livesey
Robin Nicholson
Ulrich Schaad

1976

Berlin: Hotel in Meineke Strasse

p 36

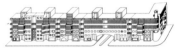

James Stirling/Michael Wilford

Ulrich Schaad
John Tuomey

1976

Doha, Qatar: Government Centre

p 38

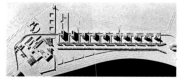

James Stirling/Michael Wilford

Russell Bevington
John Tuomey

1976

Florence: Administrative
and Business Centre

p 40

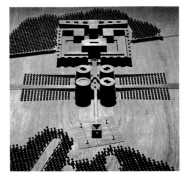

James Stirling/Michael Wilford
in association with
Castore, Rizzi, Malanima (Florence)

Russell Bevington
Thomas Muirhead
Ulrich Schaad
John Tuomey
Barbara Weiss

1977

Nairobi, Kenya:
UNEP Headquarters

p 44

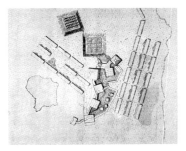

James Stirling/Michael Wilford
in association with Giancarlo de Carlo
(Milan)
and Mutiso Meuezes (Nairobi)

Peter Ray
John Tuomey

1977

Rome:
Revisions to the Nolli Plan

p 45

James Stirling/Michael Wilford

Russell Bevington
Barbara Weiss

1977

Marburg, Germany:
Dresdner Bank

p 48

James Stirling/Michael Wilford

Russell Bevington
Ulrich Schaad

1977

Rotterdam: housing study
for Müller Pier

p 52

James Stirling/Michael Wilford

Alfred Munckenbeck
John Tuomey

1977

Stuttgart: State Gallery
and Chamber Theatre

p 54

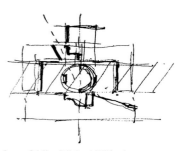

James Stirling/Michael Wilford

Russell Bevington
Jochen Bub
John Cairns
John Cannon
Markus Geiger
Laszlo Glaser
Heribert Hamann
Paul Keogh
Christopher McDonald
Alfred Munckenbeck
Christian Ohm
Alexis Pontvik
Peter Ray
Pia Regert
John Rogers
Ulrich Schaad
Peter Schaad
Rudolf Schwartz
Tommi Tafel
Shin'ici Tomoe
John Tuomey
Siegfried Wernik
Ulrike Wilke

Ove Arup & Partners/Boll & Partner
Ove Arup & Partners/
Eser Dittman Nehring & Partner
Oskar Gerber & Partner
Wilhelma

1978

Tehran: Biology and Biochemistry Institute

James Stirling/Michael Wilford
in association with
Burckhardt & Partner (Basle)

Peter Schaad

1978

Monheim, Germany: Headquarters for Bayer AG

James Stirling/Michael Wilford

Russell Bevington
Paul Keogh
Alan Levitt
Alexis Pontvik
John Tuomey

1978

New York: eleven townhouses

James Stirling/Michael Wilford

Paul Keogh
Robert Livesey
Mark Rosenstein

1979

Rice University, Texas: School of Architecture

James Stirling/Michael Wilford
in association with
Ambrose and McEnany Architects
(Houston)

Paul Keogh
Alexis Pontvik

Walter Moore & Associates
Cook & Holle
Joseph Chapman

1979

Berlin: Wissenschaftszentrum (WZB)

James Stirling/Michael Wilford

Alois Albert
Hans-Georg Conradi
Hannelore Deubzer
Volker Eich
Alexander Kolbe
Walter Nägeli
Robert Niess
Heike Nordmann
Martin Peters
Peter Ray
Peter Schaad
Norberto Schornberg
Jacques Thorin
John Tuomey
Siegfried Wernik

Polonyi & Fink
Schmidt-Reuter
Manfred Flohrer

1979

Harvard University: Arthur M. Sackler Museum

James Stirling/Michael Wilford
in association with
Perry, Dean, Rogers & Partners (Boston)

Robert Dye
Paul Keogh
Ulrich Schaad
Ulrike Wilke

Le Messurier/SCI
Syska & Hennessy
McCarron, Hufnagle, Vegkley & Bent
Claude Engel
Cavanaugh & Tocci
R. W. Sullivan Inc.
Joseph M. Chapman Inc.

1980

New York: Columbia University Chemistry Department

James Stirling/Michael Wilford
in association with
Wank, Adams, Slavin Associates
(New York)

Jeffrey Averill
Christopher McCormack
Richard Portchmouth
Ulrike Wilke

1980

London: Clore Gallery (Tate Gallery)

p **100**

James Stirling/Michael Wilford

Russell Bevington
John Cairns
John Cannon
Robert Dye
Lester Haven
Graham Jahn
Toby Lewis
Walter Nägeli
Sheila O'Donnell
Richard Portchmouth
Ulrich Schaad
Philip Smithies
Ulrike Wilke
Stephen Wright

Felix J. Samuely and Partners
The Steenson Varming Mulcahy
Partnership
Davies Belfield & Everest
John Taylor & Sons
BDP Landscape
Walker Beak Mason Partnership

1980

Stuttgart: Music Academy

p **108**

James Stirling/Michael Wilford

Ulrike Wilke

1983

Ithaca, USA: Cornell Center for the Performing Arts

p **109**

James Stirling/Michael Wilford
in association with
Wank, Adams, Slavin Associates
(New York)

Steve Bono
Robert Dye
Leonard Franco
George Gianakopoulos
Robert Kahn
Walter Nägeli
Joan Nix
Ulrike Wilke

Artec Consultants Inc. (New York)
Severud Szegezdy (New York)
Works Inc. (New York)

1983

Bologna, Italy: new town centre for Casalecchio

p **118**

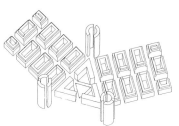

James Stirling/Michael Wilford

Thomas Muirhead
Richard Portchmouth
Barbara Weiss

1983

Turin, Italy: re-use of FIAT Lingotto factory

p **119**

James Stirling/Michael Wilford

Robert Dye
Christopher McCormack
Richard Portchmouth
Barbara Weiss

1983

Milton Keynes: Headquarters for British Telecom

p **122**

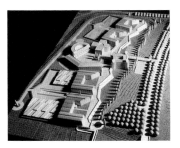

James Stirling/Michael Wilford
in association with YRM Partnership

Robert Dye
Graham Jahn
Toby Lewis
Richard Portchmouth
Peter Ray
Michael Russum

Davis Belfield & Everest
F. J. Samuely and Partners
Steenson Varming Mulcahy and Partners

1983

Latina, Italy:
Municipal Library

p 124

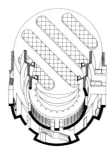

James Stirling/Michael Wilford

John Cannon
Graham Jahn
Crispin Osborne
Richard Portchmouth
Michael Russum
Barbara Weiss

Ove Arup & Partners
Davis Belfield & Everest

1984

Liverpool, England:
Tate in the North

p 132

James Stirling/Michael Wilford
in association with
Holford Associates (Liverpool)

David Jennings
Toby Lewis
Peter Ray
Leandro Rotondi
Oliver Smith
David Turnbull

W. G. Curtin & Partners
Steenson, Varming, Mulcahy Partnership
Davis, Belfield, and Everest/
J. Dansken & Purdie

1985

London: Museums of New Art
and Sculpture (Tate Gallery)

p 138

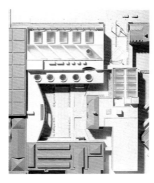

James Stirling/Michael Wilford

David Jennings
Richard Portchmouth
Leandro Rotondi

1985

Bilbao:
Abando Transport
Interchange

p 142

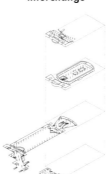

James Stirling/Michael Wilford

Paul Barke
Andrew Birds
Karl Jensen
Michael Russum

1985

London:
National Gallery extension

p 148

James Stirling/Michael Wilford

Laurence Bain
Paul Barke
Russell Bevington
Robert Dye
Felim Dunne
David Jennings
Toby Lewis
Richard Portchmouth
Leandro Rotondi
Ulrike Wilke

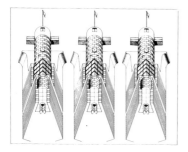
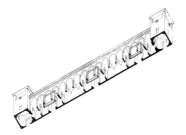

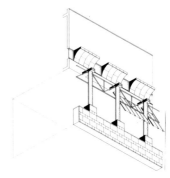

1986

London: Bracken House   p **184**

James Stirling/Michael Wilford

Laurence Bain
Paul Barke
Desmond Byrne
Ulrike Wilke

1987

Aachen: Kaiserplatz   p **186**

Marlies Hentrup and Norbert Heyers
with James Stirling

Dorette Christfreund
Marek Kisczuk
Rico Küpper
Wolfgang Brechbühl
Anja Roth
Wolf Stottele
Vefik Soyeren

1987

**Stuttgart: Music School
and Theatre Academy**   p **190**

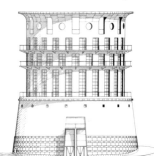

James Stirling/Michael Wilford

Russell Bevington
Birgit Class
Axel Deuschle
John Dorman
Felim Dunne
Christopher Dyson
Claus Fischer
Irmgard Gassner
Stephen Gerstner
Susan Haug
Berndt Horn
Charlie Hussey
David Jennings
Daphne Kephalidis
Steffen Lehmann
Thomas Muirhead
Toby Lewis
Esmonde O'Briain
Eilis O'Donnell
Richard Portchmouth
Ulrich Schaad
Manuel Schupp
Andrew Strickland
Charlie Sutherland
Karin Treutle
Richard Walker
Karenna Wilford
Eric Yim

Ingenieurbüro Michael Weiss (Stuttgart)
Ove Arup & Partners/Boll & Partner
Ove Arup & Partners/
Jaeger, Morhinweg & Partner
Ove Arup & Partners/
IBB-Ingenieurbüro S. Burrer
Davis Langdon & Everest/Michael Weiss
Arup Acoustics/Müller BBM GmbH
Biste & Gerling
Dr. Manfred Flohrer
Wilhelma

1987

**London: Study Centre
and Library (Tate Gallery)**   p **198**

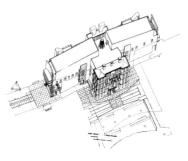

James Stirling/Michael Wilford

David Jennings
Richard Portchmouth
Manuel Schupp

1987

**Milan: Palazzo Citterio
(Pinacoteca di Brera)**   p **199**

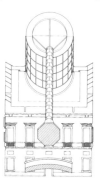

James Stirling/Michael Wilford

Paul Barke
Russell Bevington
David Jennings
Toby Lewis
Thomas Muirhead
Michael McNamara
Oliver Smith
Philip Smithies

Ove Arup & Partners/
Saini & Zambetti (Milan)
Ove Arup & Partners/
Amman Progetti (Milan)
Davis Langdon and Everest

1988

Glyndebourne, England: Opera House extension p 204

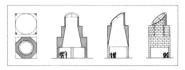

James Stirling/Michael Wilford

Laurence Bain
Charlie Hussey
Andrew Pryke
Ulrike Wilke

1988

Los Angeles: Science Library University of California at Irvine p 208

James Stirling/Michael Wilford
in association with IBI Group (Irvine)

Paul Barke
Chris Chong
Felim Dunne
Barbara Helton-Berg
Buddy Mear
Eilis O'Donnell
Richard Portchmouth
Andrew Pryke
Peter Ray
Michael Russum
Mark Tannin
Katherine Ware
Paul Zafjen

Ove Arup & Partners London/California

Adamson Associates
Burton and Spitz

1988

Toronto: Ballet and Opera House p 214

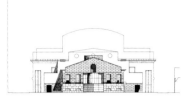

James Stirling/Michael Wilford

Russell Bevington
Luigi Ferrara
David Jennings
Martha LaGess
Toby Lewis
Christopher McCormack
Michael McNamara
Alan Mee
Eilis O'Donnell

1988

London: Canary Wharf residential development p 216

James Stirling/Michael Wilford
in association with YRM plc

Russell Bevington
Toby Lewis
Thomas Muirhead
Michael McNamara
Eilis O'Donnell
Steve Proctor
Philip Smithies
David Turnbull

1988

Los Angeles Philharmonic Hall p 222

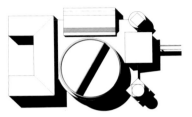

James Stirling/Michael Wilford

Russell Bevington
Luigi Ferrara
Charlie Hussey
David Jennings
Martha LaGess
Toby Lewis
Thomas Muirhead
Christopher McCormack
Michael McNamara
Eilis O'Donnell
Manuel Schupp
Philip Smithies
David Turnbull

1988

London: 5–7 Carlton Gardens p 228

James Stirling/Michael Wilford

Laurence Bain
Johan Dorman
Christopher Dyson
Charlie Hussey
Andrew Pryke
Charlie Sutherland

Ove Arup & Partners
V. J. Mendoza

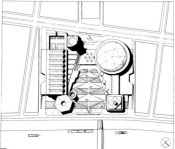
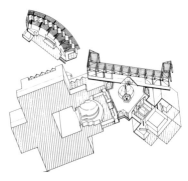

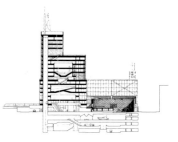
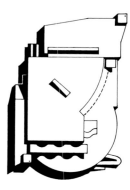

1990

London: Headquarters for Channel 4 Television

p 268

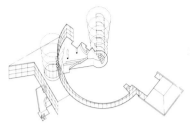

James Stirling/Michael Wilford

Laurence Bain
John Dorman
Charlie Hussey
Toby Lewis
Andrew Pryke

1991

Kyoto Centre, Japan

p 272

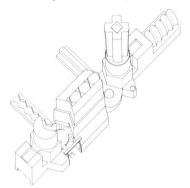

James Stirling/Michael Wilford
in association with
Mitsubishi Estates (Tokyo)

John Bowmer
John Dorman
Christopher Dyson
Charlie Hussey
Teiji Itoh
Maki Kawayama
Toby Lewis
Eilis O'Donnell
Esmonde O'Briain
Hiroshi Satake
Takashi Sugiyama
Charlie Sutherland
David Turnbull
Gareth Wilkins
Hirofumi Yamigawa

1991

Edinburgh: Museum of Scotland

p 280

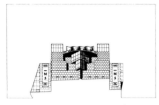

Ulrike Wilke in consultation with
James Stirling and Michael Wilford

Paul Barke
John Craig Gray
Andrew Pryke
Annette Schmidt

1991

Singapore: Temasek Polytechnic

p 284

James Stirling/Michael Wilford
in association with
DP Architects (Singapore)

Laurence Bain
Paul Barke
Russell Bevington
John Bowmer
Mark Bunting
Chris Chong
John Dorman
Christopher Dyson
Liam Hennessey
Charlie Hussey
Andrew Pryke
Peter Ray
Leandro Rotondi
Charlie Sutherland
Kit Wallace
Gareth Wilkins

Ove Arup & Partners/Ewbank Preece
Engineers PTE (Singapore)
KPK Quantity Surveyors

1992

Salford, England: Arts Centre

p 292

James Stirling/Michael Wilford

Laurence Bain
Paul Barke
Andrew Pryke

James Stirling: Biography

1926   Born in Glasgow
1966   Married Mary Shand. One son and two daughters
1992   Knighted; died in London

EDUCATION

to 1941   Quarry Bank High School, Liverpool
1945–50   Liverpool University Diploma in Architecture (with distinction)

PROFESSIONAL PRACTICE

1956–63   James Stirling and James Gowan
1963–71   James Stirling
1971–92   James Stirling and Michael Wilford

TEACHING

1958–60   The Regent Street Polytechnic, London
1960–62   Visiting Critic, Yale University School of Architecture
1961   Harvard University, School of Architecture
1965   External Examiner, The Regent Street Polytechnic, London
1967–84   Charles Davenport Visiting Professor, Yale University School of Architecture
1968–71   External Examiner, Bartlett School of Architecture, London
1977–92   Professor, Düsseldorf Kunstakademie
1977   Bannister Fletcher Professor, London University
1979–81   External Examiner, The Architectural Association, London

GENERAL

1969–   Honorary Member, Akademie der Künste, Berlin
1976–   Honorary Fellow, The American Institute of Architects
1976   The Brunne Award (National Institute of Arts and Letters), USA
1977   The Alvar Aalto Award, Helsinki
1979   Honorary Member, Accademia delle Belle Arti, Florence
1979   Honorary Doctorate, The Royal College of Art, London
1979   Fellow, The Royal Society of Arts, London
1979   Honorary Member, Accademia Nazionale di San Luca, Rome
1980   The RIBA Royal Gold Medal for Architecture, London
1981   The Pritzker Prize, USA
1982   Architect-in-Residence, The American Academy in Rome
1983   Honorary Member, Bund Deutscher Architekten
1985–   Member of the Royal Academy, London
1985   The Chicago Architecture Award
1986   The Thomas Jefferson Medal, USA
1988   The Hugo Häring Prize, Germany
1990   Honorary Member, American Academy & Institute of Arts and Letters
1990   Praemium Imperiale Award, Japan
1990   Honorary Doctorate, Glasgow University
1991   Premio Luigi Cosenza, Italy

Michael Wilford: Biography

1938   Born in Surbiton, Surrey, England
1960   Married. Two sons and three daughters

EDUCATION

1950–55   Kingston Technical School
1955–62   Northern Polytechnic School of Architecture, London
             Honours Diploma in Architecture (with distinction)
1967   Regent Street Polytechnic Planning School, London

PROFESSIONAL PRACTICE

1960–63   Senior Assistant with James Stirling and James Gowan
1963–65   Senior Assistant with James Stirling
1965–71   Associate Partner with James Stirling
1971–92   Partner with James Stirling

TEACHING

1968   Visiting Critic, Yale University School of Architecture
1968   Juror, Harvard University School of Architecture
1968   Juror, Washington School of Architecture, USA
1969–73   Tutor, The Architectural Association, London
1974–79   Visiting Critic, Sheffield University School of Architecture
1974–83   Visiting Critic, Toronto University School of Architecture, Canada
1975   Visiting Critic, McGill University School of Architecture, Canada
1975   Visiting Critic, Yale University School of Architecture
1978–79   Visiting Critic and Tutor, School of Architecture, Rice, Texas
1978–79   External Examiner, RCA School of Environmental Design, London
1980–88   Visiting Professor, School of Architecture, Rice, Texas
1980–88   Graham Willis Visiting Professor in Architecture, Sheffield University
1983–85   External Examiner, Leeds Polytechnic School of Architecture
1983–86   External Examiner, Polytechnic of North London School of Architecture
1986–89   External Examiner, Central London Polytechnic School of Architecture
1988   Royal Institute of British Architects, London Region Masterclass
1989   Visiting Fellow, University of Newcastle School of Architecture, Australia
1989–92   External Examiner, Bartlett School of Architecture, London
1990–92   Visiting Professor, University of Cincinnati School of Architecture, USA

GENERAL

1979–81   Member, RIBA Education and Professional Development Committee
1979   Jury Member, AIA Minnesota Annual Architectural Design Awards
1987   Chairman Assessor, RIBA Architecture Awards, Welsh Region
1988   The Hugo Häring Prize, Germany
1989   Honorary Doctorate, Sheffield University
1989   Chairman Assessor, RIBA Architecture Awards, Yorkshire Region
1991   Chairman Assessor, RIBA Architecture Awards, East Midlands Region
1992   Chairman Assessor, RIBA Architecture Awards, Eastern Region

PRINCIPAL PUBLICATIONS

1974   *James Stirling*. Catalogue of the RIBA Drawings Collection exhibition.
1975   *James Stirling: Buildings and Projects 1950–1974*. Verlag Gerd Hatje, Stuttgart.
1984   *James Stirling Michael Wilford and Associates*. Rizzoli, New York.
1984   *James Stirling: Die Neue Staatsgalerie, Stuttgart*. Verlag Gerd Hatje, Stuttgart.
1986   "Stirling since Stuttgart", November issue of *A + U* magazine, Tokyo.
1987   *The Clore Gallery for the Turner Collection*. Tate Gallery, London.
1987   *The Arthur M. Sackler Museum*. Catalogue of the official opening, Harvard University.
1990   *The Museums of James Stirling Michael Wilford and Associates*. Electa, Milan.
1991   *British Architecture Today*. Catalogue of the Venice Architecture Biennale.

Photo Credits

Arcaid – Richard Bryant 54, 55 (bottom right), 56, 58 (bottom left, right), 60 (left), 61 (right), 62 (bottom left, top), 63, 76 (bottom right), 79, 80, 83, 84, 85, 86, 87 (right, top left, centre left), 95 (left), 100, 101, 102, 103, 104, 105 (bottom right, centre left, top left, centre middle), 107, 110, 111, 112, 113, 114, 115, 116, 117, 132, 134, 136, 137, 168, 169, 172 (bottom), 173 (top), 175, 299 (left and centre top), 300 (left bottom), 301 (centre top)

Maria Ida Biggi 250, 251, 252 (left bottom, centre top and bottom, right bottom), 255, 304 (centre bottom)

Martin Charles 308

Country Life Library 13 (top left)

John Donat 23 (bottom), 26, 29, 31, 34, 35, 39 (top, right), 55 (top left), 66, 68, 69, 70, 71, 81 (bottom right), 98, 122, 156, 158, 159, 177 (bottom), 178, 179, 182, 185, 194 (bottom left), 208, 213, 216, 221, 224, 226, 227, 236, 240, 241, 242, 258, 261, 273, 274 (top right), 275, 286, 291, 296 (centre and right bottom), 298 (left centre), 299 (right bottom), 302 (left top), 303 (left bottom, centre bottom)

Chris Edgcombe 292 (left), 294

Richard Einzig 18, 20 (top centre)

W. von Gliszczynski 187 (right), 189

Alfredo Garuti 40, 41, 42

Reinhard Görner 87 (bottom left)

The Harvard Unversity Art Museums 92 (bottom left, right, top left, right)

Marlies Hentrup 187 (top left)

Paul Hester 76 (left, top right)

Norbert Heyers 172 (top left), 173 (bottom), 174

Wolfgang Hoyt 109 (bottom)

Alastair Hunter 58 (top centre, right), 59 (right), 61 (bottom left, centre), 88 (right), 93 (left), 95 (right), 105 (top right)

Timothy Hursley, The Arkansas Office 55 (top right, bottom centre), 88 (left), 89, 92 (bottom centre), 93 (bottom right), 94

Jeffersons Air Photography 292 (top right)

Kandor Modelmakers Limited 15 (bottom right), 124, 126, 128, 130, 138, 140, 141, 143, 228 (left, centre right), 229, 230, 300 (centre top)

Waltraud Krase 10, 81 (top centre)

Kunstsammlung NW Düsseldorf, Bauwettbewerb 23 (top)

Thomas Muirhead 199, 200

Jon Reis 109 (top)

Steve Rosenthal 90, 93 (bottom centre)

August Sander 30

Richard Sibley 269, 271

Morley von Sternberg 20 (top left, right), 21, 296 (middle centre)

Hiroshi Ueda 272

Peter Walser 8 (bottom), 58 (top left), 59 (left, bottom, top), 60 (bottom right), 62 (bottom centre), 191 (bottom centre), 195 (bottom left, middle centre), 197

First published in Germany in 1994
by Verlag Gerd Hatje, Stuttgart

First published in Great Britain in 1994
by Thames and Hudson Ltd, London

First published in the United States of America in 1994
by Thames and Hudson Inc., 500 Fifth Avenue, New York, New York 10110

British Library Cataloguing-in-Publication Data
A catalogue record for this book is available from the British Library

ISBN 3-7757-0416-7 (Verlag Gerd Hatje)
ISBN 0-500-34126-5 (Thames and Hudson)
Library of Congress Catalog Card Number 93-60420

Printed and bound in Hong Kong

James Stirling and Michael Wilford in 75 Gloucester Place in 1985